MATHEMATICS AS A CONSTRUCTIVE ACTIVITY

Learners Generating Examples

STUDIES IN MATHEMATICAL THINKING AND LEARNING
Alan H. Schoenfeld, Series Editor

Artzt/Armour-Thomas • *Becoming a Reflective Mathematics Teacher: A Guide for Observation and Self-Assessment*

Baroody/Dowker (Eds.) • *The Development of Arithmetic Concepts and Skills: Constructing Adaptive Expertise*

Boaler • *Experiencing School Mathematics: Traditional and Reform Approaches to Teaching and Their Impact on Student Learning*

Carpenter/Fennema/Romberg (Eds.) • *Rational Numbers: An Integration of Research*

Cobb/Bauersfeld (Eds.) • *The Emergence of Mathematical Meaning: Interaction in Classroom Cultures*

Cohen • *Teachers' Professional Development and the Elementary Mathematics Classroom: Bringing Understandings to Light*

Clements/Sarama/DiBiase (Eds.) • *Engaging Young Children in Mathematics: Standards for Early Childhood Mathematics Education*

English (Ed.) • *Mathematical and Analogical Reasoning of Young Learners*

English (Ed.) • *Mathematical Reasoning: Analogies, Metaphors, and Images*

Fennema/Nelson (Eds.) • *Mathematics Teachers in Transition*

Fennema/Romberg (Eds.) • *Mathematics Classrooms That Promote Understanding*

Lajoie • *Reflections on Statistics: Learning, Teaching, and Assessment in Grades K–12*

Lehrer/Chazan (Eds.) • *Designing Learning Environments for Developing Understanding of Geometry and Space*

Ma • *Knowing and Teaching Elementary Mathematics: Teachers' Understanding of Fundamental Mathematics in China and the United States*

Martin • *Mathematics Success and Failure Among African-American Youth: The Roles of Sociohistorical Context, Community Forces, School Influence, and Individual Agency*

Reed • *Word Problems: Research and Curriculum Reform*

Romberg/Carpenter/Dremock (Eds.) • *Understanding Mathematics and Science Matters*

Romberg/Fennema/Carpenter (Eds.) • *Integrating Research on the Graphical Representation of Functions*

Schoenfeld (Ed.) • *Mathematical Thinking and Problem Solving*

Senk/Thompson (Eds.) • *Standards-Based School Mathematics Curricula: What Are They? What Do Students Learn?*

Sternberg/Ben-Zeev (Eds.) • *The Nature of Mathematical Thinking*

Watson/Mason • *Mathematics as a Constructive Activity: Learners Generating Examples*

Wilcox/Lanier (Eds.) • *Using Assessment to Reshape Mathematics Teaching: A Casebook for Teachers and Teacher Educators, Curriculum and Staff Development Specialists*

Wood/Nelson/Warfield (Eds.) • *Beyond Classical Pedagogy: Teaching Elementary School Mathematics*

Yoshida/Fernandez • *Lesson Study: A Japanese Approach to Improving Mathematics Teaching and Learning*

MATHEMATICS AS A CONSTRUCTIVE ACTIVITY

Learners Generating Examples

Anne Watson
University of Oxford, Oxford, UK

John Mason
Open University, Milton Keynes, UK

LEA LAWRENCE ERLBAUM ASSOCIATES, PUBLISHERS
2005 Mahwah, New Jersey   London

Lawrence Erlbaum Associates, Inc., Publishers
10 Industrial Avenue
Mahwah, New Jersey 07430
www.erlbaum.com

Cover design by Kathryn Houghtaling Lacey

Library of Congress Cataloging-in-Publication Data

Watson, Anne, 1948–
   Mathematics as a constructive activity : learners generating examples /
Anne Watson & John Mason.
       p.   cm.
   Includes bibliographical references and index.
   ISBN 0-8058-4343-4 (cloth : alk. paper)
   ISBN-0-8058-4344-2 (pbk. : alk. paper)
      1. Mathematics—Study and teaching—Methodology.   2. Example.
   3. Concept learning.   I. Mason, John, 1944–   II. Title.

QA11.2.W39   2004
510'.7'1—dc22   2004050657
                                                                          CIP

Books published by Lawrence Erlbaum Associates are printed on acid-free paper,
and their bindings are chosen for strength and durability.

Printed in the United States of America
10 9 8 7 6 5 4 3 2 1

We dedicate this book to the 1952 founders and early members of the Association of Teachers of Mathematics, whose vision of mathematics as a creative and constructive endeavor, and of all learners as active constructors of meaning, inspired and informed the thinking and practice of generations of teachers, and whose influence is still felt by teachers, teacher educators, and curriculum designers throughout the world.

Contents

Preface

This book is about the teaching strategy of asking learners to construct their own examples of mathematical objects. Anybody who teaches mathematics could find it useful, because it describes and elaborates on an important and effective pedagogical strategy whose potential is rarely exploited yet which promotes active engagement in mathematics. It arises from a perspective that mathematics is a constructive activity and is most richly learned when learners are actively constructing objects, relations, questions, problems, and meanings.

An immediate response might be that learners are not in a position to construct objects for themselves. In this book, however, we show that not only can all learners construct mathematical objects, but the act of construction can engage learners who might otherwise be passive and uninterested. Making choices for yourself is energizing; being trusted to make choices is empowering.

We describe a range of practices in which teachers give responsibility to learners for producing the examples that generally illustrate, model, and demonstrate mathematical ideas. We claim that the examples learners produce arise from a small pool of ideas that simply appear in response to particular tasks in particular situations. We call these pools *example spaces*. We present ways in which these spaces can be explored, enriched, and extended—a pedagogical focus that is a powerful way of working mathematically.

- Teachers will find ways to transfer initiative to learners by getting them to construct mathematical objects, extending their sophistication and deepening their understanding. It is surprising how learners can be energized and intrigued by simple adjustments to standard classroom tasks.

- Researchers will find ways to reveal learners' depth and breadth of understanding of mathematical concepts.
- Curriculum developers will find general strategies for creating engaging and concept-deepening questions for use by teachers.
- Teachers and educators will find general strategies for engaging preservice teachers in exploring, enriching, and extending their appreciation of mathematical structures, concepts, and connections among topics.
- Lovers of mathematics will find new ways to think about familiar topics that they can use for themselves.

The material on which it is based comes from research and from our own experiences of teaching, learning, and working with mathematics. In particular, it arises from our earlier work from which we accumulated a range of questions and prompts for mathematical thinking (Watson & Mason, 1998) and from responses to workshops. From this we have gained insights that inform our teaching and our work with other educators. Their responses have also contributed to the book. They have told us about their experiences in doing the tasks we offer and about things they do when teaching or learning that seem to relate to what we are saying. Hence, this book is derived from the accumulated wisdom of many practitioners, teachers, and learners of mathematics.

Throughout the book reference is made to the research of others for the following reasons:

- As researchers, we wish to relate our work to what others have found out and look systematically at what is known.
- As teachers, we wish to find out if our instincts are supported by research; as writers, we value the writings of others.
- An important part of our approach is that we continue to question, refine, and critique the distinctions we make and to find out what further questions need pursuing.

However, it turns out that remarkably little has been written about the specific use of the strategy of getting learners to construct their own examples, even though example construction is a vital part of a mathematician's coming to understand a topic and despite many teachers at all levels reporting to us that they use some version of this strategy in their own teaching. It was heartening therefore, as we finished writing the book, to come across a paper by Orit Hazzan and Rina Zazkis (1997) who promoted learner construction of examples as a useful pedagogical device and who made some of the same arguments that we have also developed.

It is impossible to learn mathematics without doing some mathematics, and it is also difficult to learn about the learning of mathematics without some intense work with mental images of mathematical tasks, learners, and classrooms. For this reason, the book contains over 60 mathematical tasks to provide immediate experience and access to past experiences. Throughout, we try to use a range of mathematics from elementary to tertiary. It is essential that you try some of our tasks for yourself to get a feel for what we are talking about.

What would you do if you find a task that involves ideas you have never had or just seems mysterious? The first and best advice is to try to simplify the task or specialize it in some way. You will find suggestions for some tasks in Appendix B. Based on extensive experience, our advice would be to carry on reading because there may be something more immediately appropriate to follow or there may be some support in the commentary. However, it may not be necessary to understand the mathematics to grasp the point we are trying to make. If you can see the structure of the task, then try using it on a more familiar mathematical topic.

What would you do if you think a task is too simple or familiar? Try applying the same task structure or device to a topic that is less familiar or more challenging for you. But be warned; as many of our colleagues have found, some apparently simple mathematics can give some interesting surprises.

Each task functions on at least two levels: as an interesting bit of mathematics (if you do not find it interesting, then try to imagine someone who might) and as an example of pedagogy. You might find yourself responding to some of the tasks with "I couldn't do that with my class" or "I already do that with my class" and moving on without pausing to consider them further. Such instant responses of rejection or acceptance may block access to insight. Instead of being swept up in a stock response, sticking with the tasks can allow them to become useful starting points for critical reflection; they can be reexamined in the light of considered imagination.

We expect readers who have engaged with the tasks to emerge with a deeper and more connected sense of mathematical topics as well as of the use of examples in teaching.

WHAT IS IN THE CHAPTERS?

By doing some mathematics and reading about other teachers' practices, and by experiencing and reflecting on that experience, we want you to form your own conjectures, theories, and understandings. We insert results from research throughout the book and especially in Appendix A, but by the time you read others' comments (apart from our own) you will be fairly knowledgeable about the possibilities, potentials, and pitfalls.

Chapter 1: Introduction to Exemplification in Mathematics

We offer two useful exercises for readers that show ways in which a learner can be encouraged to generate examples. We say what we mean by *examples* and relate our work to the thoughts of Plato, Giambattista Vico, John Dewey, Augustus de Morgan, George Polya, Ference Marton, and Edwina Michener.

Chapter 2: Learner-Generated Examples in Classrooms

We describe some ways in which teachers ask learners to generate their own examples and identify some underlying principles.

Chapter 3: From Examples to Example Spaces

Drawing on documented responses to our requests for exemplification and the reader's own experience working on several tasks, we identify some central themes of example construction and introduce the concept of example spaces.

Chapter 4: The Development of Learners' Example Spaces

We theorize on the idea of example space and offer several examples of learning through exploring and extending personal example spaces. Exercises and illustrations lead to the development of a range of theories and tactics about such extensions.

Chapter 5: Pedagogical Tools for Developing Example Spaces

We identify structural features of example spaces and devise ways to move learners away from dominant images to explore other possibilities.

Chapter 6: Strategies for Prompting and Using Learner-Generated Examples

We present a panoply of illustrations of classroom events in which teachers have used their belief in the ability of all learners to create mathematical objects for themselves. This chapter ends with a reference list of ways to prompt learners into generating examples.

Chapter 7: Mathematics as a Constructive Activity

We draw together the threads that emerge during the development of this material, introduce a few more related ideas, and report on a workshop with mathematics educators. Finally, arising from our work, we offer a set of questions with which to interrogate task design.

Appendix A: Some Historical Remarks on Teaching by Examples

We review the use of examples in textbooks through history, leading to a sense of the roles exemplification takes in mathematics pedagogy.

Appendix B: Suggestions About Some of the Tasks

We make a few suggestions in case you get stuck.

NAMES AND GENDERS

Some of the names in the text are real; some were changed. When we changed names, we may not have used the same alternative name that we used for that person elsewhere. We were not always able to check if people wanted their names used or not, and we were also aware that sometimes people change their minds and do not want to be associated with something they said or did casually in the past. We tried to respect this, but we also wished to celebrate openly the inspiring moments we experienced in classrooms. Use of gender throughout the book is faithful to what really happened. When we made up genders, we tried to do it randomly.

IN BRIEF

We enjoyed working on the tasks in this book, and every group of teachers we worked with have been similarly excited by the possibilities they afford. Many have reported to us later that "their teaching was transformed" and that learners became active questioners who were eager to understand more. Seeing mathematics as a constructive activity liberates teacher and learner from the deadliness of predetermined answers, and turns it into creative activity. We found it rewarding for our own mathematical understanding to use the strategies to modify and develop tasks.

No matter how profoundly one thinks one understands, it is always possible to probe more deeply and to discover more connections and complexities.

We are always keen to hear about more ideas, additional examples of exemplification, critical comments, stories about practice, and so on. We are also willing to offer further suggestions about the mathematics if you are really stuck or to enter into discussion if you find mathematical errors. We can be contacted at anne.watson@educational-studies.oxford.ac.uk and j.h.mason@open.ac.uk

ACKNOWLEDGMENTS

Several colleagues at Linacre College, Oxford, U.K., and at the Open University, Milton Keynes, U.K., have unwittingly given us material. More wittingly, many groups of people have been involved, particularly the 1999 to 2001 cohorts of pre- and in-service mathematics teachers at the Department of Educational Studies, Oxford, U.K.; staff of the National Center for Mathematics Education in Goteborg, Sweden; staff, students, and visitors of the University of Alberta Mathematics Education Centre in Edmonton, Canada; participants of the Annual Institutes for Mathematics Pedagogy which we organize; the Mathematics Learning and Teaching Support Centre at the University of Birmingham; participants in sessions at Association of Teachers of Mathematics and the British Society for Research in the Learning of Mathematics conferences and various teacher workshops; Lara Alcock, Dave Askew, Richard Barwell, Anthony Broadley, Bob Burn, Patricia Cretchley, Lorna Denham, Jackie Fairchild, Jan Goodall, Jonny Heenan, Nathan Hill, Nevil Hopley, Sara Howes, Nick Jackiw, Ed Mann, Ference Marton, Quentin Mason, Tim Mason, Jim Noble, David Pimm, Ulla Runesson, Chris Sangwin, Shannon Sookochoff, Vicky Spratling, Malcolm Swan, and Kate Watson. At the 26th Annual Conference of the International Group for the Psychology of Mathematics Education, we were aided by some 60 participants in our workshop, many of whom wrote comments for us, in particular: Dan Aharoni, Shahrnaz Bakhshalizadeh, Lorna Bateson, Willi Dörfler, Maria Doritou, Tommy Dreyfus, Dietmar Kuchemann, Peter Liljedahl, Joanna Mamona, Heather McLeay, Elizabeth Oldham, Pat Perks, Margaret Sangster, Nathalie Sinclair, Roberto Tortora, Ron Tzur, Gaye Williams, and Peter Winbourne. We are indebted to Adrian Pinel, Melissa Rodd, Tim Rowland, and Orit Zaslavsky who read early drafts of some or all of the book. We particularly thank Alan Schoenfeld for his encouragement and detailed comments and suggestions, and Naomi Silverman, Lori Kelly, Erica Kica, and Barbara Wieghaus at Lawrence Erlbaum Associates for their efforts and care in getting this book to publication.

1

Introduction to Exemplification in Mathematics

We start with a task that concerns factors of whole numbers:

Task 1a: Two Factors

Think of some integers that have only two factors.

Nothing amazing will have happened yet! You might have to decide what you mean by *factors*. Do you include or exclude the number itself, and what about 1? However, because you are reading this without us you do not have to worry about our definitions; just use your own definitions, and stick to them. Whatever you decide, it gets more interesting when you develop this task:

Task 1b: More Factors

Think of some integers that have only three factors.
Only four factors.
Only five factors.

As we said in the preface, reading a task and then moving directly on to our commentary may be tempting, but it may not give you an experience of full participation in or an appreciation of the ideas of this book.[1] You may want to read no further until you have considered the numbers you have just produced. What do they have in common? How do they differ? Are these classes of objects useful or interesting in any way?

A central theme of the book is that mathematics is learned by becoming familiar with examples that manifest and illustrate mathematical ideas and by constructing generalizations from examples. The more of this we can do for ourselves, the more we can make the territories of mathematics our own.

A higher level question that we expect teachers to ask themselves is "would I use this task with students? If so, with whom, why, and how? If not, what adjustments would be needed?" It is very tempting to reject tasks found in books as inappropriate for your situation. The tasks that we offer are not just specific tasks but rather illustrate possible task structures that have proved at least interesting and productive. So rejecting a task immediately may block access to potential value.

Task 2 addresses the issue of helping learners distinguish among several technical terms by working explicitly on what distinguishes them.

Task 2: Mode, Median, and Mean

Construct a data set of seven numbers for which the mode is 5, the median is 6, and the mean is 7.

Alter it to make the mode 10, the median 12, and the mean 14; alter it to make the mode 8, the median 9, and the mean 10.

Is it possible to preassign any value to each mode, median, and mean independently and restrict the data set to just five data points?

How small a data set can achieve any preassigned mode, median, and mean? How much choice of data set is there then?

A common approach is to start with the mode because it has to be repeated, tinker with adding extra data values so as to make the mean work, and then adjust those values to achieve the median. One pedagogical aim of the task is to promote awareness of the range of possibilities and to raise questions about what it is about a data set that is captured by each of the three statistical summarizers.

But what was your experience of doing this task? How did you choose to start, and why? If you started with particular numbers, why those? If you started with some general relationships, what was the pathway by

---

[1]There is some support for *Tasks 1a, 1b,* and *2* in Appendix B.

which you moved toward particular data sets if, indeed, you bothered to do that? You may have chosen to stay with the generalities. You may have become aware of generalities as you did the task; if so, what did you do with this awareness? What choices were you making, and how were they linked to your knowledge of underlying relationships?

Similar tasks could be used to emphasize the difference between products, sums, and differences (e.g., for pairs of numbers) as well as between commutativity and associativity in groups and rings.

Having promoted your reflection, perhaps it is already time to address a fundamental question.

WHAT IS AN EXAMPLE?

In this book we focus on the learner's experience rather than on definitions. Because most of what is offered to learners in schools and colleges is intended to indicate some kind of generality (a concept, a class, a technique, a principle, etc.), we use the word *example* in a very broad way to stand for anything from which a learner might generalize. Thus, example refers to the following:

- Illustrations of concepts and principles, such as a specific equation that illustrates linear equations or two fractions that demonstrate the equivalence of fractions.
- Placeholders used instead of general definitions and theorems, such as using a dynamic image of an angle whose vertex is moving around the circumference of a circle to indicate that angles in the same segment are equal.
- Questions worked through in textbooks or by teachers as a means of demonstrating the use of specific techniques, which are commonly called *worked examples*.
- Questions to be worked on by students as a means of learning to use, apply, and gain fluency with specific techniques, which are usually called *exercises*.
- Representatives of classes used as raw material for inductive mathematical reasoning, such as numbers generated by special cases of a situation and then examined for patterns.
- Specific contextual situations that can be treated as cases to motivate mathematics.

There are deep and significant questions concerning just how examples actually illustrate or exemplify, and these will be addressed later in the book. We use *exemplification* to describe any situation in which something specific is offered to represent a general class with which the learner is to become familiar—a particular case of a generality. For instance:

- A trial examination question may be offered to represent the kind of questions learners will have to answer.
- A specific object may be used to indicate what is included and what is excluded by a condition in a definition or theorem; for example, a drawing of a particular rectangle to accompany a definition of rectangles given in a textbook.
- A specific object may be used to indicate the significance of a particular condition in a definition or theorem by highlighting its role in a proof or by showing how the proof fails in the absence of that condition; for example, using $f(x) = |x|$ to indicate how continuity on its own is not enough to ensure that every value of x has a derivative associated with it.
- A specific object may be offered to indicate a dimension of variation implied by a generalization; for example, in *Task 1b: More Factors* we could have offered or been offered 25 and 225 as numbers that both have odd numbers of factors, are both square, but do not have the same number of factors; thus, they offer some ideas about a possible generalization and also put limitations on what can be claimed.
- An object may be chosen to illustrate a complex structure but is made up of simpler objects familiar to the learner; for example, the expression $3(4 + 5)$ to introduce distributivity.
- A generic diagram may be used to indicate something that remains invariant while some other features change; for example, as suggested earlier, a drawing of one generic triangle (that does not look equilateral, isosceles, or right-angled) can be used to illustrate the coincidence of medians.

All of these situations require the learner to see the general through the particular, to generalize, to experience the particular as exemplary to appreciate a technical term, theorem, proof, or proof structure, and so on.

Possibly you already find yourself disagreeing with us about some of these matters. For instance, textbooks typically give examples of rectangles whose sides are parallel to the edges of the paper, often in the ratio 2:1 and with the longest side horizontal. How, then, can such a diagram represent all possible rectangles? One diagram of a triangle does not convince learners about *all* possible triangles, so why not use dynamic geometry software instead of a static drawing? The first numbers you find with 3, 5, and 7 factors are all squares, but will this always be the case?

These are precisely the kinds of questions that we have been asking ourselves for some time. Clearly, one special example may not enough to give learners an idea of the full extent of what is possible, and it may indeed be misleading in its details.

In this book we develop the idea of *example spaces*: collections of examples that fulfill the kinds of functions just listed and suggest that these collections might be seen as central in the teaching and learning of mathematics. We have found ourselves using and extending language introduced by Ference Marton to describe the structure of example spaces in terms of dimensions of possible variation (our adaptation from Marton & Booth, 1997; see also Leung, 2003), which constitutes a generality that can be read into or through examples, and the associated notion of range of permissible change in each of the dimensions of variation. These terms appear through the book and are elaborated in chapter 5. A different way to describe the structure of example spaces is in terms of detecting invariance of some features while others are changing, which is powerfully accessed through use of the prompt "what is the same and what is different" about a collection of objects (see, e.g., L. Brown & Coles, 2000). Again, this notion is developed through the book.

At the start of this chapter we offered a task with variations that was intended to trigger an exploration of an example space emerging in your response to the task itself. You may have made use of decomposition of multiples into their prime factorization and stated that only prime numbers have precisely two factors—themselves and unity. You may have been on familiar territory. Then we asked for numbers with three factors. You may have continued to look at prime factorizations and tried to construct numbers using three factors including unity; but then you noted that the number created also has to be a factor as well, so every time you multiply two of the factors you get a new factor! How can you have two factors that, when multiplied together to make the final number, do not produce a new factor as well? Or, you may have used a decomposition approach and listed the factors of various numbers systematically, noticing that they occur in pairs. Aha! If they occur in pairs, how can you ever have an odd number of them? But as you decompose several numbers you may begin to group them according to the number of factors they have and thus create classes that you may not previously have recognized as classes. What do 15 and 21 have in common? What do 12 and 18 have in common? Eventually, you may have extended your search to some numbers other than small integers.

If counting factors is familiar territory, you could have asked yourself whether a prime number of factors produces a recognizable class or whether you can characterize cubes or higher powers in terms of numbers of factors. Any task can be opened up to further exploration by altering constraints.

Notice how working on this task invites an interplay between what is familiar and what is unfamiliar. Every now and then you may have experienced a rush of recognition as a new idea took shape and, maybe, was recorded in some way. The numbers you used as examples are all old friends, but you looked at some of them in new ways perhaps. You may even have chosen to use particular numbers because of properties you already knew, like choosing 24 because it has several factors, 81 because it is a square of an odd square, 1,760 because it is a larger nonprime number, or $2^2 \times 3^4 \times 5^2$ because you can "see" how to count factors (Campbell & Zazkis, 2002). But 1,760 may not have been big or complex enough, so you may have had to construct particular numbers that have the desired properties. You have explored your example space, looked at what you know in new ways, and constructed new objects to occupy new or extended example spaces.

At the heart of this approach to teaching lie two important pedagogical principles:

- Learning mathematics consists of exploring, rearranging, and extending example spaces and the relationships between and within them. Through developing familiarity with those spaces, learners can gain fluency and facility in associated techniques and discourse.
- Experiencing extensions of your example spaces (if sensitively guided) contributes to flexibility of thinking not just within mathematics but perhaps even more generally, and it empowers the appreciation and adoption of new concepts.

These principles are illustrated in what follows through tasks and commentaries. You can examine your own experience throughout this book, either by trying the tasks yourself or with learners or by imagining what would happen in your usual teaching situation to get a sense of the effect of such prompts.

ON WHOSE SHOULDERS ARE WE STANDING?

We ground our work in a well-established tradition of questioning the relations between experiences, ideas, and knowledge as well as in the pedagogical wisdom of friends, colleagues, and others. Authors' expressions of this wisdom can be found in every period of recorded history.

Plato wondered how we could come to understand color, shape, or indeed any abstract noun. If we see examples of *white* and hear them being called *white*, we will eventually construct our own understanding of what it means to be white and will be able to use the word in ways that others understand. How, he asked, can color be explained to a blind person who has to rely on definition and abstraction? Thus, he highlighted an apparent paradox that must be resolved by any constructivist view of learning: How can we construct what we do not already know? This is only a paradox if you assume there is a fixed meaning for *white* that is independent of the knower, and a true meaning the learner has to strive to understand. Similarly, learners of mathematics strive to make sense of the examples they are offered, use the terms their teachers use to describe generalities, and ultimately are expected to construct new objects and understandings that match those of their teachers.

George Polya (1981) was prolific both as a mathematician and as a reflective and articulate educator. He made use of the terms *extreme*, *leading*, and *representative* as types of examples (p. 10), which other authors also use. Extreme examples involve going to the edge of what usually happens within the particular mathematical context and seeing what unusually happens. For instance, young children might believe that multiplication makes things bigger; but even if we restrict multiples to positive integers, we find that multiplying by one does not make things bigger. Furthermore, multiplication by zero obliterates everything! Extreme examples, therefore, confound our expectations, encourage us to question beyond our present experience, and prepare us for new conceptual understandings. Multiplication by zero prepares us for new understandings of multiplication just as treating a circle as an n-sided polygon when n grows very large prepares us for work with limits.

Drawing on Polya's ideas, Edwina Michener (1978) experimented with the explicit use of several different types of examples of mathematical concepts in her teaching of undergraduates. We draw particularly on the notion of a *reference example* in chapter 5. A reference example is one that becomes extremely familiar and is used to test out conjectures, to illustrate the meaning of theorems, and to appreciate how the proofs of theorems work. For example, consider the following statement: If two numbers sum to one, then the square of the larger added to the smaller will equal the square of the smaller added to the larger?

You are very likely to want to check it first using something familiar, such as $\frac{1}{3}$ and $\frac{2}{3}$ ($\frac{1}{2}$ and $\frac{1}{2}$ is probably not worthwhile!).[2] This could function as a reference example for fractions that sum to one. You may also want to

---

[2]Some readers who are familiar and confident with algebra might express this in symbols immediately. They might like to try this instead: Must a finite group in which every element is of order 2 be of order 2^n? Looking at groups of order 6 as reference examples could be an informative place to start.

test this statement on some extreme like 0 and 1 or even –1 and 2. Note that we have shifted from making sense of examples to creating examples to make sense.

A shift toward generating one's own examples is implied by the perspective of Giambattista Vico (1990) who probed what it means to know, concluding that we can only know for certain what we have made: Other kinds of knowing are not certain in the same way. When we make things with our hands, we have objects we can show to others to say "this is what I know"; but when we make mental objects, it is not so easy to offer them to others to check out or to use. The aim of learning is to construct meaning for ourselves, not to attain external, preexistent meanings, while conforming to social practices. In education, this belief was most notably taken up by John Dewey (1902) who said that education should involve the use and development of what learners bring with them to their learning, thus drawing a picture of active learners taking some kind of personal roles in their construction of meaning.

In mathematics, Zoltan Dienes (1963) articulated further a philosophy of mathematics as a constructive activity that closely corresponds to many of the ideas in this book:

> Constructive thinking takes place when one aims at a set of requirements and attempts to build a structure which will meet them. . . . What we call one construction is largely arbitrary, as practically every construction can be built onto as well as taken down from, and it may be difficult to say where one construction ends and another begins. . . . Abstraction is essentially constructive in character. We start with elements and eventually build them up into a class by becoming aware of the defining attribute that must, perhaps not very consciously, have induced us to class the elements together in the first place. (pp. 95–96)

Larry Sowder (1980) summarized some of the research into the importance of examples and instances in the teaching and learning of mathematics. One view that emerges from research, and from our own experience, is that a learner's passive acceptance of given examples, or given definitions, does not necessarily result in deep understanding of a concept. Sowder drew attention to a phase in which, once they were adept at distinguishing examples and nonexamples, learners need to construct their own examples prior to stating and using formal definitions meaningfully.

What pervades and informs our practices in teaching is the image of active, arguing learners engaging with examples and, when possible, constructing their own examples and their own objects.

A particularly strong version of this image is given by Augustus de Morgan (1831/1898) who wrote:

He cannot learn that a particular fact holds good for *all numbers* unless by having it shown that it holds good for *some numbers*, and that for those *some numbers* he may substitute *others*, and use the same demonstration. Until he can do this himself he does not understand the principle, and he can never do this except by seeing the rule explained and trying it himself on small numbers. (p. 22)

He recommended getting plenty of experience with examples before applying a given algorithm: "He should, until he has mastered a good many examples, continue the operation at full length, instead of using the rule, which is an abridgement of it" (p. 97). Rather than being given a theoretical exposition as an introduction to a topic, he recommended an inductive approach: "draw his rules from observation of many results, not from any theory" (p. 104).

Further, de Morgan suggested that learners could usefully create their own examples:

On arriving at any new rule or process, the student should work a number of examples sufficient to prove to himself that he understands and can apply the rule or process in question. . . . He may choose an example for himself, and his previous knowledge will suggest some method of proving whether his result is true or not. (p. 177)

For now, we trust that you are sufficiently convinced that there is something to what we have to offer that makes it worthwhile to read the rest of the book, which is about active engagement with multiple exemplification and how it might promote learning.

SUMMARY

We have raised the issue of just how and under what conditions an example is seen or experienced by learners as exemplary. We have introduced ever so briefly some of the technical terms that will unfold in their use and meaning, including example space, dimensions of possible variation, range of permissible change, extreme examples, and reference examples. We have hinted at deep historical roots concerning the use of examples in teaching and learning mathematics and how learners can be encouraged to be active constructors (which is elaborated in Appendix A). Most important, we have already invited you to participate, and in the following chapters that invitation will be stronger and more insistent! In the next chapter we describe some classrooms in which learners are asked to construct their own examples of mathematical objects.

2

Learner-Generated Examples in Classrooms

In this chapter we describe some classroom incidents in which responsibility for the direction of the lesson shifts from the teacher or textbook to the learners. We are interested in particular kinds of shift: those that involve learners in generating and creating the material on which part of the lesson is based. In some of the cases we report some of the effects of this shift, but we do not claim that such shifts will always have such effects. Rather, we think that readers will respond to the stories in personal ways by finding themselves thinking "I could use that" so that our examples may be catalysts for using some new strategies. Alternatively, your response might be "That would never work with my students," in which case any recommendations we might be tempted to make would be little more than ripples on a stream that may be flowing in another direction. In these cases, we hope you will at least imagine how it could have worked with some students but might not work with yours. If necessary, simplify or complexify each task to suit your interests.

One way to work with the stories is to engage with the mathematics first, to try to do the task yourself, perhaps pretending to be a learner, in order to get a sense of its potential for promoting learning. Before we start on the collection of stories, try this:

Task 3a: Alternating Signs

Make up an infinite numerical sequence with alternate positive and negative terms, and state a rule to generate all the terms.

People are sometimes perplexed by the openness of the phrase "make up a sequence." Possibly you wondered why we are asking you to do this: Why should I engage in this task at all? How do I chose one rather than another? What will I have to do with it? Do the authors have something in mind for which I should be striving or guessing? Is there any way in which my work is going to be labeled *right* or *wrong* or, even worse, *useful or not useful* or *interesting or not interesting*, which are euphemisms that teachers use when they pretend a question is open-ended but really only want certain responses? You could be frozen into inaction by a desire to produce the best example you can think of for the unknown next step. Thank goodness that you are in the privacy of this book and do not have to perform the task in public!

If you went beyond these suspicions, you may have had further problems with the idea of a rule. Could I just include the phrase "alternately positive and negative" in my rule? Do they want a single symbolic expression? How would I write it in symbols?

Perhaps you decided to think about the task as a pedagogical device rather than engage in it yourself. This task could be used to encourage learners to multiply by negative numbers or to defy instant assumptions that all patterns are linear. But if the rule they eventually express includes the phrase "alternately positive and negative," would these two goals have been achieved? How can you channel their energies into thinking about multiplying by negative numbers without taking away the genuine exploratory aspects of the task and the realization that multiplying by -1 is, indeed, multiplying by a constant even if it does not feel like it?

We could give more support by suggesting the following method:

Task 3b: Alternating Signs Again

Make up an infinite sequence of numbers with alternate positive and negative terms by multiplying each term by a constant to get the next term.

What would have been the advantages of this more tightly constrained approach, and what are the disadvantages? Often in mathematics the action of adding constraints to a problem opens up new possibilities for the learner and promotes creativity. But this potential is usually only accessed after learners become aware of the greater freedom from which they are being constrained. Our aim here is to produce an experience that encourages comparison of the effects of applying more or less constraint.

The set of stories that follow all involve deliberate decisions by teachers to ask learners to generate examples, and nearly all of them are of lessons we have observed. The rest have been reported to us. In our observations of teaching in a variety of learning environments we have frequently used a combination of personal response and pedagogical critique to make sense of what we see.

TEACHER-INITIATED, LEARNER-GENERATED EXAMPLES

In this section we briefly describe and consider practices found in eight classrooms.

Sarah's Practice

Sarah was the mathematics coordinator in a middle school, teaching 9- to 13-year-old children. She frequently asked children to make up their own examples to rehearse newly learned techniques. For example, she asked the children on one occasion to "make up your own examples of subtraction, using addition to check your answers." Sometimes she suggested to individuals that they work with a particular range of numbers. After the lesson, she stated the following:

> A lot of the children think that they can do things that they can't. Even today we were doing subtraction and then checking using addition, inverse operations, and one boy decided he was going to do it in thousands, and even though he understood the concept of inverse operations and checking he couldn't operate above . . . he couldn't operate with numbers in the thousands. He just couldn't; he didn't have the place value for thousands. . . . They all operated at what they *thought* they were comfortable with, what they *thought* they could do, so one child, he was subtracting multiples of ten from other multiples of ten. Another child . . . in fact I did target one group and told them to just use numbers below ten and choose from that. The most able children were choosing intrinsically very simple subtraction sums . . . under-operating, if you like, but the objective of the lesson wasn't to do the hardest subtraction sum possible, the objective was to use the inverse operation to check.

In this case, even though learners were used to being asked to exemplify the use of techniques, the teacher's intention was not carried through into all the learners' interpretations of the activity. Those she described as "most able" were working closely with the teacher's intention (perhaps this is a component of what was identified as "ability"). Indeed, it seems that they have constructed tasks for themselves in which they have made deliberate decisions about the focus. Another learner had chosen to use much larger numbers than he could actually handle and, hence, failed to communicate his understanding of inverses to the teacher through this task; her knowledge that he did understand inverse operations came from somewhere else. We can only guess at his motives for choosing large numbers.

Given that making up examples was the norm in this classroom, perhaps he had picked up an unintended idea of hierarchies or status in mathematics, missing the real purpose which was to make up examples that would allow him to focus on the new or tricky bits of a topic.

Task 4: Same and Different Tasks

What is the same and what is different about the following two tasks?
Make up your own examples of addition of two-digit numbers.
Invent examples of addition with a vertical layout, with carrying.

There is an important difference between these two tasks. The second requires more than just practice. It would be possible to produce appropriate examples involving carrying by trial and error, and it would also be possible to develop such examples conceptually or systematically by using appropriate pairs of digits. The act of creating examples by trial and error might itself bring about the realization that certain pairs of digits lead to carrying. Example creation can provide an arena not only for practice but also for conceptual learning.

With every construction there is also a question: How much choice do I have? Mathematicians typically pursue this by then asking whether they can characterize all such examples in some way. For example, in how many different ways can carrying occur when adding two-digit numbers, three-digit numbers, and so on, and can I characterize those three-digit numbers that can arise as the sum of two-digit numbers, three digit numbers, and so on?

The addition tasks could also be dressed up a little to be more motivating:

- Make up examples that show you know how to do addition with carrying.
- Make up some hard examples that could be used to test someone else's addition.

Now try these yourself:

Task 5: Practice Tasks

Make up your own examples to rehearse turning percentages into
fractions. Make up an example that makes it hard to see how to
turn a percentage into a fraction.
Make up your own examples to rehearse integration by parts. Make
up an example that makes it hard to see that integration by parts is
a suitable method.

Prompts like these raise further questions: What are the issues here?
What are the tricky bits? What would be easy, typical, and hard examples?
In the second question we may have been forced to think about what has
to be present for a function to yield to integration by parts.

Ed's Practice

Ed was a student teacher who had decided to ask learners to develop their
own examples to generate practice exercises for the whole class. Because
this lesson was to be observed, it is unlikely that he made this decision out
of laziness! The learners were mainly 13-year-olds and were generally
considered to be just above average in mathematical achievement.

The lesson was supposed to be about solving linear equations in one
unknown when the unknown appears on both sides of the equation. Previous lessons had been about simpler linear equations with unknowns
only on one side. The specific task he used was:

- For this task x is 4. Write this as $x = 4$. By doing the same thing to both
  sides of the equation, gradually build up a more complicated version
  of this equation in which x appears on both sides.

This was not a familiar request for these learners, but they were used to
student teachers working in unfamiliar ways.

Before he set the task he asked individuals to come to the board to develop a line-by-line example: $x = 4$. The first wrote: $x + 1 = 5$. The next
wrote: $x + 2x + 1 = 5 + 2x$. The next wrote: $3x + 1 = 5 + 2x$, and this line was
taken to be final. Then they all created their own equations; the value of x
remained the same throughout. The 33 examples produced were written
on the board. Some were solved individually during the lesson, and the
rest were assigned as homework.

In discussion after the lesson, Ed said that his intention was that, by going through the process of building up the equation, they would have a
better sense of how to solve each other's equations. That is, they would ex-

perience the rules for solving equations in the context of making increasingly complex statements for themselves.

The lesson was successful in terms of creating an enthusiastic work atmosphere, and most of the class were able to undo each other's equations correctly, either during the lesson or later for homework. Also, already knowing the answer helped them concentrate on using appropriate methods to achieve it. There was no point in resorting to getting the answer from a neighbor. Overheard discussions were about how to undo what had been done at each stage or about making harder examples. For example, one learner asked "can I get x to have a negative sign?"

As well as the obvious motivational benefits, learners are more likely to be able to solve someone else's tasks if they know how those tasks are constructed. Using structure to increase complexity facilitates their use of the same structure reversed as a means of simplification. Task reversal is a technique that many teachers have used for some time, and it is one of the strategies that Hazzan and Zazkis (1997, 1999) found powerful.

Ed's approach acts on both affective and cognitive aspects of motivation. However, exposure to structure does not on its own guarantee either facility or reconstructability, especially when the learners are used to following algorithms rather than thinking mathematically. We are not saying that this lesson is all that was needed for learners to know and remember how to solve such equations. In fact, Ed reported that he was disappointed to find that 2 weeks later several of them had forgotten how to solve such equations. Nevertheless, the initial experience of structure made it easier for them to reconstruct methods later on, because they had more to recall than just a set of manipulation rules.

We came to think of this kind of task as "burying the bone"—hiding an answer in the successive layers of operations that generally have to be undone in conventional mathematics questions. The notion can be extend to the construction of almost any example: Can you create an example that is so complex that it might be hard for others to "unpick" it to see what it exemplifies?

Linda's Practice

Linda teaches children in their first year of primary school. It is common for teachers of older learners to assume prior knowledge when they start to teach a topic. Fortunately, that is not generally true of those who teach very young children, and in the United Kingdom a range of methods for getting frequent feedback to inform teaching is now employed. Linda was an experienced teacher who had been developing strategies for getting feedback over several years, and her learners were used to a high level of active participation in all lessons.

During a lesson on place value, about 15 children sat on a mat around a horizontal board lying on the floor. At the side of the board there was a mixed box of *unit blocks* and *tens blocks*, which were sticks of a length equal to 10 of the unit blocks.[3] Children could choose whether to add or remove individual unit blocks or tens blocks from a display on the board and report the result of their actions in terms of the total value of blocks on the board. Children could also decide for themselves when to take part. Linda asked "who would like to start?," and there were several volunteers.

Child 1	Placed a tens block to start the display	Said "10"
Child 2	Added a tens block	Said "20"
Child 3	Added a tens block	Said "30"
Child 4	Removed a tens block	Said "20"
Child 5	Added a unit block	Said "21"
Child 6	Added a unit block	Said "22"
Child 7	Removed a unit block	Said "21"
Child 8	Removed a unit block	Said "20"
Child 9	Added a tens block	Said "30"
Child 10	Added a tens block	Said "40" and so on

This continued until all the children had contributed an operation.

There are obvious ways of taking part with minimal effort or of playing safe, and Linda intervened occasionally when she thought this was happening, asking "is there anything else you could have done?" or "can you do something different?" to encourage engagement at a deeper level.

It seemed that some children (3, 6, 8, and 10) participated by following a pattern initiated by others, some children (4 and 7) by undoing what the previous person had done, and some children (5 and 9) by breaking a pattern and introducing another aspect of number structure. Learners were displaying different awareness levels about the freedom of choice available to them. Some seemed to be following someone else's lead; others appeared to be deliberately acting differently as to what had gone before. In addition to revealing confidence about place value, this activity can also reveal who is working empirically by following patterns the learners detect and who is working more structurally by making use of other possibilities. Linda's additional challenges could encourage learners to shift from local patterning to structural generalization.

In her skillful hands, this task had the potential to promote shifts in learning about number structure and to have the positive motivation and feedback functions of learner-generated exemplification.

---

[3]These are sometimes called multibase, Dienes, or structural apparatus.

Task 6: Further Development

What might be the effect of saying: "You can now choose to add or
  remove more than one block at a time"?

This next sequence of tasks may have some similarities with Linda's
task.

Task 7a: How Different?

Give an example of a linear equation.
Change your example in some way to give a different straight line.
Make further *similar* alterations to get new straight lines.
Now make a different kind of change. How does the new straight
  line differ from those achieved so far?
What other kinds of change can be made, and what is the effect of
  these changes?

And this sequence may have similarities as well.

Task 7b: How Different Variation

Write down a function that is continuous except at one point.
Write down another.
Write down one that has a different kind of discontinuity at a point.
What other kinds of discontinuity can you make?

What did you notice about being asked to generate examples that are
different in some way compared with generating your first example? You
might, for example, have found yourself wondering what features you
could change and in what way you could change them.

Jeff's Practice

Jeff's class of mixed ability 12-year-olds had been working with the inputs
and outputs of functions using flow diagrams. They were familiar with
using number lines for recent work with directed numbers. Jeff had

drawn several diagrams of number lines and a function machine on the board like this:

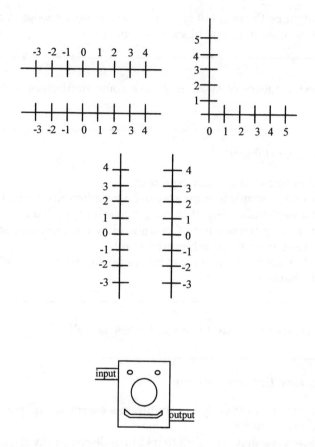

He asked them to suggest ways in which they could use these diagrams to represent the function inputs and outputs they had been working on during the previous lesson. He reminded them that one of the functions they had worked with was Output = Input + 3. Learners first indicated actual numbers as inputs and outputs for the function machine. There was much laughter about the apparent face on the machine. Then the contributions became more serious, and there were various attempts to join output and input values on the parallel number lines. Jeff asked learners to comment about each attempt without comment himself. They noticed that the lines joining input and output values made a set of parallel lines, but then Jeff introduced some counterexamples for other functions they had worked on previously: Output = Input × 2 and Output = 6 − Input.

Eventually, one learner drew a nest of rectangles in the orthogonal number lines in which each horizontal edge was three units more than the vertical edge.

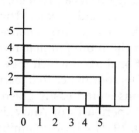

Another learner noticed that it would not be necessary to draw the whole rectangle, because dots for the only vertex that was not on an axis would be sufficient. Jeff was aware that they were not using the standard convention in which the horizontal axis is used for input and the vertical for output. Rather than immediately introducing the conventional order of coordinates, Jeff stayed with this line of reasoning and let the dots be drawn to represent the function.

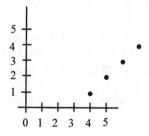

It was agreed that this was the best representation so far, and it also worked for other functions. Some learners said "it's like graphs."

Throughout the lesson Jeff let learners do most of the talking and all of the boardwork, apart from his original diagrams. His most directed intervention had been to introduce two functions that challenged a learner-generated regularity that he knew was not generalizable or generic. He was content to let learners develop the representation for themselves so that they understood the principles behind graphical representation in general and the conventional version he would use later. In the next lesson, he pointed out that the convention was to use the horizontal axis to represent the input. This did not seem to be at all problematic for the learners. He reported that they were quite pleased to have developed something so acceptable for themselves. It is noticeable that to make this lesson work Jeff, who was in his second year of teaching and working with a new class, had to trust learners to generate desirable ideas and comments. He did not see this as a problem; he had thought through a range of possible responses and predicted what would happen fairly accurately, believing they would first choose to work with the drawing, then to work with the more familiar number lines, and finally to work with the conventional axes, which they had already encountered but not very recently. His confidence that learners who had constructed their own representations would easily grasp conventional representations is similar to the experiences of Andy diSessa (diSessa, Hammer, Sherin, & Kolpakowski, 1991) whose commitment to the importance of constructing objects has led them to produce some stimulating educational software.

In this story, it is not the exemplification of functions that was handed over to learners but the exemplification of modes of representation. The exploration helped learners connect number patterns to graphs so that several ways of seeing such structures might be available to them in the future. Creation of representations enables learners to make more sense of conventions and the reasons for them.

By looking beyond the specific context of graphs, it is possible to imagine similar tasks. One could ask learners to invent various ways of expressing "square one number, then multiply the result by another number" and then compare their different representations to see which is best according to the criteria of usefulness, clarity, lack of ambiguity, efficiency, and so on. They could include calculating the area of a circle as one of the test items. In this way, they might come to understand how to use πr^2 correctly even if they originally thought their own expression had been better.

Farah's Practice

Farah, an experienced and highly qualified teacher, was working with her class of 11-year-olds on their understanding of multiplication. They had been assessed as having average attainment in their previous schools. In United Kingdom parlance they were classified as *middle ability*, which means that on tests they tended to come somewhere in the middle range.[4]

---

[4]We see *ability* as (at best) an attribute of behavior in a specific situation, not as an attribute of a person. Categorizing learners by past attainment is the usual measure by which they are grouped for teaching mathematics, but it is difficult for learners to break out of the mold. The phrase we use here is the usual one in the community of teachers' practice.

She had been explicit about the use of the distributive law to deal with different place values of the digits used in large numbers. For example, they had been taught, or reminded, through calculator exploration that 7×65 was the same as $7 \times 60 + 7 \times 5$ or $7 \times 50 + 7 \times 5 + 7 \times 10$ or other such representations. Learners were asked to contribute examples of multidigit multiplications and show how they would calculate them to the whole class. Some learners used a traditional approach of dealing with separate digits, such as $37 \times 9 = 30 \times 9 + 7 \times 9$, but others used ad hoc decompositions that suited the specific numbers being multiplied, such as $37 \times 9 = 40 \times 9 - 3 \times 9$. Farah particularly praised these decompositions. Her aim was for learners to develop flexible methods and mental methods for multiplication, as well as to understand distributivity. The examples were shared within the class. Two weeks later she repeated the exercise. There was a significant increase in most learners' use of flexible approaches based on characteristics of the numbers involved, rather than just separating the digits, although there had been no work on this area of mathematics meanwhile. Farah took this to be a sign that some learning had taken place as a result of the emphasis she had placed on interesting decompositions in the earlier lesson.

Exemplification of methods and public discussion valuing such methods can encourage learners to become more resourceful and flexible. Here the development of exemplification is not explicitly forced by the teacher imposing constraints but by sharing, making other possibilities available, and publicly valuing examples of what the teacher hopes others will be able to do later. A range of ways of seeing the mathematics was introduced into the public domain of the classroom, and this appeared to have an effect on learners' creativity in arithmetic.

Bob's Practice

Task 8: Comparing Squares

Give an example of a number c such that given $0 < a < b$, then $ca > cb$
and an example to show that $a < b$ may be compatible with $a^2 > b^2$.
Will your c work for any a and b meeting the specified constraints?

Bob used this idea to illustrate how he tries to get advanced learners away from their very strong tendency to think of number in terms of the behavior of positive integers. These requests are intended to alert learners to the (possibly surprising) fact that multiplication and squaring do not always preserve order. Whether giving one example is sufficient to eradicate these misimpressions is another matter.

This task is also an induction into the practices of sophisticated mathematicians in setting up challenges for themselves and questioning assumptions. Many common preconceptions or challenges to intuitive notions can be explored in this way. The assumption is that these learners do have considerable knowledge of the number system, but they need to be jolted out of established patterns of behavior that limit their approach to advanced concepts.

John and Anne's Practice

We have given the following task to many groups of learners, teachers, and others:

Task 9: Quadrilateral Sequence

Draw the following in sequence:

- A quadrilateral.
- A quadrilateral with a pair of sides equal.
- A quadrilateral with a pair of sides equal and a pair of sides parallel.
- A quadrilateral with a pair of sides equal and a pair of sides parallel and a pair of opposite angles that are equal.

Now go back and check that, at each stage, your example would not satisfy the next constraint. If necessary, produce a new example that does not fit the next constraint.

The intention is to prompt people into awareness of geometrical properties as constraints on freedom of choice and to encourage them to have a range of images available when someone says "quadrilateral." This pattern of questioning conflicts with a tendency to offer rather particular examples. In every group with whom we have done this task, many have started with a rectangle and stuck with it for the entire first sequence of requests. Often, undoing self-imposed restraints for the last part of the task proves to be quite hard. We can be blinded to other possibilities by the dominance of one image. The task reinforces familiarity with different objects and the properties that distinguish them, so that in the future more examples might come to mind from which to choose.

Bernita's Practice

First-year undergraduate mathematics learners were reminded of the theorem that a continuous function on a closed interval takes on its extreme values. Then, for each condition in the theorem, they were asked to construct an example that satisfied all but that condition and to show that the conclusion then fails. The idea was to get learners to focus on the necessary conditions for the theorem so that they knew why they were there; they did not just learn the theorem statements by rote. This exercise revealed that several learners did not see *continuous* as a condition. It was an integral part of their concept of *function*. Then they were asked to provide a discontinuous function that satisfied all the other conditions and did not attain its extreme values. The exercise also led learners to explore whether all discontinuous functions fail the theorem and, hence, to try to characterize a more general class of functions satisfying the conclusion of the theorem. It is common experience that learners are so eager to apply a theorem that they do not bother to check all of the conditions. Constructing their own examples engaged learners in making sense of the import of the theorem and the significance of the conditions.

Summarizing the Tasks and Their Underlying Beliefs and Purposes

What do these stories tell us? When observing classrooms and listening to reports from teachers, it is impossible to avoid getting caught up in comparing what is said and done to the norms of other classrooms. What we have tried to do is focus only on the exemplification task together with the teachers' intentions and learners' actions associated with it, when known. In this way, we are able to offer a collection of beliefs and purposes for which asking learners to generate examples might provide a useful pedagogical practice. Before you read our summary you may like to look back and decide what you think the teachers might have achieved in each case and what implicit theories of learning mathematics might be demonstrated by these practices.

Sarah asked learners to create their own practice examples and self-check their solutions. This was motivating for the learners who responded well and revealed to the teacher something about what they thought was the purpose of the task. Making up examples that need particular techniques to solve them can focus learners on the mathematical structures that relate to those techniques.

Ed asked learners explicitly to make up equations to hide a value of x, which they already knew, with the aim of helping them understand the rationale for the technique they would use to solve such equations in future. We noted that understanding does not guarantee fluency or recall of technique.

Linda allowed learners to decide what to add and subtract from a pile of tens blocks and units blocks. She intervened to encourage students to make more adventurous moves. We noted that some learners followed patterns, whereas others were prepared to disrupt these patterns and work with deeper structures—at least when encouraged.

Jeff believed that by letting learners design and evaluate their own notations they would be better able to accept and understand the conventional notation of graphs.

Farah's learners showed that by sharing different examples of multiplication using distributivity, with the teacher praising certain types, they could become more creative with their ideas.

When John and Anne asked people to construct quadrilaterals, many start with a rectangle. Thus, they become perplexed by the further constraints, at least until they meet the requirement that their examples cannot all be the same, at which point they start using more general quadrilaterals. They become aware of a wider class of general quadrilaterals than they first thought.

Bob and Bernita asked learners to find examples of objects that have, in their opinions, unexpected properties. Often learners' expectations of properties are based on a limited range of possibilities or a limited range of experiences.

In all of these stories, the generation of examples of questions, techniques, actions, notations, and mathematical objects by learners provides the material for the lesson. In some, the act of creating the example seems to involve construction or extension of meaning; in others, reflection on a range of examples seems to affect cognition. In all of them, there is sense of a range of possibilities being explored; a general structure or "truth" that lies behind the examples produced. Furthermore, these stories encompass all ages and so-called abilities of learners. Each teacher believed that learners are able to exemplify for themselves and that to do so contributes to their learning.

Our aim as educators is to maintain a principal focus on the development of mathematical thinking, rather than acquisition of facts or algorithms. If learners are used to thinking mathematically and choose to do so for themselves instead of being dependent on authorities, they will learn mathematics more easily and more effectively because they will have developed a structured understanding of the subject and a network of meanings through which new experiences can be perceived and into which they can be assimilated.

This is not as far-fetched as it may sound at first. Although there are few descriptions of such learning in the literature because most teachers and curricula are bound by a fragmentary knowledge-based approach to the subject, there are some notable examples. Jo Boaler (1997, 2002) compared data from two secondary schools that had similar socioeconomic status and very different mathematics curricula. She found that the learners at one of the schools found learning mathematics and tackling unfamiliar examination questions easier than at a more traditional school because they had learned all their mathematics in a problem-solving, investigative, and meaning-making way. There is also evidence that those who approach the subject, whether it is explicitly taught or encountered through other activity, as an arena for meaning-making learn it more successfully (see, e.g., Dahlberg & Housman, 1997; Ginsburg, 2002; Krutetskii, 1976; Maher, 2002; Schoenfeld, 2002).

LEARNERS USING EXAMPLES, COUNTEREXAMPLES, AND EXTREME EXAMPLES

The classroom accounts so far have all been teacher initiated. Would learners exemplify for themselves even when not prompted by a teacher? We have observed that exemplification, one feature of mathematical thinking, can arise spontaneously from learners in learning environments of various kinds and that this practice is certainly not confined to the cleverest mathematicians. This is illustrated in the following classroom accounts.

Story 1

Two learners in a class were given eight questions to rehearse the distributive rule with numbers before stating it algebraically. They answered the questions quite quickly, talked about them, and started inventing their own questions using much larger numbers than the teacher had provided. They said that they were doing this to make it harder for themselves and to show "that it always worked." Asked what "it" was, they responded that they had developed a conjecture about the structure (a correct one, as it happens) and saw themselves as testing and demonstrating it with difficult numbers.

Story 2

A class of 14-year-olds who had been placed in a low-achievement group were asked to make posters showing what they had learned about Pythagoras' theorem. It was a hot Friday afternoon on the day when England (where this story takes place) had been eliminated from the World

Cup, so teachers were expecting disaffected behavior. Nearly all of the learners chose to do this using self-generated examples. A group of four learners cut out right-angled triangles from paper to stick onto the poster. They decided to measure the sides and "do Pythagoras." Of course the sides turned out to have lengths that involved one or two decimal places and approximations but they persevered, stating "we decided to do it, but we got stuck, but we had to finish it." While doing the calculations there were useful discussions about "nasty" numbers and what happens when you square them and round them. In another part of the room two learners drew isosceles triangles to demonstrate how you could find the height using Pythagoras' theorem. There was discussion about whether, if you knew the base, the height was always the same. One learner claimed it was, but the other countered this by offering two alternatives, one short and one tall, to demonstrate that heights could vary. All learners in this class were deeply engaged with the task and reluctant to stop at the end of the day.

Story 3

A 14-year-old, Indira, had been taken out of her low-achievement class to work with a support teacher. The rest of the class was working on 20 quick questions at the start of the lesson, and the support teacher had decided to go through the same questions with Indira and discuss each answer with her. One of the questions was:

Task 10: What is a . . . ?

What is a prime number?

We have posed this as a question for you, because, in the context of exemplification, you might like to think how you would answer it. You could choose to define the term or exemplify it.

Indira chose to answer it by giving 11 as an example. The teacher asked "why is 11 prime?" Indira thought for a while and then said: "Well, 6 is not a prime number because it is 2 times 3, and 12 is not prime because it is 4 times 3." She had tried to answer by exemplification and realized that giving examples of what is not a prime might be more effective than trying to describe the characteristics of a prime. Creating examples and counterexamples for the purposes of explanation seemed like a sensible approach to her.

Of course, the teacher could have pushed her further and asked "is a prime number one that is not 'times 3?' " but instead accepted the answer as evidence of Indira's understanding. For us, it is evidence that exemplification and counterexemplification might be natural ways for learners to argue and explain; hence, the task type illustrated here might be useful in many mathematical settings. We have seen learners who were asked "what is a point of inflexion?" respond by generating a mixture of exemplification and counterexemplification.

Story 4

While running workshops in Colombia in South America, John was taken to a small village to sample a particular fruit indigenous to the area. In the huge main plaza that seemed entirely deserted, there was one little shop where the fruit could be obtained. Outside two little girls of about 9 or 10 years old were playing with cards. On closer inspection, they were found to be writing questions on the cards and giggling about the answers they were putting on the back. The questions were all mathematical! One would write a question and then challenge the other to answer it. Questions included: What is .00000000000000000345 in scientific notation? What is the use of scientific notation? What is the theorem of Pythagoras?

In addition they had a stack of blank cards which they said were for interesting questions when they arose. The activity had all the hallmarks of a spontaneous game devised by the children themselves. This would be a wonderful way to review mathematics lessons.

Story 5

A student teacher, Fiona, was teaching reflective symmetry and had decided to start the lesson by offering an example and asking learners to say how they would tackle it. The lesson was observed by the usual teacher, Jean. Fiona drew the diagram on the left on a chalkboard with a background grid and asked learners to tell her what to do.

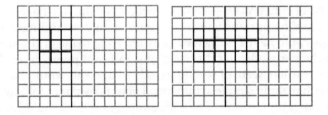

Fairly quickly, learners told her what to draw, and she produced the finished diagram as shown on the right. She then asked "how did you decide this was the right answer?" and received a reply from Student A "I count the squares beside the line and then make sure I have the same number on the other side."

Almost immediately, Student B called out "but that won't necessarily work, that isn't helpful. Can I show them?" He was given the chalk and drew the following diagram, indicating by tapping on the board that he had drawn nine squares.

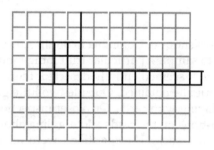

Fiona thanked him and then asked for explanations that would account for shape as well as size.

Student B had spontaneously used counterexemplification to demonstrate that Student A's explanation was incomplete. Jean commented afterward that she had been pleased to see this because she explicitly encouraged learners to give their own examples and join in discussion. This spontaneous use of counterexemplification showed that, at least for some, the habit was becoming part of their normal behavior in a mathematics classroom; thus, even with a different teacher, it was a strategy that some learners thought to use.

But there is more than this to be gleaned from the story. The incident reveals the paucity of Fiona's original example. The shape was very simple, the mirror line was vertical, and the shape could have been reflected by construing reflection as having something to do with doubling. Also, the learners had squared paper, so the reflection could have been achieved in a variety of other ways—some of which would not have been about square counting or translating. Even with an understanding of reflection, the shape could have been achieved by referring to the grid squares rather than to the perpendicular distances of significant points from the mirror line. The learners were of secondary school age and would have been familiar with making simple symmetrical objects by paper folding for many years. Fiona's philosophy of offering simple examples could lead to learners having the kind of impoverished experience of reflection that leads to problems when the mirror line is not parallel to the edge of the page, the shape is not regular, and so on. Her habit of welcoming learners' ideas and thanking them without comment may, without Student B's interven-

tion, have led to Student A continuing to think that her way of understanding the task was as valid as any other.

This story shows that, with the right encouragement, exemplification
and counterexemplification might become habits in classrooms even
when the usual teacher is not in charge, but it also illustrates what can go
wrong with teachers' choices of examples. We could tell a similar story
about use of $10\% = \frac{1}{10}$ used as an example for converting fractions to decimals and the consequent belief that $13\% = \frac{1}{13}$.

Story 6

Some student teachers with mathematics degrees but no background in
formal geometry were asked: Are there any relationships between any of
the lines in the following diagram, and if so, what form do the relationships take?

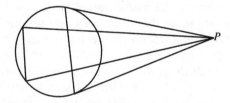

The two lines from P that looked like tangents are, in fact, tangents, but
the two almost parallel chords are not, in fact, parallel!

The aims were to get them to experience geometrical reasoning in an ill-
defined situation, think about what flawed reasoning could arise from a
learner's interpretation of a teacher's diagram, and think about the assumptions a learner makes. Most of them drew diagrams that imitated the
given one with two nearly parallel chords. This led them, as the teacher
had expected, to speculate incorrectly about relating angles and parallel
lines, similar triangles, and so on. Many conjectures about ratios were
generated.

One student then produced an extreme example of the diagram in
which P is on the circle, thus effectively showing that there were no relationships of the general kind that they were seeking, namely equal ratios,
arising from similar triangles. The only invariant relationships are the
equality of tangents to a circle from a point and the tangent–secant relationship.[5] There were some doubts voiced about the role of this diagram
and whether it was permissible to move P until it is on the circle.

---

[5]The square of the tangent is the product of the segments from P to the circle.

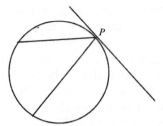

We were struck by the power displayed here of using an extreme example to explore geometric relationships. Surface features can lead to false conjectures; extreme examples can expose these. One way to find interesting examples is to push given variables to extreme positions. On the other hand, extreme examples can be too simple; in this case, many of the features of the problem were lost. This extreme example could have been an example of many other geometric situations. But we were also struck by how most of the learners, all mathematics graduates, seemed unable or unwilling to draw anything that did not closely resemble what they had already been shown. Being stuck with one image can be so misleading and result in incorrect proofs. There are similarities with the earlier example of John's and Anne's practice in which people stuck with one rectangle when asked to draw quadrilaterals with various characteristics. The use of construction tasks to prompt learners to go beyond their first constrained thoughts is a major theme in the unfolding story of this book.

INITIAL THEORIZING: SHIFTING RESPONSIBILITY

It is widely accepted that encouraging learners to take responsibility for aspects of their work has positive effects on learning and motivation. Usually this is discussed in terms of organizing work, choosing what to do and how to do it, self-assessment (e.g., Bell & Swan, 1995; van den Heuvel-Panhuizen, Middleton, & Streefland, 1995), problem posing (e.g., S. Brown & Walter, 1983; Cudmore & English, 1998; Ellerton, 1986; Stoyanova, 1998; Winograd, 1997), raising workable questions (e.g., Streefland & van den Heuvel-Panhuizen, 1992), developing metacognitive awareness (e.g., Flavell, 1979; Garofalo & Lester, 1985; Pimm, 1994), and so on. Among these ideas is the somewhat woolly notion of helping learners gain ownership of their mathematics. Because mathematics is an agreed system of symbolic representations of abstract relationships, often manifested by manipulations that can be ascribed values such as right and wrong, it is hard to see what *ownership* might mean. How can I own mathematics if what I write down as a result of my cogitations can be rejected by the teacher or examiner? However, if learners are being asked to bring their own experience to bear on the lesson, to search their experience mathematically, and to be creative with what they find, then they are more likely to achieve the kind of mental empowerment that good mathematics learners seem to have intuitively.

We strongly agree with Dewey (1943) who said:

> The pupil [should] have a genuine situation of experience—that there be a continuous activity in which he is interested for its own sake . . . that a genuine problem develop within this situation as a stimulus to thought . . . that he [sic] possess the information and make observations needed to deal with it . . . that suggested solutions occur to him which he shall be responsible for in an orderly way . . . he have opportunity and occasion to test his ideas by application, to make their meaning clear and to discover for himself their validity. (pp. 190–191)

Our interpretation differs from some because we see all these activities as possible within mathematics itself, in a world of abstract structures, rather than merely in real applications. When we learn something we develop a structure, a schema, which relates the current topic to other knowledge we have (Skemp, 1969). The way this structure develops is personal, because our interactions with the world and with others (with text and with teachers) are personal. Therefore, it helps us reflect on our learning to get a sense of how our knowledge is structured or how it might be structured. In doing so, we look at knowledge from a different point of view, perhaps trying to link events into a story or asking new kinds of question.

Reflection is also a mathematical term that is used for reflection in a point, line, plane, and so on. But to effect a mathematical reflection physically (as a rotation), it is necessary to move through an extra dimension: You need two dimensions to reflect a point in a point as a rotation about that point, three dimensions to reflect a point in a line as a rotation about that line, and four dimensions to reflect a point in a plane as a rotation about that plane. Using this mathematical fact about reflection provides a useful metaphor for psychological reflection, which requires "moving into another dimension" from the current activity, to get an overview of what has been experienced and how it links with other experiences.

Our theory is that asking learners to exemplify aspects of what they have studied encourages them to search through the structure from varying points of view, using a new dimension, and hence see, perhaps for the first time, what might be there by discerning features and aspects. Thus, learners might find that being asked to exemplify gives them an opportunity to search in unfamiliar ways through what is familiar to get a more complex sense of the range of possibilities in the topics studied.

SUMMARY

We have offered numerous examples of classroom practice in which teachers have invited learners to construct their own examples, suggesting at least that it is possible to do this and even that it can be effective pedagogically. We have also offered some accounts in which learners spontaneously constructed examples for practice, contradicting a conjecture, and understanding through taking extreme cases. All of these ideas will be developed in later chapters. We suggest that the use of examples in these ways is entirely natural, but underused in mathematics lessons, and that learning is greatly enhanced when learners are stimulated to construct their own examples. Indeed, we could go so far as to say that until you can construct your own examples, both generic and extreme, you do not fully appreciate a concept.

In the next chapter we probe more deeply into the experience of constructing examples before we look at the structure of emerging spaces of examples in chapter 4.

From Examples to Example Spaces

In this chapter we move from individual examples to the space of examples triggered in a learner. In the process we aim to describe some of the features of what it is like to construct an example of something. We begin by asking you to reflect on this for yourself and to engage in some tasks that we have found effective when offered to various groups of learners and colleagues. We use their reports to locate and elaborate significant aspects of example construction. In particular we find that examples are interconnected and can be perceived as members of structured "spaces," and we begin to explore what those structures might be like.

Before you read this chapter you may like to draw on your experience of the tasks in chapter 2 to describe what finding examples is like for you. Your experiences of example creation may vary according to the kind of prompt you used or your familiarity with the topic. Responses to tasks so far may easily have had emotional as well as intellectual aspects. It is often useful to try to crystallize experience in one or more metaphors or similes, as in the next task.

Task 11: What Is It Like to . . . ?

What comes to mind as you complete these phrases?
 Finding an example of something I already know about is like . . .
 Creating an example to fit someone else's rules is like . . .

People have told us that finding an example of "something I already know" is like:

Choosing what to wear	Greeting a friend	Recognizing a tune
Reorganizing the larder[6]	Putting loose socks in pairs, with none missing	Saying something that seems obvious while fearing it might be silly

Creating an example to fit someone else's rules is like:

Putting on a jacket and finding the sleeves sewn up	Giving a present and needing to know if it is appreciated	Not having the right size drill and having to improvise instead
Getting started in a cryptic crossword	Going into the dark with a torch but no battery	

We offer these sample responses to stimulate you to go beyond your first thought and to offer some surprises that you might, on reflection, find appropriate to your own experiences. These responses reveal a range of issues about confidence, emotion, knowledge, and familiarity (as well as insight into other people's lives). We focus on intellectual and conceptual features, although we recognize that "the feeling of what happens" (Damasio, 1999) is often a significant influence on classroom activity.

A DIFFERENCE OF 2

Try this before reading further:

Task 12a: Difference of 2

Imagine asking your students to write down two numbers whose difference is 2.
What do you suppose they would do?

---

[6]Equivalent words might be *food cupboard* or *pantry*.

Of course your answer depends on the kind of learners you are teaching, the relationship you have with them, and whether this is a new kind of question for them. Or does it? At first glance, you may think this task is only suitable for very young children. They may visualize numbers on a line and think about making jumps of 2 units. They may think of a number track and a "train" 2 units in length going along it and stopping at various places. Where can it stop? Is it allowed to stop between whole numbers; if so, what are the two numbers they have to write down? And, is it important which number is written down first? When we asked a group of mathematics teacher–educators to do this, some wrote the smaller number first, perhaps thinking their way along the number line, and others wrote the larger first, perhaps thinking of subtraction. This task could raise the question of whether one can have positive and negative differences.

Now do this task yourself, step by step:

Task 12b: Difference of 2 Again

Write down two numbers that have a difference of 2.
Now write down another pair.
Now write down another pair.

You can probably see that this task may trigger several different ways of thinking; it can generate several different kinds of answers in a classroom. Some choose two smaller whole numbers; others may choose bigger numbers. Depending on their previous experience in mathematics, some may include simple fractions or decimals in their suggestions. Would any have bridged zero and included some negative numbers?

Not all learners will use an image of a number line to generate their first answers. They may have had other images—perhaps sets of objects to be counted, mental pictures of some written mathematics, or 10-by-10 number grids, and so on. Their past experience will have given them some dominant images to which they automatically refer and that limit other choices they can make.

Here are some responses that illustrate how different people responded to the same task.

7, 9	6, 8	198, 196	"The first two were boring, so I chose a 'harder' pair the third time."
6, 8	14, 16	39, 41	"I wanted to jump over a 10 on the number line."

5, 7	28, 30	17.5, 19.5
2.653, 4.653	$-8\frac{1}{3}$, $-10\frac{1}{3}$	

Here the task had been extended (this person continued writing until we stopped her) to see how many different kinds of interesting answer could be produced. We see her as demonstrating confidence in a variety of forms of number.

17, 19	11, 13	3, 5

"I wanted to stick to prime pairs." (By severely limiting the range of change, an area of number theory is addressed.)

401, 399	100_2, 10_2
2×9, 2×8	

This last person wrote the larger number first because that is the order in which the numbers appear in a subtraction sum; then, he went on to give answers from as many areas of mathematics as he could. Later, he also responded "11 and 1" on a clock face as two numbers whose difference is 2 hr, or should he have said "1 and 11"? He worked well beyond the boundaries of the number line.

The psycho-emotional nature of the responses is typical.[7] Learners turn the very open task into something that is meaningful for them and provides areas for further exploration. They also challenge themselves to some degree, and when offered a similarly structured task in the future, they tend to respond more playfully and creatively. Thus, an apparently simple task becomes a field for rich mathematical activity. The richness is not in the task; it is in the range of response from the learners.

Task 12c: Least Obvious Difference of 2

Write down two numbers that differ by 2, but for which the fact that the difference is 2 is as obscure as possible.

We have been offered pairs such as −1 and 1, and 999 and 1001, illustrating that because of the base 10 number notation, there are some pairs

---

[7]Hazzan and Zazkis (1997) also noted affective factors: "Students exhibit and acknowledge emotional difficulty to deal with degrees of freedom" (p. 4-305). Their students used a range of strategies to construct examples of random or informed trial-and-error, of algorithmic approaches or creation of algorithms by adapting a known one, of finding trivial examples that avoid conceptual challenge, and of constructing objects from principles. The last of these created most need for reassurance.

that may seem less obvious than others to learners who have not yet achieved full facility with arithmetic.

Although we have been discussing outcomes, you probably have been thinking about the generalities that could be developed from the examples. One of the principal effects of tasks like this is that they open up learners' minds not just to more playful and extreme possibilities, but to awareness of a whole, usually infinite class of possibilities from which to choose. This marks a significant development from being grateful for one answer coming to mind when asked a question by the teacher!

Task 12d: Difference of 2 Generalized

Describe the class of all pairs that have a difference of 2.

It would not be a huge leap for learners to say "I could write down any number for one of the pair, and add 2 to it to get the other number." This prealgebraic statement can be readily symbolized, using symbols chosen by the learner to stand for "any number." Are there any other ways to find the second number? You could, for example, subtract 2 instead of adding, and learners can be asked to invent a notation for symbolizing "any number, add or subtract 2."

Here are some responses:

- The number and the number plus 2.
- The number and the number minus 2.
- $[x, x + 2]$
- $[a, b]$ where $a - b = 2$
- $[x - 1, x + 1]$

Such attempts at generalization can be discussed as a whole class. Are all cases included? Do learners think the symbolization makes sense and expresses what they know?

Note that some people will respond with a description of the class when asked for more than one example, and some may imagine they have finished the task. However, rapid generalization can block experience of the possible range of examples.

Varying the Task

A slight change of task leads to this variation:

Task 12e: Fractional Difference

The difference is $1\frac{1}{2}$; one of the numbers is $2\frac{1}{3}$. What could the other number be?

What is the relationship between the $1\frac{1}{2}$, the $2\frac{1}{3}$, and the other numbers?

In this version of the task the arithmetic is much less open, as there are only two answers, but the interpretation of the relationship is open. Note that you have experienced a shift from an extremely open and unconstrained task (*Task 12a: Difference of 2*) to an increasingly constrained task (as in *Task 12e*). By experiencing movement from the more free to the more constrained, learners have access to a residual sense of the contrast between the original freedom of choice and the effect of adding further constraints, which is an important theme throughout mathematics.

Here are some descriptions of responses we have received:

- $2\frac{1}{3}$ is the mean value of the two possible answers.
- $2\frac{1}{3}$ is the midpoint of the two possible answers.
- The difference between the two possible answers is 3, which is twice $1\frac{1}{2}$.
- I saw mine as manipulating fraction cakes, seeing an image on a poster we had in school inside my head.
- It's a symmetry.
- You can jump each side of $2\frac{1}{3}$.
- Once I had $\frac{5}{6}$, I saw immediately the other was $3\frac{5}{6}$.

Notice the amount of work you have to do to understand, to "see," what different people report. By working on these tasks we extend our knowledge of possible articulations and ways of seeing. Specifically, sharing these different descriptions could allow people to relate the graphical idea of "midpoint" to the arithmetical idea of "mean" and to the spatial idea of symmetry. Different ways of visualizing the task enable learners to make links between different areas of mathematics and different representations of the same mathematical structure. Notice also that the traditional core image of a fractions "cake" does not relate easily to the other representations in this context. The task is naturally extended by asking whether there is anything special about the numbers $1\frac{1}{2}$ and $2\frac{1}{3}$.

Some people try to make the task more constrained for themselves to create further challenges: "I tried to find something which kept the three values together—trying to find a new system"; "I changed the difference to negative 2." We have noticed this desire to create personal challenges frequently, and this kind of task makes it easy to do so. Elizabeth Oldham, doing a similar task in a workshop with us (personal communication, July 2002), commented that she deliberately chose between the "obvious and the odd."

Perhaps *Task 12a: Difference of 2* is not a task that you would think of giving to advanced learners, but we were pleasantly surprised when someone offered us 11_2 and 1_2 as numbers differing by 2. This led us to muse on how learners might be indirectly prompted to think of two complex numbers whose difference is 2 or to decide that difference could mean "distance"; thus, they could think in terms of magnitude or modulus. Where would all the complex numbers be whose distance from a fixed number is 2? Could both numbers be irrational? Could one be rational and the other irrational? How could I find vectors whose difference in magnitude from a given vector is 2? What about two functions for which the integral of their difference over a given interval is 2? Would it make sense to ask about figures whose areas differ by 2 or perimeters?[8]

Notice how the task is altered when we ask "does this task make sense with higher level concepts?" We have moved away from the real line. In fact, when this task was given to some mathematics undergraduates it was only necessary to wait and wait and wait for them to start asking these kinds of question for themselves. A task that sounded trivial generated some new understandings of vaguely understood concepts. Learners who tried to create examples of integrals used fairly simple functions and tried to generalize the limits while asking deep questions about the meaning of 2 in this context. They suggested trying to construct a dynamic image of an area of 2 for the region between the curves over all intervals of a fixed length. This is a similar idea to younger learners visualizing the difference as a fixed length that moves along the number line.

The activity generated by these prompts has given us insight into the processes of generating one's own examples. We will categorize some factors in example generation after we describe some responses to the next task.

INTER-ROOTAL DISTANCES

A group of experienced mathematicians was asked to describe families of polynomial functions of degree two which had in common the horizontal

---

[8]This reminds us of an activity used frequently in classrooms in which learners find shapes whose areas and perimeters are numerically equal. Asking if area and perimeter differ by 2 makes, of course, no sense because one would have to ask what units are being used. This makes us wonder about the purpose of the common equality task.

distance between their roots; we call this the *inter-rootal distance*. Before we describe what happened we urge you to take some time to think about this to get a personal sense of how to bring to mind, construct, and explore examples of this phenomenon.

Task 13a: Inter-Rootal Distance

We have decided to call the horizontal distance between neighboring roots of a polynomial function the inter-rootal distance.
Imagine a quadratic equation with two real roots. What families of quadratic curves have the same inter-rootal distance?

There are, of course, many kinds of response to this task. For some, the context and the phrase "inter-rootal distance" might be an obstruction; for others, the task may seem trivial; yet others might find it intriguing.[9]

One mathematician, Donald, reported that he first imagined one example and quickly saw that if he translated it he could generate a family of such curves. He then paused, satisfied that he had finished but aware that he ought to be searching for other possibilities. After mulling for a while, he found another way to vary the curve, by stretching it in the *y*-direction, which also preserved the inter-rootal distance. However, finding this second way to generate the curves felt more difficult and rather surprising. There was an "Oh yes!" feeling of realization once it came to mind.

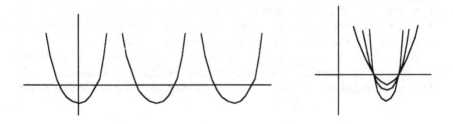

Another mathematician, Neil, whose recent experience of doing mathematics was largely based on work with dynamic geometry software, did not contemplate sideways translations because he saw these as "all the same curve." Of course, he was aware that he could move them sideways,

---

[9]If you found it an obstruction, it may help to think about a bowl-shaped curve going through two fixed points on the *x*-axis and seeing what range of similar curves could go through the same two points. What are the possibilities if you slide the points along the axis but keep the same distance between them?

but he did not see the results as a family. Seeing translations as not altering the curve meant that he focused on other kinds of transformation and, hence, arrived at stretching in the y-direction very readily as a way to generate an exemplary family.

Before considering other responses to this task, we want to look in more detail at Donald and Neil's responses. These will inform some conjectures about exemplification that introduce a language of description that we find useful.

Reflections on Donald and Neil's Responses

Example Creation Is Individual. These two mathematicians, each of them thoroughly familiar and competent with the concepts involved, displayed different ways to search for examples. We suspect that this is because their experiences had created different frames of reference for the concept. For Donald, the positions of both axes were worthy of attention, together with an interaction between the axes and a fixed shape; for Neil, the shape and how it could change were worthy of attention. Of special interest is that the contents of their example spaces may have been similar, but the structuring of them in terms of classification, similarity, and availability was different in this instance.

This may be similar to your response to the earlier task of giving two numbers whose difference is 2. Your answers may well have been limited to numbers used in your recent teaching experience even though you are perfectly capable of using other numbers. In other words, what you have access to at any time is circumscribed by recent experience, among other things.

This exercise was an invitation to think about a different way to structure one's understanding of quadratics. In a sense, Neil was already heading toward such a classification by taking a dynamic geometric approach to the task. Donald, taking a more algebraic approach, may have been less able to reclassify immediately, but he was more able to recognize connections with other features of quadratics. For instance, attention to coefficients highlights the relationship between the inter-rootal distance and the more familiar discriminant. For Donald, varying the shape required a different way of seeing the challenge; for Neil, recognizing the possibility of different axis positions helped him to see his one original shape as an infinite family.

In these two responses we see similar groups of examples being created, uncovered, or "coming to mind" by two different routes, each involving an interplay of algebra and geometry but starting in different places. Why did this happen? Certainly Neil's recent immersion in dynamic imagery could explain where he started, just as Donald's immersion in work with secondary teachers could explain his starting place. But we are wary of saying glibly "it depends on experience" because attraction for a dynamic approach may be an underlying characteristic of Neil's career choices as well as his mathematical choices. All we can say is that examples are structured and accessed differently by different people at different times and in different situations. Being a mathematician includes being able to question one's first response and seek alternatives, searching algebraically, geometrically, and in other ways to find as many examples as one can.

Without this insight, we might assume that it is only a lack of knowledge of possibilities that restricts learners' findings. Instead, we are reminded that flexibility of thinking and being dissatisfied with a single answer lie near the heart of mathematical competence. Looking for alternative ways of thinking about a problem or concept and developing confidence in multiple representations and multiple perspectives is likely to increase one's effectiveness as a mathematician. We are also sensitized not to expect that having an example come to mind in one situation automatically means that the same example will come to mind at another time or in a different situation. Part of the purpose of this chapter is to elaborate on these issues more fully.

There was further evidence from the group that creating examples happens in different ways. People reported having different starting places. Some used peculiar examples. There were different views of the specificity or generality of examples. Some started with algebra, others with geometry, and for some others a sense of infinity played a role. For many the search soon shifted to one of finding examples of operations that change the quadratic but preserve inter-rootal distance as an invariant.

Starting Places. The task began as "imagine a quadratic with two real roots." Both Donald and Neil started with images of curves. We might conjecture that the wording of the challenge led them to this, but not everyone started in that way. Another mathematician said: "The word *root* was fixed for me; everything started from there."

She then constructed quadratics as pairs of factors, $y = k (x - a) (x - b)$, for values of a and b that were 2 units apart. For her, it was the word *root* rather than *curve* that triggered a way to proceed. Her examples, which started off looking algebraic, might have ended up looking like those of Donald and Neil, but initially they were very different and were entered differently. To shift from one to the other would have required working with at least two modes of representation side by side.

In any group, different learners will respond more strongly to different features of the question. For many, a first response had been to draw or imagine a bowl-shaped curve. For this learner, it was the algebraic representation of intersections on an x-axis that was the first object of attention.

Role of Peculiar Examples. Donald reported being stuck for a while, knowing there ought to be more alternatives but not knowing how to find them. Did he know this from his mathematical experience, or was it his suspicion that any question from us would have more to it than appeared at first thought? The circumstances in which questions are asked can certainly influence the search, but how can you get beyond your first thoughts? Being aware there might be more to find is the first step. One mathematician said: "I needed to think of a peculiar example to get out of being stuck and into another range of possibilities." There is a symbiosis between examples and classes, with each new example indicating a possible new subclass. But how do learners first find peculiar examples without having a sense of the class that is to be exemplified?

Task 13b: Inter-Rootal Distance Constrained

Find three different examples of quadratics whose roots are 1 and 2.

Notice how the wording of this request constrains the search. By giving less freedom and by fixing some aspects of the search, the teacher is also indicating that it is possible to vary some other features of the curve. What constitutes *different*? This is an extremely productive mathematical question, and the answer usually changes during the exploration, as what seemed to be new at one stage is next incorporated into new categories subsuming previous ones.

The pedagogical prompt "Find me an example of . . . such that . . ." can indicate a new subclass as a possibility. Learners who are used to looking for what can be varied will search actively for the freedom they are given in the prompt. Those who are used to being given exact instructions may not be able to decide what to do.

Of course, once we know we can vary the curve by stretching it in the y direction the word *peculiar* no longer applies. The class of quadratics we have found is very familiar. The use of the word *peculiar* by this mathematician indicates the restrictions she was unintentionally imposing on herself. It tells us something about the extent and structure of the space from which she can pull out appropriate examples.

Why did we ask for three examples, one after another? The main reason is to force the learner beyond the realization that suitable quadratics exist in pairs by reflecting in the x-axis. If we had only asked for two examples, some learners may have only ended up with one very simple example, such as $y = (x - 1)(x - 3)$, and its reflected partner. In chapter 5 we develop further the pedagogical role of asking for multiple examples, one after another.

Did you think about reflections? Of course, if the aim is to get learners to think about the reflections, we could further restrict the earlier request:

Task 13c: Inter-Rootal Distance Further Constrained

Find a quadratic whose roots are 1 and 3 and whose x^2 coefficient is ±1.

This prompt is much more specific than the others. In fact there are only two answers. It is, to use Liz Bills' (1996) words, a request for *particular* examples, and it indicates a possible link between finding examples and answering closed questions. There is an important sense in which every statement beginning with *find* is a request for construction of an example, even if it is intended that the learner use a well-rehearsed technique for carrying out that construction. (We shall have more to say about this in chap. 5.) But inserting parameters and expressing constraints in terms of them is a rather mechanical approach. We are not denying its power, but such a method is unlikely to lead to the creation of wildly exciting, hitherto unknown mathematical objects.

In this commentary we use peculiar to mean unfamiliar, unexpected—an example that does not fit with what I already know—and a nonintuitive response to the task. Bills also uses peculiar in this way. But *peculiar* examples, according to this definition, cannot be so strange as to be unconnected with anything that is already known. Rather, the aim of working with peculiar examples is that they could become familiar and easily available for future use. Further, they push learners to extend the range of permissible change in various dimensions of possible variation of which they are aware. For example, when thinking about inter-rootal distance as a dimension of variation, the values 0 or i may initially appear to be peculiar,[10] but eventually they can be seen as extensions of the range of change that the learner sees as permissible. Similarly, the fraction $\frac{1}{1}$ seems peculiar the first time it is encountered, but it is necessary to "fill out" all the fractions as numbers.

A significant force of asking for peculiar examples is to shift from seeking any isolated particular example that will fit to becoming aware of the choice and particularly the range of such choices. This can serve as a pre-

---

[10]For i read the imaginary number, the square root of minus one, $\sqrt{-1}$.

lude to appreciating the entire family of examples meeting the conditions, which might even be expressed algebraically as a generality.

A more colloquial meaning of *peculiar* is something that is odd, does not seem to fit any expected frame, and can be relied on to act in unexpected ways. In this sense a peculiar example could be one that acts so strangely that it embeds itself rapidly into the memory and might be dragged out in future when strange behavior is required.

For example:

Task 14: Large Interior Angle

Can you create a quadrilateral with an interior angle greater than 180°?
Is it possible to create a quadrilateral with two interior angles greater than 180°?

Perhaps the wording of this task makes you suspicious, because previously we have simply asked for examples and not whether it was possible. Some teachers think it is important that learners encounter tasks that are impossible to develop their inner criteria rather than simply making assumptions about the kind of tasks their teacher will pose.

In *Task 14* there was no example available. You had to start from scratch. A classic problem-solving heuristic[11] is to work backward as well as forward. You may have noticed yourself using this technique, even alternating between forward and backward. Tasks like this can be useful for bringing heuristics to the surface and labeling them to make them more likely to be used by learners in the future.

The second question was decidedly odd: But how did you justify your answer? Can you imagine learners trying to find such a polygon? Did you find yourself beginning to wonder what *interior angle* means in the context of nonconvex polygons?

Generic or Specific.   One of the comments from the group of mathematicians was "I used generic sketches on paper and in my mind, but for the equation I felt I had to 'go specific.'" Images are perhaps more inherently general than symbols, although not for all learners at all times. De Morgan (1831/1898) commented that in geometry reasoning is commonly applied to one example, whereas in algebra it is a mixture of general and particular statements (p. 192). The safety of reasoning on one case, wheth-

---

[11]Other heuristics can be found in Polya (1957), Schoenfeld (1985), and Mason, Burton, and Stacey (1982).

er in geometry or algebra, depends on seeing the particular case as a generic one, which requires awareness of what is permitted to change and what is not. Features in spatial images are often taken as general features. Dynamic images help us explore what changes and what stays the same as we change the shape in certain ways. One thing that has been learned from dynamic geometry software is that single diagrams on a page have an implicit hidden structure (what can be changed and what has to remain in the same relationship) and implicit order (which objects are constructed first and which are based on previously constructed objects). For an expert, a single diagram speaks of a whole space of diagrams, the single diagram is generic; for a novice, each diagram is particular until the novice has been shown how to look *through* a diagram generatively rather than just looking *at* it.

The mathematicians in this activity had a choice (whether they used it with awareness or not) of working in spatial or symbolic form or a mixture. To work in symbolic form, we have to think about whether a feature is general or not and to represent it so that it can be changed or not, as appropriate. In each approach there is the need to make small changes and see what stays the same. In geometry we can then describe constant features of the shape; in algebra we can reduce the representation of variables and parameters to its most efficient form and symbolize their relationships.

A very elementary example of the interplay between generic and specific examples can be found using apparatus such as Cuisenaire rods.

If two rods are placed as a train and a single rod is selected of the same length, then removal (subtraction) of either of the original two lengths leaves the other behind. From this come multiple perspectives (addition and subtraction are related to each other) and multiple sentences for the same situation. If this relationship is always the case and not just for these particular rods, then we can symbolize the relationship in such a way that any pair of rods can be used. Interestingly, one choice of symbolic representation is to give instructions in words, as we just did.

But why did this respondent to the inter-rootal task feel that to use algebra required specificity? After all, algebra is the language of generalization. What seems to be being expressed here is the duality of algebra. Algebraic expressions can be constructed by substituting letters for numbers in specific cases—an inductive process—but can also be developed by expressing a structure that is already known in some other form—a deductive or expressive process. This mathematician may have been following the second route. When we gave the same prompts to a group of secondary teachers whose pedagogical tradition with quadratics was to draw curves through points plotted from equations (using shape merely as a means to check the calculations), not only were they very stuck to find any examples, but when they did so their generalizations were of the inductive kind. In other words, they needed to generate, share, and inspect several examples before focusing on what relevant features were the same in each of them.

We deduce that whether an example is seen as a special case, a generic model for other cases, or a generalization depends on the learner, the situation, and the representation. When learners construct examples for themselves they know what mathematical role is being played, although a teacher can suggest shifts in that role. When a teacher offers an example, do the learners always know what role and status it is supposed to play? If prompted by the teacher to become aware of their choices, they become aware of the class of objects from which they have chosen a single example. The example is then experienced as being exemplary because they have made their own choice.

This might be another place to pause and consider for yourself the role that examples have played for you, conceptually, in this and the preceding chapter. Probably the role has been quite complex, depending not only on your mathematical knowledge but also on whether you acted as a knowledgeable mathematician, a teacher, a researcher, or a learner with respect to each task.

Algebra or Geometry.   Some respondents wanted their equations to focus on inter-rootal distance; thus, the structure of the algebra brought $(a - b)$ immediately to attention, where a and b are the roots. This search led some to the realization that inter-rootal distance is basically the square root of the discriminant[12] divided by the coefficient of x^2. People who are familiar with quadratics and have recent teaching experience with them might have known this immediately. However, if they only knew an algebraic derivation of the discriminant (possibly from "completing the square"), the connection could easily be a surprise. One person said: "I knew I needed to write an equation in a form that connected the algebra with what I wanted to see. Different forms of the equation lead to different generalizations." We took this desire to express the main feature of the question algebraically to be an indication of the mathematical sophistication of the group. It is a beautiful, yet complex, instance of expressing structure with algebra, with the added challenge of trying to relate the expression of the inter-rootal distance with more well-known forms of

---

[12]The discriminant of the quadratic function $ax^2 + bx + c$ is $b^2 - 4ac$, which must be nonnegative for the function to have real roots.

quadratics. In other circumstances a task could be set asking learners to transform the expression for a quadratic function so that the inter-rootal distance was obvious. You may like to ponder on the different experiences of those who used expressions such as $ax^2 + bx + c$ and $k(x - a)(x - a + d)$ in making the connection. Further ways to connect algebraic and geometric images would be to classify quadratics according to their inter-rootal distances and to ask what inter-rootal distance could possibly mean in cases with complex roots.

The opportunity to express structure is not a rare one in mathematics classrooms. It is around most of the time, although it may not be used by learners or teachers. The common school exercises that require learners to express spatial patterns algebraically can be viewed as rehearsals for the kind of awareness expressed here, but often the formula that learners find is seen as the goal of the task rather than an algebraic model that can be used for more exploration. In the work of Laurinda Brown and Alf Coles (1999, 2000) the need to express mathematical ideas in algebra arises naturally for learners from their own questioning.

By way of contrast, consider the following task, which illustrates a vast range of similar counting tasks:

Task 15: T Shapes

Displayed below are the 2nd and 5th pictures in a sequence. Describe in words a way to make any picture in the sequence.

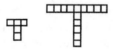

If a single square is made from four toothpicks, how many squares and how many toothpicks are needed to make the 37th picture and the nth picture?

Although the activity has some features of mathematical thinking, in that a generalization has been generated from some examples, it is a rather mechanical exercise. What was the point of expressing this structure? Do we know more mathematics than we did when we started? Do we now have access to some insights that we did not have before? In fact we do, because we can compare several different versions of a general formula for the number of squares needed to make the nth picture. Learners can generate their own formulae, not just the particular cases that led them there. Thus, they can equate:

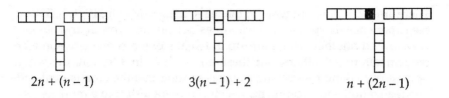

$$2n + (n - 1) \qquad\qquad 3(n - 1) + 2 \qquad\qquad n + (2n - 1)$$

and hence learn some of the rules of algebraic equivalence, the role of brackets, how to multiply, and so on. Learners can also try to construct a way of seeing the T shapes that corresponds to the simplest expression, $3n - 1$.

However, it is hard to think of further uses for this structure in its own right as a mathematical object that might enable us to develop more complex understandings. Working with structure does not necessarily lead to higher mathematics.

Sense of Infinity.   There were some responses to the inter-rootal distance task that shed light on the power of prompts to evoke mathematical wonder: For example, "once I had seen two in the family, I had a sudden sense of infinity." Requests for examples can be used to direct learners toward infinite classes of objects that they have not previously considered. Caleb Gattegno (1984) remarked that mathematics is "man's awareness of its capacity to generate entities shot through with infinity" (p. 20), which we assume means that infinity is always potentially present when there is a generality and that mathematics is concerned with generalization. But the existence of multiple examples is not sufficient in itself to give this sudden sense of potential or actual infinity of generalization. There may have to be some recognizable similarity in the act of creating the examples, as well as similarity in the examples themselves, that provides a doorway to seeing structure rather than detail—a kind of inductive intuition that one could go on and on and on producing examples by varying one aspect or systematically varying more than one aspect.

By contrast, the task of fitting together the 12 different pentomino tiles to make a 6 × 10 rectangle sheds hardly any light on how to make a 4 × 15 rectangle, much less on other tiling problems.

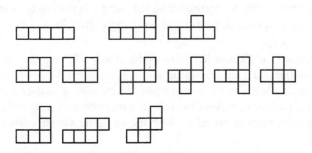

There are 3,719 different ways to make rectangles (Martin, 1991, p. 57), yet the experience of finding one way does not prepare you in any obvious way to find another. There are small tweaks one can make to some arrangements to get others, but these are ad hoc. In addition, the whole process of making the rectangles takes so long that the emotions of sudden realization and excitement, which can mark a shift to a more general level of awareness of structure (if there is such a generality to be had), are unlikely to be sustained. The fitting together of pentomino tiles does not offer obvious possible infinities of ways of tiling rectangles to experience and describe, although the rectangles themselves could then be used to tile the plane. The task, if completed, might be seen as that of a collector, not a mathematician, at least in Gattegno's terms.

Contrast this to *Task 14: Large Interior Angles*, which is about quadrilaterals. The second question is in some sense finite, because the kinds of possible quadrilaterals are very limited and could therefore be considered nonmathematical, yet the idea on which it is based can be extended infinitely by considering all polygons. Infinity might be glimpsed not in a sudden gestalt of solution, but in a painstaking application to more polygons with more and more sides to get a sense of what is possible. The dimension of possible variation here is the number of sides, which is effectively infinite, whereas the number of possible reflex angles for each case is finite.

Emerging Mathematical Themes

Several major themes of mathematical thinking emerged spontaneously from the exemplification experiences of these groups. Here are some brief observations arising from the reports and remarks made so far, which will be elaborated in the next section.

Exemplification Is Individual and Situational. Exemplification is dependent on the knowledge, multiplicity of experience, and predisposition of the learner, but it is also framed by the wording of the prompt, who is making it, and under what circumstances; different learners may respond with different examples in the same learning environment, and the same learner may respond differently in different situations.

Perceptions of Generality Are Individual. A request to exemplify may bring to mind a single example or a class of examples or a "flavor" of possible examples. The same example can be seen as either a special case or a representative of a class by different learners in the same learning environment depending on what they see as being variable and how far it could vary.

Examples Can Be Perceived or Experienced as Members of Structured Spaces. Examples are usually not isolated; rather, they are perceived as instances of a class of potential examples. As such they constitute what we call an *example space*. In terms of the observations so far, learners experience access to an example space that emerges in response to the situation, prompts, and propensities. Some aspects may become habitual, whereas others are conditional. Example spaces are not just lists; they have an internal, idiosyncratic structure (in terms of how the members and classes in the space are interrelated), and it is through this structure that examples are produced. Their contents and structures are individual and situational; similarly structured spaces can be accessed in different ways, which is a notable difference being between algebraic or geometric approaches. There are often classical or conventional examples that teachers show learners and that are useful if, and only if, they gain familiarity with them, internalize them, and integrate them into their example space sufficiently that they come to mind in different situations.

Example Spaces Can Be Explored and Extended by the Learner, With or Without External Prompts. These example spaces, which become available to the learner in response to particular prompts, can be explored or extended by searching for situationally peculiar examples as "doorways" to new classes, by being given further constraints to focus on particular characteristics of examples, by changing a closed response into an open response, and by glimpsing the infinite. Of course, standard mathematical heuristics assist in carrying out explorations suggested or stimulated by the kinds of task questions being developed here.

HOW DO THESE THEMES RELATE TO OUR WORK WITH OTHER GROUPS?

We described and commented on the responses of one group in some detail, but we have worked with many groups of educators and students on exemplification, both explicitly and implicitly, in the course of our roles as teachers, researchers, and teacher educators. On the basis of these experiences we can elaborate further on the aforementioned ideas.

Exemplification Is Individual and Situational

When people have told us how they create examples, their descriptions are given in personal terms. However, we are aware that there are often common features about the examples they produce. Try these:

Task 16: Freedom

Draw a hexagon.
Give a convergent sequence of numbers.
Construct a number between 1 and 2 using all the digits from 0 to 9
   once each that is as close to 1.5 as possible.

Partway through chapter 3 in a book with exemplification as a focus
you are probably not just writing down the first thing that comes to mind.
However, we expect you will recognize what we say about what usually
happens. In the first case people usually draw convex, symmetrical hexagons with an edge parallel to the bottom edge of the paper. They may
even attempt to draw a regular hexagon but what often emerges appears
squashed. In the second case they usually give a positive sequence, converging to zero, probably written as fractions. In either case we would
have to impose more constraints to get anything less obvious. In the final
case there are lots of constraints, but in our experience people usually give
a decimal number and rarely a fraction,[13] such as

$$\frac{9+8+7+2+1+0}{3+4+5+6}.$$

If exemplification is individual, why are these responses so similar
even in such open situations?

Learners make sense of mathematics from what is available to them. If
their experience in normal classrooms is dominated by examples used
repeatedly by authorities, these can be seen as conventions. In this way,
learners may be enculturated into a mathematics of misleading simplicity in which examples always have special features that they acquire un-
consciously.[14] Fractions are always pizzas, hexagons are always symmet-
ric about a vertical axis, and functions are always continuous and
smooth. Familiarity with a limited class of examples may also lead to ignorance of the range of permissible change. The hexagon drawing may
also be influenced by early attention to neatness and by use of the word
hexagon outside the math classroom. The sequence might be influenced
by a faulty understanding of convergence derived from only having seen
examples with the characteristics they have reproduced. The use of decimals in the third case, rather than fractions, might be due to a belief that
decimal questions demand decimal answers or because a teacher has deliberately given this impression. All these possibilities show the influ-

---

[13]We thank Alan Schoenfeld (personal communication, June 1, 2003) for this example.
[14]Research on the ways beliefs are enculturated and sustained by classroom practices can
be found in Schoenfeld (1989) and Alba Thompson (1992) among many others.

ence of classroom and textbook cultures on how individuals construe their experiences.

But not everyone gives these standard responses, perhaps because they have learned to avoid clichés, or found other examples to be more useful, or made a decision not to talk about the first thing that comes to mind and to be a bit more original. Furthermore, if asked for a second example, people make very different decisions depending on how they search for examples: starting from their first thought and varying it somehow or starting from somewhere fresh.

Perceptions of Generality Are Individual

When teachers offer examples, they need to be aware that learners may see them as individual specific objects or as special cases, not just as examples of something more general. In addition, even if learners do see them as representatives of a larger class, they may have a different class in mind than the teacher. Sophisticated learners will know that examples are representative of general classes, but they may not think to ask what it is that is being exemplified. Gregory Bateson (1973) reported that he was surprised when suddenly his students asked him this question: "we know they are examples of something . . . but of what?" Imre Lakatos (1976) argued that mathematics develops as people question the implicit assumptions that limit the examples offered or that come to mind. Novice learners may not even question the status of an example or may see the generality it represents on a very mundane level, such as a template into which other numbers can be fitted.

Suppose a teacher works through an example in front of learners. Some learners may see the working as all of a piece, a single action that they are supposed in some way to learn. This happens despite the teacher pointing and pausing, emphasizing, or sliding rapidly past. You can test your own reaction to worked examples for yourself:

Task 17: "Do Thou Likewise"

Here is a worked example of a calculation on some abstruse number-like objects represented as pairs of numbers:

$$(a; b) + (c; d) = (ac; bc + ad)$$

so

$$(4; 6) + (3; 5) = (4 \times 3; 6 \times 3 + 4 \times 5) = (12; 18 + 20) = (12; 38)$$

Now cover up everything above, and do (1; 2) + (3; 4) yourself.

What could you recall? Perhaps you had a sense of component parts or perhaps of some relationships between components. But perhaps what was happening was a mystery. Perhaps there was some resonance with past experience, whether faint or strong. Without a sense of overall mathematical structure or purpose, it is difficult to detect and remember details. If you had recognized the operation as an upside-down version of adding fractions, you would have had little trouble in performing the operation. Here, the generalities to be learned are both the method and the concept represented by the structure of the ordered pairs.

If learners can find only one example of what is required, a particular case, then either the question was closed or the learner perceived it as being closed. Most learners' experience in school is of closed questions, even after curricular reform, so their perception of closure on getting one example is not surprising. They are embedded in a culture in which the teacher sets tasks, and the learners' job is to complete those tasks more or less correctly (Brousseau, 1997). Prompts beginning "Find . . ." are particularly confusing. For instance, try this task and think about how the instruction "find" is being used:

Task 18: Finding

Find a prime number that cannot be expressed as $4k \pm 1$ for any positive integer k.

Find a prime number that cannot be expressed as $6m \pm 1$ for any positive integer m.

Find a prime number that cannot be expressed as $8n \pm 1$ for any positive integer n.

A novice learner does not know whether the approach should use arithmetic or algebra. It is a very common response to try to use algebra if the task seems to be algebraic. In these tasks, however, it may be a better plan to try out some particular prime numbers, such as 7 or 11. When people try numerical approaches, they often start with low, but not very low, positive whole numbers. The reason for this seems to be that they want to avoid the oversimplicity implied by very small numbers and introduce a sense of generality while keeping the problem manageable. In fact, in these tasks it may be advisable to start systematically with very small whole numbers, with the "generalness" of bigger numbers depending more on their multiplicative structure than on their arithmetical size.

Having found one answer, does the novice think to ask if it is one of many or the only possibility? What are learners to do if they find no answers? If you tackled the tasks yourself (or if you already knew what they were about), you will have found that there are quite limited choices in the first two cases; by the third case, you may have used a general argument to explain what is going on rather than give examples. Here one cannot use single cases as templates for generating further results; instead learners would have to work with number structure, possibly to transform their images of numbers, to argue what is or is not possible.

We chose those tasks about primes deliberately to demonstrate that when authorities ask learners to find something, they often have a hidden agenda: either that the search itself is the focus of the task, the example found is supposed to represent a generality, or it is a special case. In each of these agendas, what the learner is supposed to learn is different, but the overt instruction is the same. In the first situation, the learner has to find the only possible example; in the second, there are two possibilities that can be described as a finite class, "factors of 6"; in the last, the class is potentially infinite. This is indeed very confusing.

You may like to consider an alternative form that does not begin with *find*:

Task 19: Is It Possible to Find?

Is it possible to find a prime number that can be expressed as $4k$, as $4k + 1$, as $4k + 2$, as $4k + 3$ for any positive integer k?

We leave it to you to imagine how learners' responses might be different. For instance, is this task more likely to prompt engagement with number structure, perhaps by classifying integers into four sets?

A different illustration of the personal nature of generality is given by Anna Sfard (2002). She reported on a learner who could not accept a very long thin triangle as a triangle because she wished to call it a *stick*.

For Sfard, this is an example of the importance of mathematical discourse; for us, it provides an illustration of different senses of generality.

It would be interesting to explore, using a dynamic model, when triangles with, say, one side varying in length cease to be called *triangles* and start to be known as sticks. Such an exploration of the boundaries of the example space done with the learner might reveal and alter the learner's sense of the generality.

Examples Can Be Perceived as Members of Structured Spaces

In people's responses to our prompts, there was often a clear sense of searching for something. For example, they reported:

- Feeling happy to find one appropriate object and then recognizing it as one of a class; for instance, finding a straight line that goes through a given point and then realizing that, apparently, "rotations" about that point give all the others.

- Trying to create a general description of all possible objects; for instance, saying that the only prime numbers which cannot be expressed as 6k ± 1 are the factors of 6 or that all the points which are the same distance from a given point as they are from a fixed line are those on a particular parabola.

- Looking for new types of object that have similar properties or that fulfill the requirements in some other way. Often this happens after listening to other responses. When asked for two numbers whose difference is 2, learners began to think of strings of operations in brackets as numbers, for example, $(5 + 9 - 3) - (3 \times 3)$; others began to look for constant differences between definite integrals of functions.

- Getting a sense of how different examples relate to one another, such as matching an algebraic example of a quadratic equation to a graphical example or converting a convex example of a pentagon to a concave one by reflecting one vertex in the line joining its two adjacent vertices.

Indeed, what is described here is the discovery or construction of a space consisting of elements and their relationships. For Michener (1978), the process would be one of discovery, because her idea of examples spaces was that they exist for particular mathematical definitions and theorems. For us, the process is a combination of discovery of what is conventional; of what is already known but can be restructured into new relationships; and of the construction of new objects, new relationships, meanings, and personal understandings out of old and familiar components.

What brings an example space into being? Even with a variety of influences acting on the creation of an example space, some spaces seem to be almost universal and shared by many people. For instance, there are many situations (games, tricks, gambling, etc.) in which one is asked to "think of a number." It is expected that one will choose a small, whole, positive number; only mathematicians would think a fraction or a negative number is an appropriate choice. Universally used spaces can act as starting points for further extension; just as in any learning, the learner can only start from what is already known. In example creation, learners tend to start from what they are comfortable with, which may be a proper subset of what is known. For instance, if you are asked to give two numbers that add to 12, you may start by thinking there are only 11 or 12 possibilities; then you might begin to include negatives, decimals, and fractions. In fact you can find an infinity of answers—a wildly liberating experience but one that could become unmanageable if not systematically handled. Whether you regard these as extensions of the range of permissible change of your original dimension of variation, or entirely new dimensions, is a product of your familiarity with numbers and whether the first examples to present themselves to you were on the real number line or seen as counting numbers or in some other grouping.

Example Spaces Can Be Explored and Extended by the Learner, With or Without External Prompts

Exploration and extension of example spaces, which we see as being a crucial component of learning mathematics, will be examined in more detail in the next chapter. From the experiences we have reported so far, there seems to be an overarching distinction between the kind of examples that can be found easily, which exist as accessible images in their own right, and constructed examples, which have to be made from available information, including past experience that comes to mind.

SUMMARY

In this chapter we have invited you to probe more deeply into the question of how examples and the spaces to which they relate are constructed. We have drawn out four main threads:

- Exemplification is individual and situational.
- Perceptions of generality are individual.
- Examples can be perceived or experienced as members of structured spaces.
- Example spaces can be explored and extended by the learner, with or without external prompts.

The structure of constructed example spaces is personal, and it relates to knowledge, experience, and predisposition. The wording of the prompt influences the nature of the example space that comes to mind and the entrance to such a space. Spaces are often dominated by strong images, some of which may be almost universal. Less dominant images and relationships between images that are accessible in one situation may not be so readily accessible in another. Even strong images may not come to mind everywhere they may be appropriate. What then triggers one form of example space instead of another? Perhaps the experience of constructing examples for oneself contributes to increased sensitivity to trigger richer example spaces.

Whatever the teacher's intention, different learners are likely to see the same example as representing different classes or as special cases of different generalities. Some special cases turn out to be examples of generalities that are new to the learner.

Example creation can give a sense of structure. One has to search structures to find classes of examples. One may have images of certain examples as if they belong to certain structures. To sense structure one may need an experience of the infinite. Constructing examples can be seen as a way of systematically exploring the structure of example spaces implied in conventional mathematics.

Spaces can be explored by finding out what can vary and how far it can vary, identifying new variables, working from first principles, building objects from definitions, and using alternative modes of representation to see what is possible in one and relating it to another and in other ways.

In the next chapter we consider how example spaces develop in complexity.

The Development of Learners'
Example Spaces

Having introduced the notion of an example space to try to capture our sense of where examples come from, in this chapter we consider what sorts of things might be found in an example space, nonexamples, and counterexamples. Our particular interest is in how learners' example spaces emerge and develop as they look for particular examples in response to prompts. We identify six ways in which spaces develop.

REMINDER: WHAT IS AN EXAMPLE SPACE?

The example spaces of interest come into being when learners are invited to engage in mathematics constructively. Whereas there may be a large potential space of examples arising from past experience, what comes to mind tends to be fragments of that potential which are resonated by the current stimulus and situation. The learners' potential space is likely to be a subset of what is taken to be conventional by mathematicians and textbooks, and it is likely to have different emphases.

Being a learner in a classroom, reading a book, searching for a suitable task for learners, or being in a professional development workshop are likely to trigger different features and, hence, to afford access to different possibilities. Thus, a learner who is frequently expected to contribute numbers for calculation purposes in class (as in Sarah's practice in chap. 2) is likely to choose numbers from a wider range and with more awareness of possible use than someone being asked to choose a number for a conjuring trick. Furthermore, the contents and structure of each person's space will be influenced by their recent mathematical experiences, what else comes to mind concerning the topic, memory, and assumptions about what is required. Some elements in the space may be linked, but in general a space may be fragmentary and disconnected. The wording and circumstances of the request for an example trigger a particular example space, with a particular configuration of contents and a particular point or points of access to it.

For instance, in your response to some of the tasks in the previous chapters, you may have recognized a number space in which positive integers and positive decimals are closely linked, related by order or magnitude; fractions can be hauled in if required, but these involve rational relationships of integers, not just comparisons of magnitude; and some peculiar numbers like π and e can be included if necessary, but they tend to interrupt the regular tramp of giant strides off toward infinity. You may have some other arrangement in mind. We are not suggesting that there are natural, unique, or even easiest ways to see relationships and organize example spaces.

There is some similarity here to the metaphor of *problem space* representing a solver's understanding of a problem and the strategies, knowledge, and subgoals that might be used to effect a solution (see, e.g., Greeno & Middle School Mathematics Through Applications Project Group, 1998). Annie Selden and others (Selden, Selden, Hauk, & Mason, 2000) also saw problems as triggering particular mental structures that include knowledge of collections of possibly similar problems, and she and John Selden (personal communication, May 25, 2003) suggested that these could be seen to be example spaces of problems of varying similarity and routineness. Rather than categorizing textbook questions either as routine (to be answered by mimicking the given worked example) or as nonroutine (to be tackled with a problem-solving heuristic), it makes more sense to see the range of possible questions as varying from routine, through moderately routine, moderately nonroutine to totally unfamiliar. Their example space of problem types can be explored and extended in the ways we describe throughout this book, in particular by learning that each question could itself represent a class of questions. Similarly, exercises seen as collections of problems or questions can also be explored structurally.

METAPHORS

The phrase *example space* suggests a spatial metaphor, in which different examples play different roles within some sort of structure or topology that offers positions and relationships in which to play. The term *space* also suggests enclosure: inside and outside. Although the universe might be considered as a space with no "outside," no one has access to all possible elements and features of a potential example space associated with a specific topic. Even the conventional, Michener-type example spaces prevalent at a given time may be extended or altered in the future.

In the discussions so far we have assumed that there are mathematical objects inside and outside an example space. Some of those that are inside may be lurking in dusty corners, and their links with other inside objects may not be very clear. The examples that leap into the mind as clear, central images do not necessarily provide access to everything in the space. The space consists of contents and connections, and availability of the whole space, as well as individual elements in it, is subject to being triggered by cues in the prompt. There are also objects that may have once been familiar but are not in the example space as generated at this particular time and place. These can be considered to be outside the current situated space even though on another occasion they will be considered to belong inside. We find it more helpful to stress the experienced, situated phenomenon rather than to imagine the contents of some larger personal example space that may only be accessed in parts. This is not a psychology of all knowing but a metaphor for our experience. Each learner could be seen as having access to a subconscious global example space from which local example spaces, of the kind we are working with here, are temporarily drawn.

We realized that the spatial sense of example space suggests a landscape, with some very familiar examples acting like easily accessible pastures in the valley, whereas less familiar or more complex examples are like pastures higher up on the slopes or hidden behind hedges and hence more difficult to see and reach. Guy Claxton (1984) similarly described knowledge as a territory with signposts. Familiarity with neighborhoods and aspects of how they link together grows and complexifies as different parts become more familiar and more and more links between them are experienced. Indeed, James Greeno (1991) described number sense as having these kinds of properties. But the example spaces we describe do not exist independently of the learner: They emerge from the situation.

Another way to think of example spaces is as a toolshed containing a variety of tools—examples that can be used to illustrate or describe or as raw material. Some tools are familiar and come to hand whenever the shed is opened, whereas others are more specialized and come to hand only when specifically sought. An old but familiar screwdriver may come to hand more readily than a new-fangled, multibit driver. A jar of assorted screws may rarely be opened, but it may contain exactly the right object for the current task.

A metaphor that we find particularly apposite is example space as a kitchen cupboard or larder. Clustered at the front are frequently used and familiar items. There is a sense that further back there are other items, but reaching them usually means pushing other things aside. When some things run out, they are put on the shopping list, and sometimes while shopping something catches the eye and is purchased for some imagined future use. This corresponds to the way in which many examples are first encountered from some other source, but then they are appropriated and modified for your own purposes later.

In Michener's (1978, p. 362) view, a conventional example space grows by *constructional derivation*, that is, new examples are obtained by adapting or extending old ones—a process we examine more closely later when we consider how construction can also lead to the growth of personal example spaces. She calls the combination of examples and their constructional potential an examples space. In her hands it is more like a directed graph than a larder, more like a preexisting structure than something emerging or created in the moment. The directed graph metaphor implies fixed relationships, whereas the larder metaphor allows for different relationships to be noticed according to how the observer is attuned to the search and for other things to be unexpectedly sighted out of the corner of one's eye.

We realize that these are highly spatial metaphors and would not describe everyone's experience; but when we have worked with others on these matters, we have found that many people use spatial metaphors to describe their searches for examples even when we have not used the word *space*.

CENTRAL EXAMPLES

Figural Examples

It is important to emphasize that most people's examples are modified versions of examples they have encountered elsewhere, whether in texts or lectures, or for some other purpose. Mathematics texts are littered with classic examples handed down from generation to generation, to the extent of becoming core elements of theories. Examples include 2 as a number with an irrational root, von Koch's continuous but nowhere differentiable snowflake function, the Sierpinski gasket, and the Mandelbrot set, which are all classic examples of mathematical objects in higher mathematics (see, e.g., Peterson, 1990), and their images are familiar to many who do not know the details. In this way they have become figural images that stand for and constitute the associated concepts (indeed some of them have a decorative life of their own).

The way in which images become icons for concepts has been studied in detail by Efraim Fischbein and colleagues. Fischbein (1993) coined the expression *figural concept* for concepts derived from paradigmatic figures that may be inappropriately abstracted due to stressing unintended attributes. Such examples are said to have *prototype ambiguity* by Baruch Schwarz and Rina Hershkowitz (2001). For example, in school, most triangles are acute and have one edge parallel to the bottom of the page, as do most parallelograms; rectangles are the most familiar quadrilateral; and most fractions have numerators smaller than the denominator. Patricia Wilson (1986) discussed learners' struggles with examples in the context of polygons depicted with one edge parallel to the base of the page. Such a presentation can lead learners implicitly to the reasonable assimilation of that property into their sense of polygon. Learners who have abstracted *triangle* as requiring one edge parallel to the bottom of the page, have excluded the first object in the following diagram because it is a stick and not a triangle (Sfard, 2002; see chap. 3, this volume), or consider that the second figure in the following diagram is a square but the third is a diamond have developed figural concepts that are at odds with the terms as used by their teacher. Therefore, one of the important roles for tasks inviting learners to construct examples is to broaden their range of permissible change in the images they associate with concepts.

The sequence of squares (1, 4, 9, 16, . . .) and the sequence of triangular numbers (1, 3, 6, 10, . . .) are deemed sufficiently important to have a place in some school curricula so they can be recognized. The Fibonacci sequence (1, 1, 2, 3, 5, 8, 13, . . .) also appears as a sequence with many fascinating properties that can be easily explored and, in some cases, proved. The concept of sequence could remain attached only to mathematical descriptions of the special features of these few sequences, and little more learned through their study. Alternatively, they could be seen as examples of classes ("make up one of your own that is in some way like this"). The broader your experience of sequences, the more likely you are to recognize one in a novel context; the more familiar you are with how to work on sequences, having done more than just learn results about a few, the more likely you are to be able to study any unfamiliar sequence effectively.

Michener's Classification

To understand mathematics means, among other things, to be familiar with conventional example spaces. Michener (1978) described different kinds of examples, distinguished by their use in teaching and learning, that can motivate concepts and results:

- *Start-up examples*—from which basic problems, definitions, and results can be conjectured at the beginning of learning some theory and can be "lifted" to the general case but are also understandable on their own: for example, $\frac{2}{7}$ for conversion of a fraction to a decimal and a shape with both smooth and polygonal boundaries for convexity.
- *Reference examples*—standard cases that are widely applicable and can be linked to several concepts and results: for example, using R^2 to get a sense of how things work in real analysis, which also acts as a possible source for counterexamples.
- *Model examples*—generic cases that summarize expectations and assumptions about concepts and theorems: for example, $y = x(x^2 - 1)$ and $y = x(x^2 + 1)$ for cubics.
- *Counterexamples*—intended to sharpen the distinctions between concepts and demonstrate the nonuniversality of results.

In the introduction to this list we said "distinguished by their use in teaching and learning." This is our addition to Michener's distinctions, because an authority (teacher or textbook writer) assumes a learner will use an example according to the intentions of the author. However, distinguishing between a start-up example and a model example might be beyond learners' sensitivities. The actual role, rather than the intended role, of examples is in the learner's mind, not the teacher's. There are many disturbing factors between the teacher's intention and the learner's perception. An example used to introduce a concept might also be important as a model example. Thus $y = x^2$ is, up to scaling and translation, a generative model for all quadratics, whereas $y = x^2 + 5x + 6$ used as a start-up example may look more general than $y = x^2$, but this equation has special relationships between its coefficients that might be distracting when it comes to using it as a model for other, or all, quadratics. For cubics, $y = x^3$ can be very misleading as a start-up example, and it offers little as a model either. If the learner has met the start-up example before, but in some other context, then it is likely to be used as a model example from the onset because the learner starts the study by thinking "oh, this is about so-and-so" and thus links everything new to a bunch of other knowledge already structured.

Michener reported that learners began to use the reference and model examples she had used repeatedly in her course when they answered questions such as "tell me everything you can about. . . ." They were also able to search the given reference example to find counterexamples to certain assertions. In other words, when examples were frequently and explicitly used for clear pedagogical purposes, learners were likely to pick up this habit and use the same examples for exploring and expressing their understanding.

Bob Burn's (e.g., 1993, 1996) expositions of undergraduate mathematics use reference examples deliberately to build up images to which meaning and knowledge about a whole topic domain can be attached. Christopher Zeeman (personal communication with B. Burn, April 12, 2001) observed:

> I look for an example that captures the quintessence of a whole branch of mathematics, that you can constantly refer back to fruitfully as you go deeper into that subject. Each example should naturally generate a few theorems around itself to prove its key properties. But even before you do this, it should be sufficiently intriguing to capture the attention.

NONEXAMPLES AND COUNTEREXAMPLES

Finding a number that is not rational is finding a nonexample of rational numbers (e.g., $\sqrt{3}$ or π). They show that not all numbers are rational. So if we have the conjecture that all numbers are rational, then $\sqrt{3}$ and π are counterexamples. Nonexamples are examples that demonstrate the boundaries or necessary conditions of a concept. Counterexamples are examples that show that a conjecture is false.[15] Thus, $\frac{1}{5}$ is a nonexample of a fraction that is a recurring decimal and a counterexample to a conjecture that all fractions with nonrecurring decimals have even denominators.

The following tasks illustrate a structure that can be used to confound naive conjectures and assumptions as well as to extend conventional mathematical knowledge beyond the confines of the ordinary syllabus.

---

[15]Thus, a nonexample can become a counterexample in response to a conjecture that some condition is not necessary.

Task 20: This But Not That

Find an even number greater than 4 that is not divisible by 4.
Find a fraction that is not the sum of two unit fractions (numerator of 1).
Find a number that leaves the size (absolute value) of a number unaltered under multiplication.
Find two different triangles with the same angles.
Find a triangle whose altitudes do not meet inside itself.
Find a plane that does not intersect at all with $x + y + z = 0$.
Find a surface on which the sum of the angles of a triangle do not add up to 180°.
Find an infinitely differentiable function that is not identically zero but whose Taylor series is identically zero.

Each of these objects is a nonexample (indicated by the presence of *not*). Consequently, each is a counterexample to an implicit conjecture. For example, the first subtask implies a conjecture that all even numbers are divisible by 4; the second implies that all fractions can be presented as the sum of two unit fractions.

It is very common for learners to identify concepts with one or two early examples they have been shown by a teacher. Because these early examples are often simple ones, the learner is left with an incomplete and restricted sense of the concept, and even the presence of a few nonexamples makes little impression. Learners are very good at dismissing examples and objects that do not fit with their current conceptions.[16] This can be subconscious, so that awkward examples are just not seen, or are dismissed as being totally different. Janet Duffin and Adrian Simpson (1999) described these examples as "alien," so far outside the learner's current frame of reference that they do not make an impression at all. Des MacHale (1980) suggested that learners often simply dismiss uncomfortable examples. Alan Bell (1976) reported that school learners often do not recognize the significance of counterexamples and would not necessarily alter their conjectures or proofs if a counterexample cropped up.

Dismissal can also be a conscious act, such that people can act in mathematics as we do in other areas of life and admit the existence of exceptions without seeing the rule as having been challenged. The existence of three-legged cats does not challenge the rule that they have four

---

[16]For example, Bruner, Goodnow, and Austin (1956) found that learners typically overgeneralize; but in some cases, they undergeneralize by treating some examples as if they were nonexamples.

legs, for instance. Encountering the fact that multiplying 1.5 by 10 is not accomplished simply by "adding a nought on the end" or that multiplying 4 by $\frac{1}{2}$ gives an answer smaller than 4 does not necessarily convince learners that the rules "to multiply by 10 we add a nought" and "multiplication makes bigger" are inappropriate. Rather, they stick to their familiar rules. Fischbein (1987, p. 213) went so far as to say that these primitive intuitions are never displaced, only overlaid, and that they may surface at any time.

Nonexamples need not be treated as counterexamples but as indication that there are different cases. For example, appending a nought for multiplying by 10 works fine for whole numbers but not for decimals; multiplication of a positive whole number by a positive whole number does indeed "make bigger." It would be naive to pretend that learners will not make this generalization, implicitly or explicitly, with validity in relation to their experience. Nonexamples signal the moment to restrict the scope of the generalization. They alert the learner to cases in which their previous assumptions and intuitions no longer apply to the whole class. The question is, does the nonexample indicate a class for which a new kind of statement can be made, or is it an isolated example, such as "zero has no inverse under multiplication"?

Where there is one counterexample, there is often a whole class of them; one might eventually respond by rethinking the original classification or definition. Duffin and Simpson (1999) called these counterexamples "conflicting"—those objects or experiences that force learners to rethink in order, in Piagetian terms, to accommodate the new into their schemas. For example, subtracting 6 from 4 is a counterexample to the conjecture that one can only subtract small numbers from bigger numbers, and this opens up the whole idea of negative numbers.

If learners are to be adventurous in extending their example spaces, they will inevitably meet the extremes of ranges of permissible change and, hence, bump into nonexamples that may at first sight appear to be examples or that demonstrate the importance of qualifying conditions. In other words, working with nonexamples helps delineate the example space. Deliberate searching for counterexamples seems an obvious way to understand and appreciate conjectures and properties more deeply.[17] Such a search could be within the current example space or could promote extension beyond.

However, there has been considerable controversy among researchers about the helpfulness or otherwise of presenting counterexamples to learn-

---

[17]Wilson (1986) found that counterexamples force learner attention onto relevant features of examples. Textbooks by Gelbaum and Olmsted (1964), Khaleelulla (1982), Steen (1970), and Wise (1993) focus on counterexamples.

ers as part of their concept construction.[18] In our view, learners will inevitably encounter nonexamples of concepts and counterexamples to conjectures if they are actively exploring and constructing their own spaces.

Can Learners Create Useful Counterexamples?

Learners can usefully be asked to construct counterexamples to explore the limitations of a concept or relationship, as well as to challenge conjectures. But counterexample construction turns out to be deeply problematic, especially when learners have not had a history of personal construction.

Orit Zaslavsky and Gila Ron (1998) found similar problems with novice teachers when they asked them to generate counterexamples in algebraic and geometric contexts: "Students often feel that a counter-example is an exception that does not really refute the statement in question" (p. 4-231). Learners in their study had great difficulty generating counterexamples of the type that fulfill necessary conditions yet fail to exhibit a desired property. They often gave ones that do not exist by "forcing" too many conditions on an example, or that do not satisfy the necessary conditions. They were happier with counterexamples that both proved and explained than with those that merely disproved. They concluded that learners' understanding of the role of counterexamples is influenced by their overall experiences with examples, but we suspect that they must also experience some explicitness about what counterexamples can tell us. In Randall Dahlberg and David Housman's (1997) work, which we discuss in more depth in chapter 7, some learners had counterexamples on hand but did not recognize them as such.

Sowder (1980) commented on learners' reluctance to produce or process nonexamples and counterexamples in a logical way. This reluctance may stem from the difficulty people have in overturning treasured overgeneralizations; to produce a counterexample may constitute a serious challenge to a previous belief (Tirosh, Hadass, & Movshovitz-Hadar, 1991). However, there are inherently mathematical difficulties also at work. Orit Zaslavsky and Irit Peled (1996) asked learners to construct examples of binary operations that distinguished between commutativity and associativity. In general they first tested some elementary functions, then attempted to "spoil" their properties, and only then tried to extend their example space. The task was not a success in terms of production of counterexamples, but the researchers learned a great deal about learners'

---

[18]Randall Charles (1980) suggested that "one conjecture worthy of investigation is that non-examples are more instructive for learning difficult concepts, whereas examples are more instructive for learning 'easy' concepts" (p. 19). Rina Hershkowitz (1989) found that learners pay more attention to examples than to nonexamples.

understanding of binary operations. They saw that learners were searching in a limited example space, overgeneralizing properties of binary operations, and spotting pseudosimilarities that had nothing to do with binary operations at all. In their article, Zaslavsky and Peled focused on difficulties in the production of counterexamples, but there is a further, deeper problem in that learners may not accept the logic that a counterexample refutes a rule. Further confusion is observed by Bernard Gelbaum and John Olmsted (1964) in that "*any* example is a counterexample to *something*. . . . For instance, a polynomial as an example of a continuous function is *not* a counterexample, but a polynomial as an example of a function that fails to be bounded or of a function that fails to be periodic *is* a counterexample" (pp. v–vi).

Amina Benbachir and Moncef Zaki (2001) explicitly encouraged their students to construct examples and counterexamples to support and refute conjectures. They were working on false conjectures that they knew the students would believe to be true. They found that students who constructed counterexamples to the conjectures seemed to get a deeper understanding of the concepts and of the truth and value of the conjectures than those who focused only on steps in the argument. Their study also shows the significant intertwining of independently made constructions and the empowering use of such constructions to check conjectures.

As beautifully illustrated by Lakatos (1976), it is not always obvious what is being refuted by a counterexample: a conjecture or a sequence of reasoning. A conjecture of the form "All symmetrical quadrilaterals have diagonals that bisect each other" is refuted by the existence of kites. A sequence of reasoning such as "$7n + 1$ gives a remainder of 1 when divided by 7" is refuted by making n (which has not been restricted to the field of positive integers) equal to $\frac{13}{7}$. However, the existence of a counterexample does not identify the flaw in the reasoning, it merely highlights that there is a flaw. It is not always obvious to learners that a counterexample ought to match the stated conditions and not just be vaguely from the same sort of mathematical area. Thus, if n had been restricted to integers, $\frac{13}{7}$ would not have been a counterexample. This confusion also needs to be taken into account when encouraging learner-generated exemplification.

The production of an example and an understanding of its role may cause separate difficulties. Mary O'Connor (1998) described a conversation with a child who seemed unable to produce mathematical counterexamples but who used counterexamples naturally in conversation about other areas of her life. She suggested that the discourse of exemplification is available to children outside the mathematics classroom; a child can refute a generality such as "all cats are striped" by indicating one that is not. Use of counterexamples in mathematics is limited by beliefs, experience, and a limited view of the possible example space (e.g., using N instead of

Z for examples of number). What might be required is explicit induction into the mathematical uses of exemplification and counterexemplification. Perhaps difficulties in exemplifying might then indicate a lack of familiarity with the mathematics involved, rather than an unfamiliarity with logical argument.

In Dahlberg and Housman's (1997) study, responses to their second question about counterexamples were poor and confirmed these other research results about the difficulties of generating counterexamples. However, learners had used several almost, but not quite, examples on their way to a complete understanding of all the aspects of the definition but did not think to bring some of these back into play as counterexamples. The importance of examples that can be made into nonexamples by changing one feature (and nonexamples that can be changed into examples by changing one feature) is elaborated by Mike Askew and Dylan Wiliam (1995). In Watson and Mason (1998), we called these *boundary examples*.

PROMOTING DEVELOPMENT

The important features of example spaces are their scope and their interconnectedness. Put another way, an example space functions powerfully when examples are generative and not merely figural, affording access to whole classes of similar examples. One role for a teacher is to promote the expansion of example spaces as they emerge, moving beyond the confines of initial spaces.

Having an example space associated with, contributing to, or constituting your sense of a topic or concept is potentially powerful, but your example space can also effectively limit your appreciation of scope in the same way as a single example can. This is particularly the case when a space consists of a collection of fragments rather than a network of linked examples whose structure is generative. Awareness of the notion of example spaces can remind the teacher that the scope and range, the dimensions of possible variation that define example spaces, can be probed and challenged. The teacher is then in a position to construct tasks that challenge learners to explore and extend their example spaces.

As we said in chapter 1, two pedagogical principles underpin this approach:

- Becoming familiar with and confident about a concept consists of extending example spaces and the relationships between and within them so that they trigger recognition and appreciation of details.

Through developing familiarity with those spaces, learners can gain fluency and facility in associated techniques and discourse.

- Experiencing extensions of example spaces (if sensitively guided) contributes to flexibility of thinking not just within mathematics but perhaps even more generally, and it empowers the appreciation and adoption of new concepts.

We now offer several examples of tasks that are designed to promote exploration and extension of personal example spaces.

Take a few moments before reading further to think about your own or your students' possible responses to these tasks:

Task 21: First Reactions

Task 21a: Products to 100

Find two numbers that, when multiplied together, give 100.
One of the numbers must be bigger than 50 but less than 100.
Can you make one of the numbers bigger than 100?

Task 21b: Zaslavsky[19]

Find the equation of a straight line that will cut the quadratic curve
$f(x) = x^2 + 4x + 5$ in only one point.

Task 21c: Building

Find two different polyhedra that can each be built using eight congruent equilateral triangles. Can you find more than two?

These prompts, dealing with different areas and levels of mathematical knowledge, have in common the intention to confound learners' first reactions. The first one is clearly intended to move learners beyond offer-

---

[19]Zaslavsky (1995) used open-ended tasks to give teachers direct experience of working investigationally. She structured tasks so that they became "Find examples of . . ." rather than closed prompts to apply techniques. One of the tasks, which we have adapted here, was "find equations of straight lines that have two intersection points with the parabola $y = x^2 + 4x + 5$." The learners contributed five strategies that covered most of the analytical geometric methods commonly taught at the secondary school level. Each strategy led to further questions, creating an arena in which learners needed to know methods, techniques, and formulas to solve the larger problem, rather than as ends in themselves. Learners were prompted to look at familiar mathematics in a new way and, hence, to reestablish links, relationships, and concept images. However, one can also imagine using this task with learners who are new to the concepts but can use a graph plotter.

ing factors; the second is intended to explore certain kinds of intersection and to direct learner attention to vertical lines as an available subclass of all straight lines; the third is intended to move learners beyond an octahedron.

How Might Learners Respond to These Prompts?

> Find two numbers that, when multiplied together, give 100.
> One of the numbers must be bigger than 50 but less than 100.
> Can you make one of the numbers bigger than 100?

In this case, primary school children may have the impression that 50 is the largest number you can use in such a multiplication task. Some may offer 100×1. The teacher has anticipated this, perhaps by working on the task herself first and seeing what came easily to mind. What knowledge do learners already have that has to be expressed before we can get to the real purpose of the lesson? She offered a second prompt that challenges self-imposed limitations without devaluing the immediate responses already offered. If calculators are available, learners can explore a range of noninteger answers to extend their understanding and beliefs about multiplication or about what can be offered in response to a request to "give me a number." The final task challenges the widespread belief that multiplication always makes things bigger. However, it is not always sufficient just to offer the challenge even when that challenge is met. Sometimes people need several exposures before they recognize the inconsistency with their own deep-seated beliefs and intuitions; sometimes they need a teacher to make the disparity glaringly obvious and to emphasize it as worth remembering.

> Find the equation of a straight line that will cut the quadratic curve
> $f(x) = x^2 + 4x + 5$ in only one point.

In this case, secondary students may have worked with straight lines with finite or zero gradients, but they may not think of vertical lines as members of the same class because of the lack of a y in the equation $x = k$. One intention of the task might be to promote consideration of vertical lines as special members of the class augmenting those represented by $y = mx + c$ (North American readers may be more familiar with $y = mx + b$).

This is not the sort of task found in textbooks, and you may never have thought about it before, or you may have been puzzled about the purpose of such a search. Certainly in the context of school curricula it may not be crucial to know that the class of straight lines includes those of the form $x = k$, and it is not crucial to know that they cut such quadratic functions only once, but both of these tasks add features to the learner's growing picture of what is possible in analytic geometry. The property of having each vertical line only cut a curve once is the graphical equivalent of being a function in algebra, so it does in fact have some significance; it bridges the gap between graphs and functions.

Additionally, of course, learners may interpret the word *cut* as an instruction to look for tangents. In fact, this is the usual response when we offer this task to advanced groups of learners and colleagues. Responses may include two distinct classes of object, depending on interpretation of the word *cut*. However, we have also found that people will sometimes overlook such words in an attempt to transform the question into one that is familiar.[20] Here tangency may be interpreted as "cutting in one point," but this creates tension with tangency seen as "two coincident points." What could the teacher do in this circumstance? A discussion about number of points of intersection might lead to seeing tangency as concerning two coincident points and thus not meeting the original requirements.

A natural reaction by learners is to accuse the teacher of being imprecise about the task. Why wasn't the task more specific about the word *cut*, such as saying *cut through*? Some people react strongly to such ambiguity, blaming the question setter for not restricting possible choice. Yet, the effectiveness of the task lies in exposing different ways of seeing and speaking that lie below the surface of learner awareness, as evidenced by their response to the task. Getting learners to construct objects themselves is a powerful way to expose such ambiguities and multiplicities for explicit discussion. The task could be rephrased so as to indicate a range of possibilities: "Find lines that cut the quadratic in zero, one, two, . . . points." But the teacher might be looking for learners to impose this structure for themselves in response to the single constraint of one point, which would extend their own initiative taking in further exploring any task.

Find two different polyhedra that can each be built using eight congruent equilateral triangles. Can you find more than two?

In this last case, tertiary and secondary students familiar with platonic solids may be in the habit of thinking only about these in response to the

---

[20]As we report in chapter 7, even experienced mathematicians sometimes do this.

word *polyhedra*. The prompt to find two is intended to force them to explore further and, hence, extend their range beyond the platonic subset, which is an unnecessarily constrained example space. They may wish to classify any new examples they can find.

It is very common for learners to cling to examples of concepts and mathematical classes that are, like the platonic solids, overconstrained for new purposes. We discussed this in *Task 16: Freedom*, and it can happen because previous experience has, for good pedagogical reasons, been limited to a subset of the class, as in the aforementioned multiplication task. It can also happen because the examples provided by textbooks and teachers have afforded only a limited range of images of a concept, as in the aforementioned straight-line task.

In the case of the polyhedron task, if you have not met this task before, you may have responded by thinking about platonic solids and then trying to imagine other shapes. Learners may also use what is most familiar to them not only in mathematics lessons but in other contexts: games, puzzles, design tasks, and so on. You may have given up, found some triangles and glue and started making some, or closed your eyes and imagined building such shapes, pausing to check whether particular bits of your imaginary constructions were plausible and possible. That done, you may have begun to wonder what properties these new shapes have, whether there are more like them, and how they might contribute to your understanding of what is possible in three-space. When we first worked on this task we used mental imagery to create about five apparently different polyhedra, but when we tried to classify them we began to realize that the difference was in the way we constructed them, not in the final shape.

Learners who have moved beyond the classroom games of "do what you are told" and "invest the minimum of energy" and into the practice of "take initiative and explore around" and "use the hardest maths you can" are much more effective and efficient at learning new concepts. It is an exciting pedagogical experience when learners take initiative, exciting both for them and for the teacher; although some learners may become frustrated at not finding an answer or when they realize that they failed to think of something they already knew.

In each part of *Task 18: Finding* (prime numbers), you scanned your example space to find possible objects. It is a common experience to have a sense of finding such examples in dusty corners where mathematical objects that are not frequently used are stored. They have often become detached from the central images that come to mind immediately as possibilities. You may have had a sense of this in some of the earlier exercises too, especially the ones for which you had not thought about (or taught) the topic for a while. This sounds like a crude description of how memory works that is enriched by your own awareness of struggle in searching for what you once knew. Alan Baddeley (1998), among others, developed a complex model of memory in which phonological and visual–spatial stimuli interact with each other and induce recognition. This model seems particularly appropriate for thinking about exemplification because the monitoring role of a central executive will be consciously and subconsciously influenced by the nature, language, and context of the search.

What do you do, then, when memory offers nothing substantive and when you look in dusty corners but find nothing you can use? In the next section we consider other possibilities.

How Do Example Spaces Develop?

When asked to describe his experience of example construction as a mathematician, Peter Nyikos (personal communication, April 12, 2002) offered the following. He uses the terms *lattice* and *universal algebra*, but it is not necessary to know what they mean to get a flavor of what he described:

> Like most mathematicians, I have a repertoire of "usual counter-examples" in various areas of math which I first look at to see whether they work. If they do not, I see whether trivial modifications might do the job. After that comes the hard part, trying to construct things from scratch.
>
> In logic and universal algebra, for example, lattices can serve for lots of problems. Often one needs only to look at a few well-known examples like the two lattices which are subsets of every non-distributive lattice, or at totally ordered sets with two or three elements, or the power set of a finite set, or a set of finitely many natural numbers with all gcd's and lcm's of elements included. If these don't work, a Cartesian product of two of them might be worth investigating, or one might go to other kinds of partially ordered sets, like trees and disjoint unions of lattices.
>
> As an undergraduate and graduate student I played around a lot with various finite groups and combinatorial objects like Latin squares, just for fun, and sometimes things just seemed to fall into place to give a much wealthier structure more simply than I would have dreamed.
>
> Since then my research has been mostly in topology, where I am helped along by fictitious pictures of the spaces I describe abstractly, spaces that it is really impossible to imagine precisely. The fictitious pictures often suggest properties and even proofs of those properties that work out a tolerable fraction of the time. I go down many blind alleys, but that comes with the territory, as the expression goes.
>
> The process is a bit mysterious to me even as I experience it. I wish I could communicate it better; it's a knack that develops with experience.

In our terms, Nyikos looked for standard familiar examples, then tinkered with them using familiar construction tools. He made use of objects he encountered and became familiar with in the past, sometimes finding them later in a dusty corner when they might prove to be useful. He also depended on diagrams (he called them *fictitious pictures*—thus highlighting their personal nature), which are indicators for complex structures he could not visualize directly, and made use of relationships suggested by those diagrams.

When searching the dusty corners and finding nothing that will serve the current purpose, it is helpful to look less specifically for clues from which to build a new example. If you go to a shop looking for something specific but out of the ordinary you may not find anything, but if you go with a general need in mind, you may find something that will suffice or something from which to construct what you need. Failing this, it may be necessary to go outside the familiar example space and ask "what else is possible?" This may mean waiting until something catches your attention or deliberately adjusting and probing.

We find it helpful to distinguish between several kinds of example spaces:

- Situated (local), personal (individual) example spaces (i.e., the focus of this book) that are triggered by current task, cues, and environment, as well as by recent experience.
- Personal potential example spaces from which a local space is drawn that consist of one person's past experience (although not explicitly remembered or recalled) and that may not be structured in ways that afford easy access.
- Conventional example spaces as generally understood by mathematicians and as displayed in textbooks, into which the teacher hopes to induct his or her students.
- A collective and situated example space, local to a classroom or other group at a particular time, that acts as a local conventional space.

However, all the teacher knows is what the learners express about their current example space and what the teacher herself knows about conventional example spaces.

Based on reports of experience, development of example spaces seems to happen in six ways. The first two ways are about showing objects from a conventional canon and expecting that learners will adopt them:

- By being shown new-to-you objects that are apparently unconnected or only weakly connected to anything you already know: These objects from a conventional example space may need to be worked on further to be incorporated into personal example spaces.

- By meeting counterexamples[21] that turn out to generate new dimensions of possible variation to an example space: This can be seen as learning more about the conventional example space and thus may further structure your personal potential space.

When teachers or authors work through an example that they imagine is new to the learners, their attention is on the generic nature of the work. The particular numbers or other data and the particular setting or context are downplayed or even ignored as irrelevant to the general method. But the learner may see only the particulars and has to work out which are to be stressed and which are to be ignored but without any clear criteria on which to decide. So, there is a paradox in being given something completely new, as there is no basis from which a learner can make sense of it.[22]

The remaining four ways of extending example spaces involve the learner being active in construction and construal and may involve creating examples, nonexamples, and counterexamples:

- By restructuring what you know so that forgotten experience becomes networked more clearly into your habitual ways of knowing: This can be seen as augmenting a personal local space by identifying members of a more global space that could be included.
- By realizing that things you already know can be used in ways that until now are unfamiliar to you: This can also be seen as augmenting and enriching a local, personal space but developing new structures in your personal potential example space.
- By developing new-to-you mathematical objects through tinkering with known objects, merging or gluing or juxtaposing known objects together in some way: This can be seen as enriching your local and possibly your potential example space in the future.
- By being shown new-to-you mathematical objects that relate to what you already know but could not construct unaided just by tinkering or gluing: This can be seen as encountering details of the current conventional example space.

Our work with groups and individuals on learner-generated exemplification, along with the last four ways just listed, shows strong connections

---

[21]For examples, see Gelbaum and Olmsted (1964).

[22]There is also an apparent paradox in constructing something entirely new. We return to this paradox at the end of chapter 5.

to various problem-solving heuristics (Polya, 1957; Schoenfeld, 1985) that may be used for example construction.

Restructuring Forgotten Experience and Using Old Stuff in New Ways. In workshops, when we offer prompts like those in the tasks presented so far, and someone offers an answer, it is common to hear "I should have thought of that!" or "Oh yes!" or "I would never have thought of that!" The "I should have thought of that!" seems to relate to recalling something whose usefulness is obvious to the learner once attention is drawn to it. The "Oh yes!" seems to relate to being shown a new, but not immediately obvious, context for a familiar object. The "I would never . . ." indicates recognition of the possibility once mentioned but no sense of having had access to it earlier. Whether a particular answer is "I should have thought of that!" or "Oh yes!" or "I would never . . ." depends on learners' previous images of the object, their previous understanding of its properties and potentials, and their view of themselves as learners of mathematics. We have found that "I would never . . . ," and "I could never have . . ." can turn into "but I will in the future" as people become more playful, carefree, or adventurous and get real pleasure from it. In terms of the larder metaphor, when your eye catches a less familiar object in the larder there can be a sudden rush of potential—of thoughts and images about how that object could be used—and your attention can be drawn to an unfamiliar use of an object. Learning has taken place, and an example space has been momentarily extended.

For example, the notions that decimal numbers might be woven more tightly into what is triggered by prompts about number or that equations like $x = k$ might be conceptually attached to equations like $y = mx + c$ may be a reminder to some but a revelation to others.[23] (Note how the words *remind* and *revelation* connect to the thinking and seeing implied in the verbal reactions.)

Compare your responses to *Task 21* to your response to this prompt:

Task 22a: Write Down

Write down a number.

Usually, people (apart from the youngest school children) find they cannot respond easily to this request. What sort of number is required? How might you choose just one? What criteria should you use? What might you

---

[23]Perhaps this could lead to a preference for using $Ax + By + C = 0$ as a standard form for straight-line equations.

be asked to do with this number (hence, do you want something really simple)? (See our comments regarding *Task 3a: Alternating Signs* in chap. 2.)

What would make this a more stimulating task? Possibly you would think of adding some constraints or relating it to some other aspects of mathematics or imagining what the intention behind the task might be and reframing the prompt to indicate what might happen next. What about this task?

Task 22b: Write Down Continued

Write down a number no one else in the class will (or will be likely to) write down.

Write down a number that no one else in the whole world will (or will be likely to) have ever written down.

A first response is that the second request is impossible. But a few moments' thought suggests that a finite number of people can only ever have written down a finite number of numbers in a finite lifetime, so there must be plenty left over. Do you have a sense of being sent on a searching task, the kind of quest that, in legends, would be rewarded by half a kingdom or marriage to a prince, princess, or toad? It is clear that you are being asked to delve into the dusty dungeons, unexpected corners, and insurmountable mountains to find an unusual number, and when you find it you will think "Oh yes!" If someone else finds a better one, you will think "I should have thought of that!" As a sample, what about $0.12345678987654321012345678987 \ldots$ or $\sqrt{1 + \sqrt{2 + \sqrt{\pi}}}$? Is anyone likely to have thought of these examples? Did you? Too bad: We got there first. Searching for an unusual or original object has the effect of expanding awareness beyond a single object to a whole class (a generality) from which a selection can be made. Choice is a creative act, and it is much more pleasurable than looking for a single needle in a haystack using some memorized technique.

The purpose of *Task 22b: Write Down Continued* is to prompt learners into thinking about the range of possibilities from which to select, rather than taking the first or second idea that comes to mind. We want them to become aware of choice—of selecting from an infinite range.

In the case of *Task 21c: Building*, concerning polyhedra at the beginning of this chapter, it is less likely that the new objects will be familiar to most people, so an "Oh yes!" response is not so likely. Think how different your response would be if you had been asked:

Task 21c: Building (Alternative Version: How Many?)

How many different polyhedra can you construct that each use eight
congruent equilateral triangles?

In this version, there is no information telling you to stop searching after
reaching an assigned target. Further, would you have noticed if the
words *congruent* and *equilateral* had been omitted? Would you have wondered about varying the sizes or shapes? It seems that most people need
to have some indication that there are more to be found to search beyond
the obvious.

Tinkering and Gluing and Aided Construction.   For many of the tasks
we suggested so far, people reported having to adapt or alter what they already know to fit the new requirements or constraints. In others, people
reported trying to take suitable properties from several objects and combine them to make new objects. Alan Schoenfeld (1998), in his comparison
of doing mathematics and making pasta, was explicit about the bringing
together of ingredient X to which one usually does Y and ingredient A to
which one usually does B and experimenting with doing Y to A and/or B
to X to solve a problem and create a new example.

Adjusting, tinkering with, and sticking together mathematical objects is
similar to what Claude Levi-Strauss (1962, p. 17) called *bricolage*: the ad
hoc combination of found objects and invented objects to get a desired effect. Levi-Strauss used this method to achieve an understanding of myth
making, which explains similarities between resolutions of common dilemmas across cultures. Heinrich Bauersfeld (1994, p. 144) used *tinkering*
and *bricolage* to describe the messy nature of mathematical thinking in
contrast to rule-based deductions generally expected of mathematicians.
In our experience, the bricolage of example construction can yield surprising results, because the knowledge and resources being brought to the
task are different for different learners. Although individual and idiosyncratic intuitions and insights play a role, there will also be similarities in
what people construct due to the nature of the mathematical constraints.
Rina Hershkowitz and others (Hershkowitz, Dreyfus, & Schwarz, 2001, p.
214) used the term *building-with* to describe the process of combining familiar objects as components to resolve a problem. They saw construction
as the central step in abstraction; this is when learners assemble something new from familiar pieces.

For example, when we tried to make appropriate polyhedra for *Task
21c: Building* ourselves, we eventually (literally) tinkered by gluing card-
board triangles together in different ways. We started with a tetrahedron,

then replaced one face with a tetrahedral "cap," then another, and then varied the number of triangles meeting at a vertex. What we were looking for was all possible ways of assembling them, and this required seeking some invariants, variation, and structure. Our actions of tinkering and gluing suggest a useful metaphor to describe exemplification in other situations. If you need a number with a variety of constraints, you start with something and then tinker a bit. To write down a decimal number no one else has written, you start with a pattern, then adjust it, and then perhaps adjust it again. When trying to make a function that is continuous but not differentiable at a point while avoiding the well-known $|x|$, someone tried gluing two very different but familiar functions together, a standard parabola and a straight line, translating and scaling it to make it "work" at a given point.

Willi Dörfler (2002) added an important observation, namely that the learner's construction of a mathematical object is actually a point of view taken by the learner. The notion of "point of view" is useful because it explains why two different people may act differently in mathematical interactions that appear to offer the same possibilities to each. They may envisage different potentials based on the structures of their example spaces.

The tasks we have been discussing are designed to offer opportunities to extend example spaces; but they have also been examples of example space extension task types. When offering exercises for unknown readers we have to make judgments about how far to offer straightforward tasks and how far to challenge and yet not overly daunt you. This is hard to do, and we may not always use a level of challenge maximally appropriate for you. It is particularly appropriate to raise this issue here, because when helping learners to extend their example space it is pointless to ask them to construct examples that are so far outside their experience that they cannot conceive of them, much less find them or cannot construct them or cannot recognize them, get excited by them, or relate them to anything when they are revealed. Our view of learning mathematics is that individuals make sense of the mathematical experiences they have had so far within a learning context created by teachers (and others, e.g., textbook writers) who offer new experiences. Learning takes place by constructing mathematical understandings in the form of adaptable images and networks. It arises through becoming aware of previously unnoticed dimensions of possible variation or extension of a previously conceived range of change through making new distinctions. It makes sense to us, therefore, to develop task structures that might stimulate, directly and deliberately, reorganization of knowledge.

Thus, extending example spaces involves indicating what might be slightly out of reach but attainable using what is at hand. Whether learners are able to recognize what might be useful and how it can be altered or combined usefully will vary with their previous experience and creativity. Some learners will be able to generate their own examples, whereas others may need to be shown a possibility first.

Task 23: Write Down Constrained

Write down a number between 70 and 80 that is in the "three times table."

As trivial as this task sounds, it can reveal difficulties for a child whose image of the three times table is a poster on his or her classroom wall that stops at products of 30 or 36. To find an example for the teacher, the child has to connect the three times table to counting in threes starting from zero. There is the added complication that counting in threes need not always start at zero. A child who knows that *every* positive integer (except perhaps 1 and 2) can be reached by counting in threes from *somewhere* might get even more confused than the child who does not yet know this (just as the learner who knows that tangents touch parabolae once might get confused when asked to find lines that "cut" once). To extend the example space of numbers that are in the three times table requires a subtle connection to be made between counting and multiplying.[24] What would have to be already understood for a child to get the "Oh yes!" experience from this connection?

Task 24: Constrained Search

Find an oscillating[25] function on a finite open interval that does not attain its least upper bound on the interval.

Where do you start? The word *oscillating* might trigger an image of a sinusoidal curve, or it might trigger an algebraic notation, such as $f(x) = \sin x$. But clearly this will not do, for it attains its least upper bound frequently. Having opened up a mental box of oscillating functions, your focus then shifts to the extra condition, "does not attain its least upper bound" and, hence, triggers concept images of unattainable limits. Again, you may have geometric pictures to go with your ideas, or you may have algebraic representations to look at, or some sense that is enactive, neither fully geomet-

---

[24]We are indebted to Jenny Houssart for these insights.

[25]Readers are at liberty to interpret *oscillating* for themselves. Considering more than one interpretation provides a much richer exploration.

ric–diagrammatic nor fully symbolic. Perhaps theorems come to mind about continuous functions, upper bounds, and closed intervals.

Suppose you now see the upper limit as a horizontal line on empty graph paper and an oscillating function underneath it or getting close to it, close enough that there is no other upper bound possible, but not quite getting there. What range of possibilities do we have? You may have a very strong image of increasing proximity to the least upper bound as you look to the right or left or both. Recognizing the strength of this image allows you to question it. Does this increasing closeness have to happen in those ways? Are there other ways in which the closeness of the function to the line can be shared across the graph paper? Is a graphical visualization helpful to you in this case?

Success with this question will depend on familiarity with the task domain and, to some extent, on your tenacity and commitment, on your confidence with the topic, and on your familiarity with the language we have used. If you are fully committed to a program of working with your own experience, you may actually have different experiences than those we expect; if you are not so fully committed, you may be waiting for us to tell you more. But whatever the response, you can interrogate it pedagogically. What did our questions offer you? What was the effect of your choices, especially your choice of original image? And did you realize you even had a choice?

In the account of *Task 13: Inter-Rootal Distance*, not all respondents realized at first that they had choices. The familiarity of the objects through which you are searching can limit possibilities by forming a tightly closed set that you may only ever have looked at from one perspective in the past. As someone once commented to us, "rigidity is a bad by-product of familiarity." Only when respondents examined their first ideas and began to look for others did they realize their searches had been limited by the appearance of, for them, obvious first examples. Extending their example space was initiated by suspecting that other people had successfully found other (types of) examples.

The relationship between being able to tinker and glue for yourself and needing to be shown some potentialities and possibilities is a very finely balanced one. Only the learner knows exactly how it feels to believe that he or she is being shown too little or too much and when it feels as if that is happening. To generate your own example you need to see potential in what you already know and to know possibly useful ways of expressing, altering, and combining objects to reach that potential. In other words, as in so many aspects of mathematical thinking, to be good at generating examples you need models and experience of example generation.

Pedagogical decisions about providing aid in example construction are similar to those that provide other forms of scaffolding for learners. Lev

Vygotsky (1978) coined the much-used term translated as *zone of proximal development* to describe what a learner could do with the guidance of someone more expert that they could not achieve working alone. In Vygotskian terms, the shift from "tinkering and gluing" to "aided construction" can only be made if the intended outcome is proximal to the learner's knowledge. In the discourse of personal example spaces, the requested examples have to be, in some sense, proximal to the example spaces already available and familiar to the learner but without the teacher necessarily knowing much about the learner's current spaces.

Supporting Construction Work: Scaffolding

As we mentioned earlier, there is some similarity to Vygotsky's (1978) notion of a zone of proximal development (which encompasses what can be done today with help and tomorrow without help), in the interface between creating new examples by tinkering and gluing, and having to be shown what it is possible to create so long as it is in proximity to learners' example current spaces. This obvious link causes us to think about scaffolding and what this might mean in the context of extending example spaces.

First, we want to offer an alternative image, that of the character in Samuel Beckett's (1958) play *Act Without Words* who puzzles about reaching something that descends tantalizingly from above but remains out of reach. His response is to assemble what comes to hand—boxes, chairs, and so forth—and pile them up to provide a rickety structure he can climb to attain his goal, the unknown object. This can hardly be called *scaffolding*; instead, it is an ad hoc "ladder." He uses what he has on hand to try out and test different properties of the objects. Thus, the act of reaching for a new object using what is known of existing objects and their properties enables him to learn more about the existing objects and objects in general. (Before he attempted this, all he did was use objects within reach for their usual purposes, for instance, cutting his nails with scissors.)

Task 25: Diagonally Perpendicular Quadrilaterals

Find four different types of quadrilateral whose diagonals cross at right angles.

It might be hard to find four types unless you are experienced in working with classes of quadrilaterals. If you get stuck, think about the character in the play who tried to do whatever he could with whatever he had. Can you tinker with a shape until its diagonals are at right angles? Or, perhaps you could foreshadow the quadrilateral by imagining the diagonals first, which you know about, and joining up the ends later. Construction is often achieved by "starting somewhere else" rather than in a familiar place, a standard problem-solving heuristic (Schoenfeld, 1985).

Metaphors of construction lend themselves rather well to working with spatial questions not only because they come from the same everyday discourse but also because classical geometry is constructed from axioms and rules of relationships. But the scaffolding metaphor for assisted learning, as often used, seems to presuppose a particular kind of secure, independent, external frame for a new structure. Yet, the scaffolding commonly used in many parts of the world consists of a collection of numerous wooden posts that are balanced on the concrete floor of the nth story of a building and used to wedge up the $(n + 1)$th floor.

They are internal to the structure of the building. They rise at a variety of angles, inserted like pit-props as the new floor is constructed, yet the space they occupy will eventually be spacious rooms. Their relationship to the floors and walls being constructed is symbiotic and chronologically continuous. If this metaphor is pursued, the extension of an example space can be achieved by observing the structures that already exist in your current space and exploring how they might be extended in a variety of directions, pausing at each stage to observe how the original structure has developed and changed, and particularly noticing new dimensions of variation and range of change. This is why the explicit notion of dimensions of possible variation is so useful, for when it comes to mind, it opens up possible avenues of investigation and perhaps can be coupled with posing the question: "What if . . . (something were changed)?" (S. Brown & Walter, 1983).

But what about the role of others in these processes? In the Beckett (1958) play, an unseen stagehand raises and lowers the strange object, offering the character a peek at what is possible. In the scaffolding, the pit-props enable the formation of the new rooms by foreshadowing their shapes. So, we can describe a subtle, intimate form of scaffolding by suggesting what can be reached for, offering a peek; and by foreshadowing using pit-props in the form of prompts.

In the context of exemplification, these can be achieved by asking learners to construct examples that have features they may not have thought about before and by asking students to generate their own new examples, using what they already have at hand, in the hope that, eventually, they will do this independently.

From our window, as we write, we can see a form of scaffolding more familiar in the United Kingdom. This is a well-organized, rigid, independent structure of metal poles, vertical and horizontal, that surround the shape to be formed. One cannot tell what the shape is going to be, apart from an approximate ground plan, because the scaffolding is mainly for the safety and movement of the workers, not to hold up the buildings. This image of scaffolding does not provide such an informative metaphor for learning because the interior shape that emerges can be anything that roughly fits and the scaffolding does not develop or adapt to the growth of the building.

How the Development of Example Spaces Relates to School Mathematics

The tasks in this section are similar in structure to some of those we have already used, but the commentary is more about their possible curricular purposes than the effects on example spaces. We hope that by offering a range of school-appropriate tasks and showing their potential curriculum content rather than just their affordances for mathematical thinking, we will show that learner-generated exemplification is a powerful pedagogical tool at all levels.

First, here is an exemplification task with constraints to promote awareness of the vast range of numbers, offering practice in using unfamiliar numbers.

Task 26: Named Decimals

Find a number very close to 3 whose decimal name does not use the digit 3.

Without using the digits 3 or 9, what is the closest number to 3 you can make?

Without using the digits 3 or 9, but using at least one digit 7, how close can you now get to 3?

The aim of these three prompts is to get learners to investigate infinite decimals, perhaps by looking at their position on the number line or by looking at the difference between them and the target number. The search for such numbers might entail practice with subtraction of decimals; more important, however, the whole exercise will enrich knowledge of the place value decimal system. Further, although the behavior of decimal numbers that end in recurring 9s might be known and familiar, other recurring decimal numbers are likely to be less familiar. The question of just how close you can get to 3 under this restriction can attract interest as a challenge, providing practice in summing geometric progressions and some insight into the behavior of the $\frac{1}{9}$ths that appear if you construct the recurring part as the sum of a geometric progression with $\frac{1}{10}$ as the common ratio. The task becomes a vehicle for the practice of decimal calculation techniques and conversion to fractions as well as becomes intrinsically interesting conceptually. One possibility is to extend a sense of decimal number by developing a sequence of increasing values by "sticking more 8s on the end." An unexpectedly rich line of investigation arises when someone decides to replace decimal names with fraction names for this task: $2\frac{7}{8}, 2\frac{87}{88}, 2\frac{887}{888}$ . . . . How might this shift be prompted by a teacher? Furthermore, if someone gives $\frac{6}{2}$ as an answer to the second question, how might a teacher choose between prompting further exploration and directing attention back to sequences?

Now we offer a task that focuses on the meaning and structure of equations, reminiscent of Ed's practice in chapter 2.

Task 27: Producing Related Pairs

Find some pairs of numbers called r and s so that $2r = 3s$. Make some pairs so that r is not a whole number. Find a pair that obscures the relation between r and s as much as possible and one that illuminates the relation as clearly as possible.

This question has multiple aims: to extend learners' understanding of the role of the equals sign by introducing a second variable, to extend learners' understanding of what an equation might be and how many solutions it might have, and to connect the concept of ratio with relationships between pairs of numbers. Searching for multiple examples and perhaps unusual or peculiar examples promotes awareness of what the relationship of "ratio 3 to 2" means. Thus, algebra can be experienced as a domain in which one expresses relationships in manipulable symbols. It also aims to extend learners' thinking about approaches to solving equations. Often school textbooks offer very easy equations with integer solutions as first worked examples, and the purpose of systematically worked solutions is lost on the readers who can spot solutions very quickly. The second task request seeks to move learners toward understanding a need for methods that gradually unpeel solutions from their wrappings, rather than spotting or trial-and-adjustment techniques. In addition, using letters other than x and y is a minor but important extension of their experience. This task could be extended to many other topics, such as finding functions whose integrals over all intervals are in the ratio of 3:2.

Next, we present a graphical task that is constrained to simple numbers so that learners can focus on possible relationships between expressions, factors, zeroes, and graphs:

Task 28: Zeroed Functions

The function $f(x) = x - 2$ has a zero only when $x = 2$; $f(x) = (x - 2)(x - 3)$ has zeroes only when $x = 2$ and 3. Using graph-plotting software, find, plot, and describe functions that have zeroes at other collections of integer values of x. Try collections that contain three, four, or more roots.

This task is characteristic of investigative or exploratory tasks, suggesting a starting point but not an endpoint. At first sight it might seem rather easy, in which case you can make it harder for yourself by imposing more conditions (for an example where conditions make a task much more challenging very quickly, see *Task 45a: Find a New Object*). It asks learners to construct functions, expecting them to discover cubics (at least) as products of three factors, when they are probably already familiar with quadratic curves (although perhaps not in factored form). In extending their experience to cubics, they may also connect linear and quadratic functions as members of an increasingly complex family of polynomials; they may also relate roots of quadratics to the function expressed in factorized form if they have not already done so. The insistence on integers here is rather a red herring, but it makes it easier for learners to multiply the brackets out if they wish to relate what they see to more conventional representations of the quadratic, cubic, and higher degree polynomials. Learners already familiar with slopes of functions can consider the pattern of positive and negative slopes at the roots of the functions they construct.

We have used this task to illustrate how a teacher might use learners' familiarity with one idea (quadratics) to extend their sense of how quadratics might be presented, through experiencing more complicated functions (cubics and beyond), thus encountering an infinity of possibilities (both in the choice of roots and in the choice of degree of polynomial).

Finally, we return to a slight variation of the task we used to illustrate John and Anne's practice in chapter 2.

Task 9 Again: Quadrilaterals (Variation)

Draw a quadrilateral.
Draw a quadrilateral that has two sides parallel.
Draw a quadrilateral that has two sides parallel and two angles equal.
Draw a quadrilateral that has two sides parallel, two angles equal, and two right angles.
Now make sure you have a different diagram at each stage and that the diagram at stage n would not fulfill the requirements at stage $(n + 1)$. So, at Stage 3 you need a quadrilateral with two sides parallel, two angles equal, but not two right angles.

When asked to exemplify, we often reach for an obvious example: one that comes to mind immediately. This example will usually have several special features that are not essential to the task at hand. For instance, many people will draw a rectangle in response to the first request, yet this has several properties that are not essential for quadrilaterals in general. A few start with other special quadrilaterals, such as parallelograms or trapezia. Only rarely do people start with a general-looking quadrilateral;

for them, the exercise may not be very useful, at least at first. For others, however, there is the experience of looking at a set of mental images of types of quadrilateral and examining each one to see if it could fit or could be adapted to fit. In doing so, you may be led not only to revise knowledge of types of quadrilateral but also to look at specific features of them, perhaps slightly reclassifying them in terms of how they are seen. For instance, when you think about different quadrilaterals do you bring them to mind by thinking about sides, angles, or pairs of sides? What does come to mind? How do you remind yourself that concave quadrilaterals are a possibility?

In devising tasks we have found it helpful to ask the following questions: What usual examples will learners have experienced? Are they usefully generic? What experiences outside these examples would it be useful for learners to have? How can learners be brought into contact with extensions to their existing example spaces through their own explorations and acts of construction? In addition, as we said in relation to *Task 13a: Inter-Rootal Distance*, what would have to be part of familiar experience for a learner to say "Oh yes!"?

SUMMARY

In this chapter we have focused on ways of finding, creating, and using examples within structured example spaces and for extending those spaces. Along the way we made use of figural concepts and by analogy, figural examples, as well as some problem-solving heuristics. We also considered the role of nonexamples and counterexamples that has confounded psychological research.

Learners can extend their emerging example spaces by altering familiar images, systematically searching for variables and changing them, gluing objects together, trying to construct new objects from bits of familiar objects as *bricoleurs*—in other words, by imagining and using the potential in what they already know. They may find appropriate examples in what they deem is another space (e.g., in the aforementioned decimals and fractions suggestion), so combining suitable elements of familiar spaces into a new space may be an option.

Prompts can ask for examples that highlight unusual features of objects, thus encourage learners to forge new structural links among their ideas of mathematical topics. Searches for counterexamples can be useful in helping learners come to terms with definitions and properties of mathematical objects.

In the course of the chapter we distinguished six related ways in which example spaces seem to develop:

- By being shown new-to-you objects that are apparently unconnected or only weakly connected to anything you already know.
- By meeting nonexamples and counterexamples.
- By restructuring what you know so that forgotten experience becomes networked more clearly into your habitual ways of knowing.
- By realizing that things you already know about can be used in ways that until now are unfamiliar to you.
- By developing new-to-you mathematical objects through tinkering with known objects—merging, gluing, or juxtaposing known objects together in some way.
- By being shown new-to-you mathematical objects that relate to what you already know, but that you could not construct unaided by tinkering or gluing.

We also distinguished between personal, locally situated example spaces arising in some context, personal potential spaces from which local spaces are drawn, and conventional example spaces consisting of examples appearing in textbooks. We connected example construction where outside guidance and support is required with Vygotsky's (1978) notion of the *zone of proximal development*.

Looking back at the tasks used in this chapter, we summarize the development, growth, and transformation of an example space through being asked to create examples.[26] This contributes to a theory of learning through exemplification. As with everything we say, we urge you to treat these as conjectures worthy of more research, perhaps in your own teaching and mathematical work.

In the next chapter we look more closely at the structure of example spaces and at how teachers might prompt their development and enrichment.

---

[26]A more comprehensive overview of task types is provided in chapter 6.

Pedagogical Tools for Developing Example Spaces

In the last chapter we considered ways in which example spaces develop. We now look more closely at subtle but significant differences in the effects of pedagogic prompts on the structure of personal example spaces and on the creation of mathematical objects that are new to you. Before considering types of prompts, it is useful to classify types of examples by the roles they play. We use the experience of constructing new objects to address the question of how it is possible to construct new knowledge (the learning paradox). We end by revisiting the larder metaphor, emphasizing the dynamic nature of learning and example space construction.

KINDS OF EXAMPLES

The basic structure of example spaces that we are able to delineate consists of central, generic, or dominant examples that readily come to mind; generalizations as general classes of examples; extreme, special, or "pathological" examples that make use of unexpectedly complex or unfamiliar objects; and the relations among these example spaces. We consider them in turn.

Central, Generic, and Dominant Examples

What is the first idea that comes to mind when you hear a technical term in mathematics? And how did it become so dominant?

Task 29: First Images

What sort of images or examples come to mind when you consider
the following concepts:

- Addition
- Decimal
- Linear graph
- Function

- Fraction
- Polygon
- Complex number
- Vector

A range of experiences may have taken place. People who have done
this task report the following:

- Finding themselves drawing or reliving something they learned in
  primary school.
- Being so confused by a range of possibilities that nothing specific
  came clearly to mind.
- Recalling a classical definition and writing it down.
- Not knowing enough to have anything to write.
- Knowing too much to select any one thing.
- Trying to draw some undrawable personal image that functions well
  as a mental object but does not translate to paper.
- Drawing or writing about the concept with confidence that their re-
  sponse represents a generality.
- Recalling something from a textbook or a poster on a classroom wall.
- Giving one example and then worrying about what it might not in-
  clude.
- Wondering about what is expected of them.

As we are now in chapter 5 we assume that readers are no longer preoc-
cupied with wondering what our expectations might be.

Task 30: Recalling Source

Try to recall or reconstruct the provenance of your first response.

Was it an image acquired in childhood, perhaps from a favorite teacher or
a practical activity? Was it something you had to learn by heart? Was it a

helpful example that originally enabled you to understand the concept? Is it an example that has become central through frequent use?

These questions arise from what people have told us about their central images. In a workshop, Pat Perks reported using an angle she "happened to have with her left over from a discussion during the break." Someone else reported using a sequence she had recently been thinking about as a starting example for a new task. It is interesting that they include cultural and emotional as well as cognitive provenances. As Douglas McLeod and Verna Adams (1989) pointed out with respect to mathematical problem solving and as Antonio Damasio (1999) pointed out more generally, when we work on something and when we learn something, there is always an affective dimension. From school experience, a response can be as obvious as liking or hating the mathematics teacher, recalling his or her voice telling us what is important, or disliking being "picked on" to display ignorance, or recalling how a diagram was drawn on the board or displayed in the classroom. Sensory trappings of classroom incidents may dominate the subject content of those incidents. The connection between affect and learning is not at all simple. Negativity can produce vivid recollections of incidents, self-esteem, and content; it can block such memories as well.

Task 31: Going Beyond First Thoughts

Think about your first responses to the aforementioned list of mathematical topics and try, for each, to give special cases or classes of objects that do not fit with your first thoughts.

With the help of Adrian Pinel, we went beyond our first thoughts when he pointed out how responses might change if, instead of *addition*, we had asked about *adding* or *additions*. Replacing static singular words with plural ones and/or dynamic objects makes a significant difference to the production of images. They afford access to different example spaces.

We vividly recall a university mathematics lecturer giggling when asked for her image of a vector space and demonstrating how, for her, it was like waggling all her fingers in the air! At some time in her life this had been a useful image, being three-dimensional in contrast to the images of most of her colleagues which were of two-dimensional spaces with arrows lying around on a plane. But her waggling fingers could be abandoned in favor of algebra when necessary. It did, however, give her a source of explanatory examples of the results she achieved with algebraic representation. Another lecturer saw finite groups as stalagmites, each the height of the order of an element.

What might be an equivalent or similar experience with fractions? An image of a pizza provides a source of simple examples for adding and subtracting, maybe even for other numerical operations with fractions, but becomes unwieldy for denominators that are not closely related multiplicatively. The pizza image might help a little with finding fractions of a number if the whole pizza is considered to be that number, but it is hard to see how the image itself can provide an answer. Those of us who met fractions before pizzas became so widely available worldwide may not be so limited to seeing a single circle as "the whole."

A competent learner has to know when to abandon an image and focus instead on the language and meaning of the fraction. In a recent class, when asked to write down what came into their heads when the word *fraction* was said, most learners (in upper primary school) drew quadrants, a few wrote down examples of fractions in the usual notation, but none used number lines or objects other than circles. Alarmingly, the same exercise with graduates intending to be teachers produced a similar array in similar proportions but with a few more representations of fractions as portions of rectangles, rather than circles. Again, no fractions as numbers or fractions as operators appeared, and those who wrote the usual symbols explained that this was "how we write them," rather than suggesting the symbols carried particular meaning. Only 1 of 25 graduates in this group said that the notation indicated the *division* meaning of fractions.

In our work for this book we have found very few educators in the U.K. and U.S. traditions who have reported an initial image of a fraction as point on a number line or some image that allows a fraction to be a multiplicative operator. This is true even of sophisticated mathematicians, and yet they work competently with fractions in multiple contexts, with multiple meanings, and even as numerical representatives of the class of algebraic rationals. What enables them to work effectively is the knowledge and experience of when to abandon their dominant images and when to use them—their uses and limitations.

The most useful examples for later use, which Michener (1978) called *reference examples*, may not be the ones we first encounter and are not always the first ones that come to mind. Efficient learning includes having important and useful referent examples that are available and quickly accessed, rather than being blocked by inappropriate examples as discussed in chapter 4, and having the flexibility to change examples according to the situation.

Paul Halmos (1983) emphasized similar sentiments and created his own examples:

> A good stock of examples, as large as possible, is indispensible for a thorough understanding of any concept, and when I want to learn something new, *I make it my first job to build one....* Counter-examples are examples too,

of course, but they have a bad reputation: they accentuate the negative, they deny not affirm. . . . the difference . . . is more a matter of emotion. (p. 63) [italics added]

Reference examples provide a testing ground for ideas and theorems, because they somehow contain information about a whole class of objects. The learner is expected to identify and extract relevant information to use it more widely, but this process can sometimes be blocked by unexpected obstacles apart from those due to the presence of unnecessary features. If the reference example is spatial, such as a parallelogram being overused to represent all quadrilaterals, then its special features can obstruct understanding of other quadrilaterals for people whose visual memory is very strong. When such dominant images are figures, they are the figural concepts that we discussed in chapter 4.

The idea that one example can ever embody all the information necessary to understand a concept is challenged by George Lakoff (1987) who pointed out that sometimes there are very different examples that demonstrate similar mathematical properties. If we wanted to have reference examples of numbers that have the effect of reducing positive numbers when multiplying, we might want to have more than one kind: numbers whose absolute value is less than one and negative numbers less than −1. They both reduce other numbers, but one type reduces absolute value and the other reduces in terms of position on the number line. There is also, of course, the intersection containing negative numbers whose absolute values are less than one which do both. Even in the intersection, one example does not contain the information necessary for the whole class because of compound features, which may be varied. In this case there cannot be one central paradigmatic example. Schwarz and Hershkowitz (2001) referred to this as *representative ambiguity* because no single example carries all the information required from which the whole class of examples can be constructed; that is, no example can represent all examples.

However, learners inevitably begin to see certain objects as generic and will choose members of a class that, for them, represent everything knowable about that class (Mason & Pimm, 1984). Thus, any circle illustrates and represents all circles once you are aware that the radius is allowed to change (and the thickness of the boundary and the color of the ink are not relevant). In group theory, S_4 becomes "the" symmetry group and stands for all others; the sequence $1, \frac{1}{2}, \frac{1}{3} \ldots$ becomes "the" converging sequence and stands for all others. Clearly, it is important for teachers to ensure their students have a good stock of worthwhile generic examples.

By contrast, although you might think that one ellipse illustrates or represents all ellipses, there are two characteristics that can change which make ellipses look very different: the size and the shape. However, there are single properties that characterize all ellipses (e.g., the sum of the distances from two fixed points is constant or the ratio of the distance from a specified point and from a specified line is between 0 and 1) but whether these can be gleaned from one example is debatable. In this spatial context it is easy to see that dynamic geometry software would enable a teacher to offer not an isolated reference example but a dynamic *reference family* that the learner might manipulate to get a sense of the range of permissible change. This might also be possible in some nonspatial mathematical situations where continuity is a feature and all possible examples are related through varying dimensions.

Learners are not machines. They have learning histories that encompass past successes and struggles; empathy with some teachers and hostility toward others; the past construction of useful images that may, in time, have become less useful; and a host of subconscious responses to words, diagrams, and mathematical approaches. George Lakoff and Rafael Nunez (2000) spoke about some approaches to mathematical topics being easier and more natural than others because they appear to flow from fundamental mathematical experiences and understandings ultimately based on a sense of position in space. It is quite likely that these easiest directions exist for each learner, but in our experience these are neither universal nor always predictable by others. What teachers offer, even if it turns out to be very understandable for most learners, does not work for all because of personal histories. We recall one 14-year-old student telling us "I do it the harder way because it is easier for me, but others do it the easy way, but I find that harder!" when explaining her choice of multiplication method. Although the notions of figural concept, natural approaches, and reference or paradigmatic examples are attractive, to be pedagogically useful they have to be reconstructions by the learner rather than gifts from the teacher. But the core and heart of appreciating concepts lies in the collection of examples that readily come to mind.

David Tall and Shlomo Vinner (1981) used the notion of a *concept image* to encompass all the images, definitions, examples and counterexamples, associated links, and their interrelationships that are all held together in a structured way and constitute the learner's complex understanding of the concept. As learners repeatedly construct example spaces associated with a concept, they are exploring and building a concept image by relating things that come to mind to a definition or instructions. The subset of the concept image that comes to mind in a particular situation is called the *evoked concept image* (p. 152), which may be different at different times and for different tasks. Over time, one expects emergent example spaces to become more stable as slight variations in situations begin to cue core images and examples. Learners are extending their ideas of what is possible by a complex interaction between what they know, what they can do, and what they know to be possible. We take this idea beyond conceptual understanding to exemplifying any aspect of mathematical knowledge (e.g., techniques and applications) and find that the same learning activities apply. Sometimes, as we have seen, searching can usefully be systematic, but at other times past knowledge prevents this because strong images, perhaps contrasting images, come to mind that have to be dealt with either through use or rejection. Personal reactions, situational features, and even slight linguistic differences can alter the search. There is even a difference between being asked to find three examples of something and being asked to find one, and then another, and then another (as discussed later).

Systematic extension of example spaces by identifying and altering variables is not the only way to generate examples, and we have indicated that it is not always the most productive way. Rather than thinking about systematic searching, we prefer to recognize that learners start from *eidetic* images, those that come instantly, strongly, and completely to mind (wherever they originated), and that further examples are constructed like collages from these images in ways that might be systematic but might be equally intuitive or inspired.

The word *construct* is particularly useful because it reminds us not only that all learning is considered to be the process of constructing meaning from experiences and interactions but also that in mathematics we have the habit of selecting axioms, constraints, and other elements that can be combined and operated on to construct mathematical objects.

Generalizations

Very often the best way to find an example meeting certain specified constraints is to start with a more general object and then impose constraints sequentially. In the context of numbers, the most general object is usually described in terms of variables or parameters. So, we offer this task:

Task 32: Constraining the General

Find examples of fractions that get larger when 1 is subtracted from the numerator and 2 from the denominator.

Let $\frac{a}{b}$ be a general fraction (so a and b are positive whole numbers—this itself is a constraint); then what is required is that $(a-1)/(b-2) > \frac{a}{b}$. Now it is a matter of algebraic manipulation to discover whether there are any such fractions. It turns out that this inequality forces b to be less than $2a$.

Now it is possible to choose a specific example, such as $\frac{2}{3}$ or $\frac{5}{9}$, or to stick with the generality.

Of course you might have experimented with different fractions until you found one that worked; although if you embark on such a search not expecting to find one, your search may not be sufficiently prolonged or committed to succeed.

We have found that the construction of one, two, and three examples meeting a constraint is a useful step toward the appreciation of a generality. This is developed later in the chapter.

Pip, a research physicist, was asked (as many of our victims have been) to give a function that is continuous on the real line but not differentiable everywhere. Stay with us here even if the mathematics sounds hard because his response reveals that some people work happily at a general level, looking for classes, even when individual examples are requested and come to mind.

He spotted that the last part of this request could have several meanings: Does it ask for a function that is not differentiable anywhere or for one that is only differentiable at some points? Both of these interpretations sound a bit tricky. Eventually he understood that he was being asked for one that could have regions of differentiability and places where it was not. By that time he had a general answer, rather than specific examples. So his first offering was the set of sequences of differentiable functions, piecewise continuous, defined on consecutive intervals in the domain such that the derivatives approaching the points where they joined do not converge to the same value. He only produced particular examples when specifically asked for them and took some time to decide that $|x|$ was a possibility, but one so simple he did not really want to think about it. Of much more interest were the "leftover" questions about functions that are only differentiable at single points (Wen, 2001).

Because he works with functions daily, it seemed sensible, while we had his attention, to ask him to exemplify in some other area of mathematics with which he had not worked recently. Thus, we asked him to tell us about quadrilaterals whose diagonals are perpendicular. Once again he worked from the statement rather than from triggered images. He reported mentally placing two diagonals at right angles and seeing what shapes would be produced. He offered "kite" as a generic name for these shapes and then said you could have skewed kites by pulling out one "arm" but he did not know names for these. Clearly here was someone who used to constructing generalities from properties and playing with them dynamically to find the range of possibilities. He was not seduced by our question to produce a quick contribution. Had he been aware of easy answers and rejected them before giving a generality, sensing that we wanted something more? We think not, because between offering "kite" and talking of skewed kites, he said "square, rectangle." Saying "rectangle" suggests that he was not monitoring images as they presented themselves to him in the same way as he was monitoring the construction of a generality. When asked about this he said that "square" had appeared as a dominant image and "rectangle" had "just gone with it" and been said before our reaction led him to reconsider it. It was as if leaps into consciousness of central images (which others report) were happening for him, but this was in parallel with a constructive approach that depended on the possibilities offered by first principles rather than stored facts, images, names, and their accidental contiguity. His preferred example spaces appear to be structured by mathematical definitions and properties; although they contain commonplace objects and connections, he chooses to work with generalities and unfamiliarities. Vadim Krutetskii (1976) identified the ability to generalize broadly and rapidly as a characteristic of successful mathematicians. As with many other elements of mathematical thinking, it is the search for examples and not the finished product that promotes learning, and it is important for learners to establish a dynamic between exemplification and generalization wherever they start. Hazzan and Zazkis (1997, p. 4-305) found that some of their students used a "general form" when generating examples, and they saw the application of constraints to the generality to get specific examples as almost mechanically algorithmic.

Extreme, Special, or Pathological Examples

Some examples are too extreme to be representative of entire classes, but they do show what happens at the "edges" of classes. Such examples play an important role in the structure of example spaces. If you do not have access to extreme examples, then you may be misled in your appreciation of the scope of a concept. For example, extreme examples can offer the possibility that:

1. Not all fractions have terminating decimals.
2. Subtraction and division can "make larger."
3. Triangles are limiting cases of trapezia; squares are also rectangles, trapezia, and parallelograms.
4. Multiplying by zero offers a counterexample to the belief that division always "undoes" multiplication.
5. A solid with a hole going all the way through it does not conform to Euler's formula connecting vertices, edges, and faces: $V - E + F = 2$.
6. Numbers are not only represented by simple strings of digits.

In the first case, fractions that do have terminating decimals are extreme cases because they can also be seen as infinite repeating decimals using recurring 9s; in the second case, you can bar the monsters by requiring only positive numbers or whole numbers; in the third case, it is important to include so-called degenerate cases; in the fourth case, you can explicitly exclude zero; in the fifth case, you can define polyhedra as the class of solids for which Euler's relation holds true; in the sixth case, a number might be represented as a function of some other number (see the mess of operations quote later in this chapter).

A young learner who, in the context of adding, becomes entranced with $5 + 0 = 5$ or who confidently answers $5 - 3 = 2, 5 - 4 = 1, 5 - 5 = 0$ and then stops has experienced a boundary example. It is a boundary in two ways: It lies on the border between positive and negative numbers, and it lies on the boundary of addition facts, being both simple and unusual. Similarly, $5 \times 1 = 5$ is the usual starting point for a multiplication table for the number 5 and so constitutes a boundary; concurrently, it lies at the boundary between whole numbers and fractions.

Sometimes intuition is led astray because the only examples that come to mind are well-behaved.

A function that takes every value between 0 and 1 on every interval of the real line is well beyond the experience and expectations of learners encountering functions for the first time. But this is only because most of the functions learners meet at first are specified by formulae. Others seem pathological only if you expect all functions to be specified by a formula. Similarly, a function that takes the value 0 for rational domain values and 1 for irrational domain values is well-defined, but very badly behaved in analytical terms. Because there is no formula to use, it helps learners avoid the belief that all the functions one can talk about are formula based.

Pathology is not restricted to higher mathematics. Young learners may well mimic historical experiences and treat negative numbers, fractions, irrationals, and particularly surds (roots of numbers) as pathological and, therefore, should be avoided and ignored, at least at first. Lakatos (1976) described examples that go against intuition as "monsters." In particular, he showed how the history of Euler's formula (the fifth example in the list) could be seen as a sequence of monsters arising and monsters being barred through imposing new conditions on the definition of what constitutes a polyhedron. Monster barring describes how learners usually treat what they consider to be pathological and how they cope with awkward examples: They exclude them. Attempting to ignore them will only produce difficulty; accepting them through becoming familiar and competent with them is the only sensible route. The difficulty may be with the use of the term *pathological*, because learning is about extending your sense of what is possible to incorporate the previously unheard of or unimagined.

If everything new is thought of as pathological, then learning itself is inhibited. The history of mathematics, particularly of functional analysis and non-Euclidean geometry, is peppered with searches for examples that do not behave in expected ways and with people stumbling across objects in one context and realizing that they challenge accepted assumptions in another. For instance, $0.\dot{9}$ is likely to have arisen as people thought about decimal names for numbers, not as the answer to a search for numbers with two distinct decimal names. Once you realize that 1 has two different decimal names, you can find infinitely many numbers with two distinct decimal names and even characterize all of them. A self-crossing quadrilateral (one in which two of the edges cross, but the crossing point is not a vertex) was unlikely to arise as the result of a search for a quadrilateral with uncertain meaning for interior angles or area, but it is more likely to arise as an object that someone then spotted and considered to be a quadrilateral. It is extremely unlikely that someone constructed $\sin(1/x)$ in response to search for a function discontinuous at a point; it is much more likely that someone thought of it as a possible function and then discovered that it was discontinuous at 0, in a manner different from jump discontinuities. In geometry a learner asked to think of two circles will not necessarily think of circles with zero or infinite radii or, perhaps, of two concentric circles as possibilities, yet the extension of two-circle theorems to these cases needs special consideration. However, a learner might still have the impression that all is well with the world and that their original generic examples will do, because other cases are so pathological, extreme, or special that they do not need to be pondered. Why should learners try to extend their example spaces to include such oddities?

Burn (1993) pointed out that the development of the basic ideas in analysis often depended on construction or discovery of so-called special examples that challenged or refuted conjectures. For example, Auguste Cauchy, who did much to put functional analysis on a firm footing, is said to have treated the function "x^2 when x is positive or 0 and $-x^2$ when x is negative" as pathological (not even a function) until it was presented as the formula $x|x|$.

So one reason for looking at pathological examples is to act like a mathematician by testing validity and checking the necessity of conditions. Another reason is that, as in the case of the oscillating function just noted, the techniques one uses to explore beyond current boundaries are useful mathematical techniques in other contexts. A further reason is supplied by Lakatos (1976) who used the construction of deliberately awkward examples to find the most general class of objects for which a proof works and, indeed, to challenge the theorem statement. For example, take the following theorem: A quadrilateral with three right angles must be a rectangle. This works on a plane but not in three-space; a quadrilateral in three-space therefore challenges the theorem. Another reason is that a definition, having been formulated in such a way as to make a proof work, opens up the possibility that there may be other objects that satisfy the definition.

Notice how many of the aforementioned ideas may have started as relatively extreme but have now come to serve as boundary examples that remind us of other possibilities beyond the obvious. Cases that are apparently special are seldom unique, but they are themselves representative of infinite classes of mathematical objects worthy of consideration as a class.

Some Pedagogical Implications of Awkward Cases

While the role of special and extreme examples is perhaps reasonably clear in helping learners appreciate the scope of an example space, there is always a tension for teachers. An important pedagogical judgment has to be made concerning how to deal with awkward, extreme, and pathological or unexpected cases without confusing learners. An informed response very much depends on what else learners know and how secure they are in a mathematical atmosphere that consists of questions rather than answers, with conjectures and reasoning rather than memorized techniques.

But another pedagogical judgment also has to be made about learners who generalize first and do not see a need to explore examples, because it is only by discovering the range of objects admitted under some definition that you begin to appreciate the force of any theorems or facts about objects satisfying that definition. For instance, appreciating that the area of a triangle is a special case of the area of a trapezium enriches your sense of a triangle and of mathematics being complexly interwoven, rather than a smorgasbord of isolated and disparate problems and terms.

At the university level you can ensure a vigorous debate by asking whether pathological examples have a pedagogical role. Some lecturers feel that it just confuses learners who are never going to meet the pathologies in their uses of mathematics; others maintain that you cannot appreciate the need for conditions and constraints in theorems and techniques if you do not appreciate their role, and pathological examples are why they are there.

ENCOUNTERING IMPORTANT EXAMPLES

If some examples play a reference role (i.e., useful for checking ideas), whereas others introduce previously unfamiliar objects, and if others function at the boundaries or extremities of concepts, how do learners encounter these examples, and what do they make of them when they are offered? When might one example be sufficient, when are two or three required, and what is the effect on the structure of the emerging example spaces?

Being Given One Example

Choosing to use only one example when teaching a topic means that time has to be allocated for learners to become thoroughly familiar with it, and the teacher has to use it repeatedly to illustrate and check the statements and proofs of theorems. In this way, learners see how to use the example for reference.

Gregory Bateson (1973; whose concern about exemplification we mentioned briefly in chap. 3) would probably be asking at this point, "do the learners know of what it is an example?" What is exemplary about something proposed as "an example"? What is it about the example that captures attention? Is it the relevant features of the class it represents, or is it some other feature, like its funny behavior over some range, or a nonmathematical association that will stick in the learner's mind? A simple example of this is the image of a circle cut into three congruent sectors:

To the teacher, this is an example of thirds; to a learner, it may be predominantly the Mercedes symbol, especially for students whose neighborhood heroes drive Mercedes; to a Freudian analyst, it is some damage done to a human breast; and to a pacifist, it is a peace symbol! More seriously, the use of unit fractions as general examples of fractions might mislead learners into believing that equivalence is always something to do with the numerator being a factor of the denominator. It is possible to "know" that $\frac{8}{16}$ is a half because the top number is half the bottom number, but that line of reasoning does not obviously contribute to the understanding required to know that $\frac{16}{40}$ is two fifths.

In chapter 1 we quoted deMorgan (1831) who described the relationship between experiencing several specific examples and understanding generality. This could be taken to be a demand for teaching based on demonstration and practice, but the intention here is not to achieve fluency, which is usually the goal of practice. Instead, the goal is to achieve understanding of a principle by seeing how something holds true for a variety of examples, through specialization to see the generalization, and through a generic template to see the principle. To make these shifts, the learner has to know that the cases on which the examples are based represent a class; that is, some numbers in fact represent all numbers. Learning is also about knowing what is invariant and what can change and in what way, that is, the dimension of possible variation and the range of permissible change. When learners experience making a choice from a class of possible examples, they move closer to seeing their choice as exemplary of the entire class. However, if they are satisfied with the first object that comes to mind or if they are working with objects provided by the teacher, then they are unlikely to experience it as exemplary.

We want learners to generalize broadly and rapidly, as Krutetskii (1976) suggested strong mathematics learners do. We also want them to know when the generalization applies and when it does not, and we do not want them to include irrelevant details in their generalizations. So generalization from one example might be desirable as long as it is based on underlying structure and not surface features. It is entirely possible to sometimes deduce everything that is useful from a single example. For example, in seeking to count the number of diagonals of a polygon, it is possible to treat one case as generic and replace specific reference to the number of sides and vertices by a symbol or generality—thus developing a structural generalization (Bills & Rowland, 1999). It is not necessary to produce a table of examples from which to try to guess a formula.

Consider, for example, the question of linking numbers of factors to a multiplicative structure of numbers.

Task 33a: Four Factors

The number 77 has exactly four distinct positive factors. What other numbers have the same description?

Here the teacher sees 77 as a reference example and as a generic example illustrating the structure of all numbers having exactly four factors. But learners encounter 77 cold. For them it is not yet a reference example, a familiar number about which they know a good deal and which they can use to test various conjectures about factors. Although 77 can be seen as generic concerning four factors, it is not presented structurally (7×11 seems to suggest the generic structure more clearly), and so many learners may not see it as generic.

Tim Rowland (1998, 2000) pointed out that it is not a trivial step to see a general argument in a generic example. Having used the properties of primes to prove that 1, 2, . . . , 18 under multiplication modulo 19 is a cyclic group (meaning that powers of one number will cycle round all of the others), he asked learners if they were convinced that the same would happen for multiplication modulo 29. Although most seemed convinced, one learner replied: "Although the explanation for $p = 19$ is clear and true, it doesn't necessarily follow that $p = 29$ [works]. So I'd prefer to work it through before I was convinced" (Rowland, 2000, p. 45). This learner may be confident with the work using 19 but does not yet see how or what would be changed if he or she had to deal with 29, although 29 has exactly the same multiplicative structure as 19. It may also be that the form of the argument is clear for 19, but the choice of starting number to use and how it is related to 19 may not be obvious. In other words, it is possible to see an example as potentially generic but not be clear about some details, and it is possible to see an example as an isolated individual, with no sense of how or in what way it might be generic. Where Rowland thought he was using general properties of primes, this learner thought he was using particular properties of 19. So the nature of an example provided by another depends on the learner's perception.

Being Given Several Examples

A number of mathematicians say that they need only one or two "good" examples from which to generalize. Novices are likely to need several teacher-provided examples so that their attention is drawn explicitly to important dimensions of possible variation, rather than distracted by unimportant ones. People have tried to determine the optimal number of examples, but what matters most is the actions learners perform on the examples they are given or construct for themselves.

If learners are offered several examples, they can start making sense of them by doing what comes naturally, that is, seeing what is the same and what is different about them.

Here is a variation of *Task 33a: Four Factors*.

Task 33b: How Many Factors?

How many factors does the number 77 have? How do you know?
How many factors does the number 879 have? How do you know?
  How can you be sure you have found them all *without* trying every
  prime number up to its square root? What can be learned from 77
  to help you with this?

You have to factor 879 into primes, but having done that, you do not have to try to find any other factors: The structure of a number in terms of products of primes to powers is sufficient. Experience with the more familiar 77 can be used to suggest that it is useful to factor 879 and to see that those two factors are themselves primes.

The structure of this task could be compared with *Task 1b: More Factors* in chapter 1. The specific task here is more an instruction than a construction, but we expect learners to start constructing their own examples that also have four factors and to express the structure of all possible such numbers. Here the initial task looks like a specific calculation, but the implied constraint of four factors, which might be extended to other specified numbers of factors, is intended to draw attention to the structure of numbers in terms of the products of powers of primes.

There are many other possible ways to structure this task, of course, and still lead to the construction of a class of numbers that has n factors. You could simply state that the numbers 77 and 879 both have exactly four distinct positive factors and ask "why?" You could offer pairs of numbers in factored form (how many factors do $2^2 \times 3$ and $17^2 \times 23$ have?) and invite learners to detect what is the same and what different about these two (Campbell & Zazkis, 2002). These tasks illustrate how offering two examples to compare and contrast can lead to a deeper awareness of familiar objects.

Learners' natural disposition to compare what they are offered can be used in other ways to teach mathematics. A teacher might never have to give learners a definition because they can always deduce what is being defined by seeing what the common features of the examples are. These can be superficial, such as examples of triangles that all have three sides but with different angles, lengths, and orientations. More interestingly, these can be examples of a relationship between properties, rather than just illustrations of classes of objects.

Task 34a: Same and Different Diagrams

What is the same in these three diagrams?

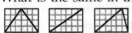

What is the same in these three diagrams?

What is the same in these three diagrams?

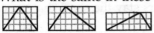

How did the variation in the diagrams influence your reactions?

These tasks (in which we gave you examples for a change!) are intended to promote thought about how a teacher can constrain the variations offered to learners to encourage a focus on the intended relationship. More strongly, if there are no discernible differences for a learner to notice, then what is there to understand? If everything were the same shade of blue, there would be no need for names of colors. Discerning the commonality of a collection of straight lines that all pass through the origin, as in the first diagram that follows, leading us to articulate "these graphs are different, but they all go through the origin," enables us to recognize the general effect of having no constants in their equations. If the graphs in the set were identical, we would have little to say about relationships within their structure. If they are all very different, as in the second diagram that follows, then we may not be able to be precise about their differences.

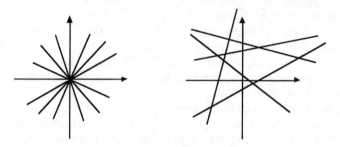

Writers have said this in many different ways (and by discerning the difference in the way they express it, we can identify what remains the same!). Our current favorite articulation is that of Ference Marton (e.g., Bowden & Marton, 1998) who, with Ulla Runesson (2001) and others (Marton & Tsui, 2004), took this belief into the classroom to look at lesson construction. Marton proposed that we learn from discerning variation in simultaneous situations. What varies in a lesson is an important influence on what is learned. The provision of examples becomes an exercise in deciding how to vary the examples so that learners will learn what we hope they will learn and trying to minimize other variations that are irrelevant or distracting. In *Task 34a* we tried to control the dimensions of possible variation that you would perceive in each set; but even so, we cannot be certain that you saw what we intended—namely, relationships between areas of triangles and areas of rectangles. The focus is therefore on one dimension of possible variation. Variation also draws attention to generality; it is because one aspect varies and others stay the same that we can make useful statements in mathematics.

For example, at any point on $y = x^2$ we can apply a technique of finding the limit of the gradient of a chord as the chord becomes very small, and it will always be $2x$. The dimension of possible variation is the value of x, and varying this shows that the relationship of the gradient to x is invariant.

Similarly, the shape of a triangle may vary as we drag it with dynamic software, but its medians are always coincident. The dimension of possible variation is the shape of the triangle, and varying this shows the constant relationship of the medians.

In each of these cases a learner could be distracted by other features that are still varying: the direction and length of medians or the numerical value of the gradient. Attention to the teacher's intention is not automatic.

Here is a further illustration of the power of focusing on a particular dimension of possible variation:

Task 34b: Same and Different Sequences

Consider these sequences:

      2, 4, 6, 8, . . .   2, 5, 8, 11, . . .   2, 7, 12, 17, . . .

What is the same and what is different about them? Can you predict
   later terms? Make up more sequences like these.
Now think about these:

      2, 4, 6, 8, . . .   7, 9, 11, 13, . . .   10, 12, 14, 16, . . .

What is the same and what is different about them? How can you
   predict later terms? Make up more sequences like these.

The teacher who was devising these tasks wanted to start on the very comfortable ground of even numbers to introduce arithmetic progressions as simple sequences. By varying one parameter at a time learners can focus on effects of change without being distracted by two things changing at once. They are also discouraged from making unhelpful assumptions associated with one sequence (2, 4, 6, 8, . . .) where the initial value is the same as the difference and where the sequence is a times table. (Focusing on extending the range of possible change could lead beautifully to negative common differences.)

Relating Personal and Conventional Spaces

Mathematical folklore includes what we have called conventional example spaces. Fragments of these appear in texts and are presented to learners by teachers as "favorite" examples. Learners then integrate some of these into their own example spaces. Teachers are responsible for careful selection of examples from conventional spaces that will enable learners to communicate easily with others. The examples teachers offer, suggest, or prompt will of course come from their personal example spaces. Thus, learners depend on teachers to be acquainted with conventional example spaces. Teaching and learning can be seen as communications between the example spaces of teachers, learners, and convention. Construction of learners' example spaces is influenced by exploration of conventional examples; conventional spaces are influenced by examples that prove to be pedagogically and mathematically informative for learners and teachers. Symbiotically, knowledge of conventional examples is constructed in the process of developing personal spaces.

CONSTRUCTING NEW OBJECTS FOR ONESELF

Is it possible to construct entirely new objects for oneself? How can you go beyond what you already know? This is the heart of the learning paradox, which we discuss at the end of this section.

We suggest that it is possible for a teacher to push learners beyond their current bounds and self-imposed constraints, to open up possibilities that are not entirely new for the learners but have not as yet come to mind in the current situation. We introduced some illustrative tasks in chapter 4 but will now dwell more on subtle differences in how tasks are presented and how these presentations might cause slightly varied responses in the structure of the learner's emergent example space.

"To Find" as a Construction Task

In an extreme leap, we begin to ask ourselves whether indeed every mathematical task is a construction problem. Traditional tasks of the "to find . . ." type are asking the learner to construct one example, usually one that is so constrained that there may be only one possibility. Consider the linguistically simple but mathematically complex differences among these three prompts:

Task 35: Same and Different Equations

Find the value for x that satisfies $3x + 1 = 0$.
Find a value for x that satisfies $3x + 1 = c$.
Find values for x and y that satisfy $3x + y = 0$.

There is no general method for "find" just as there is no general method for example generation. In the first task a learner can just "see" the required answer or use a solution method—even trial and error might work. In the second task a learner might try to solve it and give the answer in terms of c or might state that x could be anything and put constraints on c to get the inverse relationship. One could use algebraic, numerical, or graphical methods to say something useful about it. The answer can be seen as an example of a relationship or as a representative of a class. In the third task a learner might draw a graph and pick a pair of values at a point or generate values from the relationship as it is given or pick a number for x and work out what y would be. Some may even give boundary values, such as (0, 0), which exemplify special features but do not show general awareness. Each method offers different insights and uses different ways of "seeing." What is exemplified for the learner could be a technique, a class, or a relationship. Asking "make up a 'to find' task of your own like this" would reveal how it is being seen.

"To find," when only one answer is possible, can thus be seen as a special sort of exemplification task in which there are so many constraints that learners can iterate toward the one answer by applying them to a general case—assuming their initial idea is, indeed, generic.[27]

Task 36: Compounding Constraints

Solve these three simultaneous equations:

$$3x + 4y - 5z = -32,\ 2x - y + 8z = 50,\ \text{and}\ x + y + z = 4.$$

Think about what a triple (x, y, z) means or looks like graphically.
What triples satisfy the first equation? The second? The third?
What triples satisfy the first and the second equation? First and third?
What triples satisfy all three constraints?

It might be useful for students, even when they are using an algorithm to produce one desired answer, to understand that they are constructing an extremely constrained example of a general class of objects. The notion of example space supports a perception of mathematical tasks as constructive and creative, even when following an algorithm, because the student is aware that they are "homing in" on one of several possibilities.

---

[27]In his influential and unsurpassed study of mathematical thinking, Krutetskii (1976) reported that in response to the prompt "compose a problem like this one," some learners isolated specific essential features and generalized immediately without recourse to multiple examples.

Being Asked for Several Examples

> *Task 37: Several Ways*
>
> Find at least six ways to cut a square into quarters.

Did you persist until you had six?

Some learners were asked to show on the chalkboard how a square could be cut into quarters (Watson, 2001). At first learners offered four standard ways of cutting: two diagonal cuts, vertical and horizontal cuts, and three parallel cuts in two orientations.

However, there were six diagrams on the chalkboard to be quartered! The energy that accompanied getting the first four done turned into puzzled silence. The learners, not being familiar with active participation, sat and waited to see what would happen. Eventually, two more ways to cut were offered that did not result in four congruent pieces but instead focused on equal areas. A shift had been made.

There were some shouts of "you can't do that," but when it was shown that the ways of cutting could be defended and had some logic to them, there was acceptance even if understanding was not complete. Moving from the familiar to the unfamiliar required learners to alter their understanding of what was meant by quarters or, possibly, by fraction; to abandon the images of congruence that, until then, had seemed perfectly adequate; and to rethink "what else could be possible?" Of course, learners' attention may have been dominated by "what else does the teacher want from us?" rather than on "how else can you cut a square into quarters?," but once new possibilities start to emerge, everyone can construct their own version. Being asked to justify their choices (how do you know it is in quarters?) and to contemplate all possibilities from which they could choose, their example spaces do in fact extend—at least for the moment.

The point here is not that there is something special about being asked for six examples, but that they were asked for more than the number of obvious examples, which in this case turned out to be four. The teacher also had to be prepared to respond to whatever was offered. Learners might have recognized that they could use central symmetry:

which can be seen both as one of an infinite class of different examples or as a generic example of a single class (and, furthermore, the lines out from the center need not be straight, just any non-self-intersecting path from center to edge, rotated three more times through 90°).

In chapter 2, we described how the learners in Linda's classroom could choose to adapt what had already happened, continue a local pattern that someone else had started, or do something different. That each action received approval and discussion as it happened made it clear that what was wanted was not a search for one right answer but an exploration of several possible actions: movement within and extension of a shared, current example space.

This leads us to a further construct: the notion of a collective example space. Each individual (learners and teacher) has their own example space at any moment, emerging from past experience according to current stimuli. At the same time a shared, or at least taken-as-shared, space emerges through negotiation and discussion within the group. Individuals may take on more or less of that negotiated space as part of their own, and they may have quite different aspects accessible in the future. But during the development of a lesson, a temporary, situated, collective example space also emerges from which learners might draw.

Seeking More.   Although we have said that there was nothing magic about six examples, we have found that there is particular power in the way two or three learner-generated examples might be evoked.

"Find another . . ." directs attention away from a particular example, and it reminds learners that their first thought may not be an appropriate central paradigm for the whole class of objects. How might teachers plan to exhaust obvious examples and cause learners to start searching actively? Here are some accounts from practice and research.

Five experienced secondary school teachers were working on a sequence of spatial two-dimensional patterns that illustrated a quartic formula. It can be rather a surprise to find that one can draw patterns that generalize with expressions involving a degree higher than 2, because our usual understanding of dimensions may lead us to believe that two would be the maximum degree possible on paper.

Task 38: High Degree

Write down a method of generating an infinite sequence of designs
starting with the following three. Then find an expression for the
number of white squares involved in the nth design.

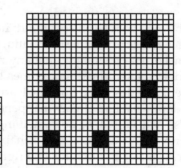

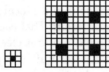

Make up more spatial sequences that can be given in two dimensions
and whose formulae involve degree three or four.

Some of the teachers found that they could only work with degree three
by drawing the usual kind of two-dimensional representations of three-
dimensional objects. It was too hard to unpick previous ways of seeing n^3
so that they could think of it in new ways. Their example spaces of possible representations needed reorganizing. They agreed that they had
learned something new about, or developed their understanding of, third-
and fourth-degree expressions but could not describe this change. One
teacher, Anthony, had developed a spatial representation by doing what
he described as "going back to the beginning." For him, this was an algebraic beginning, thinking of n^3 as "n lots of n^2" and thus seeing the possibility of drawing n lots of n^2 on paper.

Another teacher, Jim, had constructed a diagram for a fourth-degree
polynomial consisting of a different arrangement of squares to the one
given. He described his technique as "starting from what I have already
got." He created a pattern that was visually different: The squares were arranged differently, there were different numbers of them, and the counting methods one could construct from the diagrams were very different.
Yet, he claimed that it was the same as what had already been done and
hence not different. For him, the crucial part had been the representation
of multiple copies of n^2 on paper, and his meaning of "the same" was that

he had used the same basic method of representation, that is, "n^2 representations of n^2." In other words, he had an algebraic view of the problem in which all formulas of the fourth degree were seen to be roughly the same in terms of how they could be represented on paper—namely, all quartic formulas are the same up to rearranging the spatial representation using various transformations and tinkering with it. You might like to see if this is true or what it would mean for it to be true.

A geometer, artist, or designer would certainly not have thought of Jim's diagrams as the same as the given ones. However, as a general way of organizing example spaces of polynomials, categorizing them by degree, as Jim did, is often useful.

Here are some related questions about the relevance of example spaces:

Task 39: Structuring Example Spaces

For what sort of questions is it useful to see all straight line graphs as the available example space?

For what sort of questions would it be more helpful to have them divided into smaller subcategories, say those with a certain gradient or those that go through the origin?

For what sort of questions is it helpful to have them included in a larger class with other objects, such as quadratic graphs?

If "what sort of questions" throws you a bit at first, consider properties shared by all the objects in the class and then formulate questions that ask for examples of objects with those properties. For example, faced with a task devised by Sue Magidson (suggested to us by Alan Schoenfeld, personal communication, June 1, 2003)—create (in a graph plotter or on paper) a giant asterisk or starburst of straight lines—uniformity of the spacing forces attention on the slopes of the lines. What are appropriate example spaces from which to draw and cross-link to succeed?

Jim's experience illustrates three features of example spaces found in chapter 3: first, they are personal (his was constructed according to a general algebraic class); second, they emerge in response to a situation (he did not access his generalized space immediately; he had to get to it via the images triggered through the task); and, third, there is interplay between geometric and algebraic ways of seeing. In addition, it shows us some of the relationships between exemplification and insight. In his case, he saw one example and was asked to make one of his own. As he made up his own, he was thinking about essential sameness and difference between the examples, and this led him straight to a generalizing insight.

A similar thing happened in a session in which people had been asked to construct a similar question to this one:

Task 40: Marbles

If Anne gives one of her marbles to John, they will have the same number; if instead John gives one of his marbles to Anne, she will have twice as many as John. How many marbles do each of them have?

Make up a complicated version of this task using these ideas.

Some people changed the names; some people changed one or more of the numbers involved (are the two occurrences of "one" in the task the same or could they be different?); some people tried to have the same numbers and same structure but different context (comparisons of ages were popular); some people tried to generalize a class of similar problems right away, using letters for numbers and trying, using combinations of algebra and trial-and-adjustment, to find solutions. Some people altered the mathematical structure, jumping to "any context in which there are two equations and two unknowns." Within the marbles context, if the numbers are altered, will a solution still be possible? In other words, what are the ranges of permissible change for the various numbers within the marbles context?

One person wrote: "If Anne gave 'whatever-mess-of-operations-I-can-think-of marbles' to John, I can then compare what she has with John's and reverse; but the 'if' may have a solution and the reverse may not." This is clearly an example of generalization that goes beyond merely changing the numerical variables; this example substitutes functions for single values and offers a solution algorithm. The learner has seen the problem as presenting a structure rather than specific details.

Here learners have been given an example and been asked for another. In one case the construction of another led to a more abstract sense of generality. How can such insights be deliberately prompted so that more learners might experience them?

Finding Two Examples. In this section we illustrate a way in which being asked for more than one example can trigger creativity and exploration. In particular, being asked for one example first and then a further example imposing a slightly altered constraint can prompt learners to move beyond the obvious. We shall start by asking for one example and move on from there.

Task 41a: Give Me a Number With One Constraint

Construct a number that uses each digit once and only once.

You might like to recall what you felt when we posed similar questions earlier in the book (in *Task 16: Freedom* and *Task 23: Write Down—Constrained*). Here, there is no reference example from which to work. A common response is to ask "what is the trick?" Several learners tackle this task by writing the digits in order instead of thinking about the finished number, but this can lead some to write integers that start with a zero digit! Very few people use decimal points or construct fractions in the usual representation. A few impose their own pattern constraints in order "not to be random," as these comments from some learners show: "I am going to be systematic so I don't lose anything" (obviously keeping track is a problem, as some people repeat or omit digits), and "I am interested in a rational possibility, although I first wrote a decimal one."

Now try this:

Task 41b: Give Me a Number With Two Constraints

Construct a number as close as possible to $\frac{1}{2}$ using all the digits once and once only (note the similarities with *Task 26: Named Decimals*).

A former cause of insecurity (why am I doing this?) might be replaced with a new insecurity about getting it right and a sense of failure if someone else gets closer.

Some learners expressed the following: "I should have done 0.498765321," "Oh no! Has everyone got a closer one than me?," and "I never thought of that!"

Most gave decimal representations; some wrote fractions. At the very least this prompt persuaded people to use *number* to mean more than just integers. No one gave an exact answer presumably because the word *close* in the question implied approximation. In fact, it is possible to express $\frac{1}{2}$ exactly if you permit arithmetic operations. This had certainly not occurred to anyone explicitly because we tend to interpret *number* to mean the compact symbol for a number, not a calculation or "mess of operations" that represents that number in a different form. Implicitly, however, one could see fractions always as operations, either because they operate on other values (as in "two thirds of something") or because they are themselves an operation (two thirds meaning "two divided by three").

More generally, notice how the extreme openness of the first request for a number led people to be suspicious, feel insecure, and hence play safe. The second prompt led people to be a little more adventurous, although it was limited by interpretations of *close*. It also introduced a competitive edge. This led us to understand that asking for two examples might be a good way to encourage an appreciation of sameness and difference and of awareness of dimensions of possible variation and that the introduction of more constraints can increase learners' security and, paradoxically, encourage more creativity.

Here are some tasks that are structured to encourage exploration beyond the given format, to experience a wider generality:

Task 42a: Toward a Wider Generality

Calculate a percentage of a number:

$$5\% \text{ of } 20 = \tfrac{1}{2} \text{ of } 10\% \text{ of } 20 = \tfrac{1}{2} \text{ of } 2 = 1$$

Give an example of your own that is like this one.
Give a different method of calculating a percentage of a number.

How did you interpret "like this"? Are there any other possibilities?

Task 42b: Toward a Wider Generality

Here is a quadrilateral that has two pairs of equal sides:

Which vertices can you move (drag or alter) one at a time, and in which direction, and always have a quadrilateral with two pairs of equal sides?
Draw another quadrilateral that has two pairs of equal sides but could not be made by moving a single vertex of the given diagram. What about moving two at a time?

How much freedom is there in choosing such quadrilaterals? Do you think in terms of infinitely many or of there being two types that coincide in rhombuses?

> *Task 42c: Toward a Wider Generality*
>
> Here is an equation that describes the position of a particular object
>   that is moving along a straight line in a particular way:
>
> $$\text{Distance} = \text{Velocity} \times 6 + 5,$$
>
> where 6 is the time in seconds and 5 is the starting position in meters
>   away from some point.
> Make up a similar equation for yourself, and explain what it means.
> Now make up another equation for motion in a straight line that is
>   different to this one in some way, and explain the difference.

You can change the numbers without knowing what you are doing, and you can change the numbers knowing what they mean. So being asked to articulate or justify in some way is important to making contact with the full force of being asked to make up your own examples.

In each of the aforementioned tasks it is informative for a teacher to see what is regarded as similar and what as different. Pairs of learners could look at each other's ideas and say what they see as the same or different. In each case there are possibilities that arise from certain interpretations. For example, in *Task 42b: Toward a Wider Generality* it depends what might be meant by *moving* or *adjusting*; someone might see rotation as producing a different diagram due to the alteration in orientation. In *Task 42c: Toward a Wider Generality* nothing has been said about whether velocity can vary, but even if a less radical difference is proposed the learner still has to engage with the meaning of the equation to produce something different. Note how the second item in each task either requires the introduction of a new constraint or the recognition of a constraint that can be noticed and removed—that is, recognition of what can be varied. Dimensions of possible variation have to be identified and their corresponding ranges of permissible change explored.

Learners typically respond at first by (a) changing a minor feature that does not affect the structure of the example, (b) changing the operations involved in a problem, or (c) altering the context or the numbers. The teacher then asks for another example that is not like the first two. Learners have to say in what respect it is not like the first two and justify that it is still an example of whatever was requested. Thus, they explore the possible example space, and the teacher gains insight into what the learner sees as being the important features of the example.

The Role of Three.   As we commented in *Task 12b: Another and Another* (shown next), we have found that asking for three examples leads learners to push themselves beyond the mundane and create their own frameworks and questions for making the example-generation task less repetitive.

Task 12b Again: Another and Another

Write down two numbers that have a difference of 2.
Write down another pair.
Write down another pair.

In a teaching situation we have found it important not to hurry but to wait until most have done one example before asking for *another*. By the second or third time you ask for an example, most people will already be constructing several for themselves, sometimes many more than three. Here are some similar prompts:

Task 43a: Another and Another—Cutting Circles

Find a way to cut a circle into four identical pieces.
Find another.
Find another.

Task 43b: Another and Another—Continuous Functions

Find a function that is continuous everywhere but not differentiable
    everywhere.
Find another.
Find another.

We have found that when people are asked to think of an example, then asked to think of another, and then another, some of them report that the second request has encouraged them to tinker with their existing image, but the third request has sent them searching for something rather different. They find themselves asking "what else is possible?" rather than tweaking their first idea a little more. A sense of changing awareness with three examples is reported elsewhere as well. Pierre Boulez said that listeners hearing an unfamiliar atonal phrase once might think "Ouch!"; on hearing it the second time they might think "oh?"; and on hearing it the third time they sigh "ahhhh!" The first incident causes some surprise, by the second incident learners are recognizing something as familiar, and by the third time they see it as part of some bigger project—an example of a wider class. To experienced mathematicians, the first incident is an isolated example of the properties being discussed; the second suggests pattern and replicability; the third gives a sense of "here we go, listening to music, exploring mathematics, interpreting text . . ." or whatever the activity is. For some, being asked for a third example is seen as an invitation to generalize.

How might this work in classrooms with less confident learners? In a scenario in which learners are volunteering examples to the teacher, asking for another might just be interpreted as a way of saying the first was wrong. Then asking for a third might be seen as indicating that the first two had been wrong and so on. However, if the requests keep coming and if the teacher's voice tone is positive and energetic, it is more likely that learners will believe that all attempts are acceptable. Such questions reveal what learners interpret by *another*. Paola Vighe (2003) asked her primary students to "draw a triangle; draw a different triangle; draw another different triangle" and found that their notion of *different* was restricted to different sizes, orientations, or shadings of an equilateral triangle. Thus, learner-generated examples (LGEs) told her a great deal about the limitations of their concept image.

Pessia Tsamir and Dina Tirosh (2003) made creative use of the "and another" technique and the potential for variation to include incorrect examples by asking learners to "do it another way, and another way" to explore their understanding of techniques. For example:

$$\frac{6+4}{12+8} = \frac{1}{2}$$

when done another way revealed

$$\frac{6^1 + 4^1}{12_2 + 8_2} = \frac{1+1}{2+2} = \frac{1}{2}$$

Learners revealed the use of incorrect methods for getting what appeared to be correct answers. Some displayed surprise that their alternative methods gave different answers. Sometimes, sadly, learners did not seem too concerned about getting different answers as they have come to accept that "mathematics is like that" because "mathematics doesn't make sense!" Example construction is one way to try to counteract that impression. This exercise had given the tutors insight into the superficiality of their students' understanding and provided the material for working in more depth on meaning.

As with many of the strategies we suggest, new ways to question and new expectations of learners will become part of normal practice and expectations if repeated and if the outcomes are clearly valued and used for further work. Some people do not use the sequence of requests to break their current mold, but even playing safe requires some mathematical decisions in terms of defining a pattern or rule to follow. After seeing how playful and extreme others have been and after being encouraged to be extreme in some way, they usually begin to open up and even enjoy newfound freedom and creativity in choosing extreme or complex examples.

Not everyone uses requests to find more as triggers to be creative, go beyond the obvious, or step outside their comfort zone. We are beginning to believe that this task structure distinguishes between those who want to generalize, abstract, and work with classes of objects and raise more questions and those who see their task as learners as fulfilling a teacher's desires in the safest and quickest way. At first, the teacher can ask for "another that is different in some way" and then for one that is "different in another way" to stimulate exploration and playfulness. Later it may be unnecessary even to ask for a second example as learners eagerly make up several different types for themselves immediately. Another approach is to ask learners to distinguish any one of three objects from the other two and to name the quality that distinguishes them. Based on her extensive research, Carole Dweck (2000) suggested that having creativity as an explicit aim of learning can assist in converting learners who are convinced that they have a ceiling of performance into learners eager to take on challenge to learn more.

Sense of Completion.   Some learners show a desire for completeness, but this desire may not be structured by imagining what *completeness* might mean in terms of representative types.[28] For a taste of the urge to be complete, consider the following:

Task 44: Midpoint Shapes

What shapes can you get by joining the midpoints of the sides of a
    quadrilateral?

When we offered this task to an experienced group of mathematics learners who were used to being taught techniques and applying them, there was a wide variation in approaches. Some drew a few fairly standard asymmetric quadrilaterals, joined the points, and conjectured from what they saw.

---

[28]See Bell (1976).

Others drew one special shape (arrowheads like the one shown were popular undoubtedly because they have unexpected properties because they are perhaps the most peculiar of the named quadrilaterals) and tried to find out something from the diagram by using knowledge of equal lines, angles, and so on. Others drew one of every kind of named quadrilateral that they could think of, together with some less symmetrical ones, and kept on drawing while hoping something interesting would jump out at them. A few only drew rectangles. Each response is displaying at least part of their triggered example space. For each of these approaches there seems to be a different understanding of the role of examples. Most were trying to limit what they drew and hoping to apply prior knowledge to gain insight from diagrams that were to be treated as generic. Some seemed to be going for completeness by trawling through their previous classifications without a sense of what sort of categorizations might be useful for this question. Bell (1976) realized that classifying and ordering tasks were necessary to attain completeness. To achieve a general statement required a sense of completeness and insight that related to the mathematical structures under investigation.

Pattern Breaking

Being asked for another requires either adaptation of what has been already given or something different to be created—it seems as if there are no other alternatives. How do learners find ways to break patterns or to break out of familiar images? They need experience in breaking patterns to understand the important dimensions of the concept and the range of change for each of these images. Like many pedagogical practices, a teacher's first attempt to pose a new kind of question or to vary the kinds of demands he or she makes on learners may seem unproductive because learners are being asked to behave differently and are unsure about what is expected. Establishing habits takes some time and deliberate planning. But pattern breaking removes the tedium of making tiny, unimportant changes in mathematical work, such as when learners are asked to do several exercises that are exactly the same apart from the numbers so that what is being exercised is arithmetic rather than mathematical thinking about the underlying concept.

Learners will not learn to cope with complexity unless they have to cope with complexity. Learners will not learn to break patterns unless they have to break patterns. There are two types of patterns being inter-woven here: the patterns of question types and classroom expectations and the patterns of dominant images, first impressions, and limited expe-riences of mathematical objects.

Stephen Brown and Marion Walter's (1983) algorithm for breaking pat-terns often helps in example generation. They advocated identifying all the features of a mathematical problem and asking yourself what would happen if each of them were changed as the rest stayed the same. Here is a demonstration of their method of problem posing: "In the context of a per-formance in the school hall, the problem could be: How can I arrange 60 chairs in equal rows?" Brown and Walter suggested reading the problem aloud and stressing different words each time to identify what could be changed. You might then identify *60*, *equal*, and *rows* as features you could alter mathematically. Of course, you could also change *I* and let someone else arrange the chairs, but that would be managerial rather than mathe-matical! Stressing one word and consequently ignoring (relatively) the others often has the effect of raising the questions: Why that word? Why not another? Gattegno (1970, p. 136) suggested that the act of generalizing arises precisely through stressing some features and consequently down-playing others.

This could lead to variants of the problem such as: "How can I arrange 61, 62, and 63 chairs?" "How can I arrange 60 chairs in unequal rows?" "How can I arrange 60 chairs in rectangular blocks or triangles or trapezia or . . . ?"

Asking "What if it were different?" about individual words and phrases can be applied to examples of any kind, but such changes might take the object outside the current example space, depending on the con-straints required. Thus, some changes maintain examplehood, whereas others destroy it. They go beyond the range of permissible change. For in-stance, you could systematically change the features of the following quadratic equation to generate more examples with which to rehearse finding solutions: $2x^2 + 3x - 5 = 0$.

Some of the changes would create other examples, including some that are harder than this to solve. If the coefficient of x^2 changed to zero would it still be a quadratic equation? If the equality changed to an inequality it would no longer be an equation at all. Each of these changes yields inter-esting mathematical questions. In the first case we no longer have a quad-ratic; in the second case we are no longer dealing with solving equations, except as part of a more complex problem.

By carefully changing each feature, we find examples that are very close to being nonexamples and so act as a form of boundary example for that particular dimension of possible variation: Giving the coefficient of the highest power a tiny positive value takes it to the edge of example-hood. We also find objects that are very close to being examples, so close that a small change would bring them into the space: Introducing a higher power with a tiny positive coefficient would have this effect. Thus, the systematic methods of questioning presented by Brown and Walter (1983) can lead to a deep exploration and understanding of the boundaries of the meaning of a concept and a restructuring of the learner's understanding. Furthermore, attention to the features in this systematic way can lead to an awareness of pattern and generalization such as: How does the relationship between 2, 3, and 5 generalize?

Algorithmic Methods

When finding a "new" object, there are sometimes choices about the approach.

Task 45a: Find a "New" Object

Find a quadratic whose slopes at the roots are perpendicular.

There are two dominant approaches to this task: Start from a symbolic description of the general and then impose constraints or search around among particulars until you find one that works.[29] Either one can find general formulae for the gradients at the roots, force them to be perpendicular, and then backtrack to say something necessary or sufficient about the quadratic or one can start with a pair of perpendicular gradients and construct quadratics around them. One approach starts from the constraints and works toward an object; the other starts from a generality and imposes constraints. The former approach is an algorithm for making an object and others like it; the latter gives one example plucked from the air unless, of course, you start by expressing perpendicularity in a general way. Both ways produce general or specific answers, but in the second method you could start with specific gradients, produce an example, and learn nothing general about the behavior of such quadratics.

In the next task there is a more obvious choice to be made:

---

[29]Alan Schoenfeld (personal communication, June 1, 2003) noticed that because he knew the slope of $x^2/2$ is x, he could adjust this to $(x^2 - 1)/2$ to produce an example. Here familiarity affords quick access, via tinkering, to an example.

Task 45b: Find a New Object Again

Find three straight lines that meet at points whose coordinates are integers.

We could find a general formula for the points of intersection of three straight lines and then try to make them be integers, but a much easier approach would be to start with three integer lattice points and use a standard method to find the three straight lines (or take the easy route and let them go through the same suitable point!).

So searching for examples can be done by adapting standard methods to answer unfamiliar "to find" tasks, taking account of extra constraints.

We have mentioned this approach because it conforms to many "to find" tasks in textbooks, but for us it lacks the creative potential of the previous prompts. This is because, having found such an example, one may only have exemplified something that was already known and although the object itself may be new to you, nothing essentially new has been created. Note, however, that the intervention of a teacher asking questions about this new object might well guide a learner toward exploration of a new subclass that it might represent.

How Can We Build What We Do Not Already Know About?

In chapter 4 we displayed a variety of ways in which people can be induced to construct mathematical objects that are new to them: tinkering, gluing, collage, scaffolded construction, and restructuring. In each case the new object was an extension from one or more existing examples or even counterexamples. What seemed to be required is an imagination for what might be possible. This might take the form of a set of properties or criteria fulfilled sequentially as constraints on a familiar generality. It also requires flexibility to select some features or details and ignore others.

Some of the new objects created are illustrations of concepts, so there is a shift between object and concept: between object as particular and concept as generality. The word *construction* used in both contexts also suggests an analogy between object and concept construction. Given a definition, a mathematician might be able to construct a fitting object from scratch by satisfying each part of the definition, but this object may end up very unlike other previously known objects. Similarly, given an object, a mathematician routinely constructs definitions to capture some quality or property of the particular, adjusting the draft definition to make theorems elegant to state and easy to prove.

In this section we return to the issue of creating new objects and make use of the experience of object construction to explore parallels between constructing objects and constructing concepts.

Try this:

Task 46: Decagon

Construct an equal-sided decagon with as many concave vertices that jut into the polygon as possible.

School students who have become playful when asked to construct such a polygon often discover a surprise: a star! In the process, they find they have to rethink their working definitions and their example spaces of stars and polygons to include this new realization.

And try this:

Task 47: Constant Diameter

Construct a two-dimensional object that has a constant diameter but is not a circle.

It might make sense to start by rotating a stick around a fixed point on that stick, but we soon find that gives us a circle that we have to reject. It is often the case when exploring new ideas, that we have to consciously reject the old ones. Here we may decide that fixing a center point is unhelpful and maybe it would be possible to define a shape for which the diameters do not all go through the center. Rather than changing everything at once, we could rotate the stick for a while around one point, then change the fixed point and rotate it a bit more, then change the fixed point and rotate it some more, and so on until we close it up again after 180° rotation. Would this create such an object? What definition of *diameter* would work?

A further way to create objects from well-outside a current example space would be to create a description by negating features of a known definition. For instance:

Task 48a: What if Something Else?

In a geometric progression each term is a constant multiple of the preceding term. Construct a progression in which the multiplier changes according to some rule. Can you produce a formula for the nth term or for the sum of n terms?

This is a constraint on the possibilities by asking "what if not . . . ?" (Brown & Walter, 1983), a version of dimensions of possible variation. In this case we have deliberately focused attention on varying fundamental properties rather than on parameters. Here is a geometrical example:

Task 48b: What if Something Else?

Congruent triangles can be glued together edge to edge to tessellate the plane. In a sense they produce a plane. What sort of surfaces would be produced by tessellating triangles whose angle sum is greater than (or less than) 180°?

To address these questions requires more than tinkering. It requires a thorough investigation of dimensions of possible variation and some measure of fresh insight (although we have made suggestions in *Task 48a*, and there is some support in Appendix B for *Task 48b*). Once such an object is constructed it would be an interesting challenge to describe the class of which it might be an example. You would then have constructed not only an object you have never seen or considered before but an entire class—although logically it appears to be impossible.

Philosophers have been intrigued by the question "how can you construct anything new?" because it challenges theories about the growth of knowledge. On one hand, "constructing something new" seems to be necessary for knowledge to grow and, on the other hand, it seems to be impossible until you have acquired the new knowledge. Plato's entire works can be read as an investigation of this question, in which he reached the conclusion that it is necessary to have been born knowing things that are then later revealed. Subsequent philosophers have added their gloss and their alternatives. The learning paradox, the problem of how learners can construct objects that are more complex than what they already know, has also exercised educators more recently (Bereiter, 1985; Pascual-Leone, 1980). As Carl Bereiter (1985) stated: "if one tries to account for learning by means of mental actions carried out by the learner, then it is necessary to attribute to the learner a prior cognitive structure that is as advanced or complex as the one to be acquired" (p. 202).

Bereiter's attempts to resolve this paradox revolve around describing mental resources that are underused but "bootstrap" cognitive growth. Here we describe some aspects of example construction that illustrate his ideas:

- Happening to alight on appropriate examples for the wrong reasons or by chance (as in noticing something potentially useful to put in your larder).

- Using existing knowledge structures to provide likely structures for new situations: for instance, using systems and self-questioning that have already proved useful in circumstances perceived as similar (as in using familiar objects in the larder to create a new dish).
- Focusing attention on salient features in a more complex field.
- Imitating (as in following a recipe from the larder); Bereiter did not comment on how imitating behavior might affect cognition.
- An overall feeling of the sense of mathematics that enables monitoring.
- Bias, such as a tendency to give priority to certain things seen as mathematical (as in using familiar constituents in a familiar recipe).

To some extent, Bereiter's (1985) suggestion that we learn by building up complex understandings from simpler situations parallels our claim that exemplification is a central feature of learning (and teaching) mathematics. The learner is usually expected to learn about generalities through induction from given examples—to "see the general through the particular." However, we have also been suggesting deduction as a route to learning mathematics, with the learner being offered what appears to be a generalization and being asked to create examples. This is an adapted form of deduction because the learner has to have some idea of the generality in terms of image or meaning and may indeed have obtained this through earlier induction or abduction—that is, the learner generalizes from the structure and likely possibilities of a single case and brings what is already known into play (Eco, 1983). In the just-noted discussion we suggest that powerful generalizations can be conjectured. It is also clear that learners generalize from one case when they are asked to produce a similar example to one given, choosing what is meant by *similar* from what they already know and have experienced in mathematics.

Ernst von Glasersfeld (1998) resolved the learning paradox by pointing out that it depends on the view that, although learning is only inductive, the step that generates new knowledge is always creative, even if it results from empirical data such as a set of examples. Thus, even inductive theories necessarily recognize the abductive step in which the behavior of an example is seen as likely to be a feature of a more complex class of objects.

But for us there is a further question: In what way can the construction of new mathematical knowledge be regarded as the creation of more complex knowledge? Bereiter's (1985) concern depends on the belief that what is induced is more complex than the learner's previous experience, as well as on the inductive process. A learner of mathematics has to do nothing more complex than draw distinctions between objects that have similarities and differences, classify them, recognize them in different representations, understand the scope of meaning of the labels applied to them, treat classes as objects with common properties and behaviors, understand their relationships, and move to and fro between examples and generalities. Of course, some of these things take time and much experience to come to know and there are a myriad of procedures to remember that speed up transformations between representations, but the processes that enable the learner to construct new complex meanings from simpler meanings (i.e., the processes of complexifying) are already known to the learner—They are, at the very least, the processes by which language, social behavior, and early mathematics (e.g., treating a number as a noun) are learned.

Artists, architects, scientists, engineers, and certainly mathematicians all have the experience of sequentially modifying and improving, then tearing down and rebuilding. When they start afresh they incorporate improvements that have emerged so far. It is patently obvious that both individuals and communities "learn"—that is, they are able to make novel construction—by "standing on the shoulders of giants." To do so does not require knowing everything in advance. Rather, it is based on making use of previously experienced components that are reasonably confidence inspiring and can be manipulated with some facility and also on noticing interesting objects that might be useful in construction at some future time or in some other situation.

In a way, this observation is hidden in Bereiter's (1985) work: How else can one have an overall mathematical sense or a personal monitor as he suggested? The learning paradox is resolved because we do know how to complexify, how to abstract, and how to learn. In our context, we can build new examples because we know how to generalize, how to spot what varies and what stays the same, how to vary features to see what happens, how to test out examples against general statements, and how to test general statements against examples.

BEING ASKED TO GIVE EXAMPLES:
THE LARDER METAPHOR

Personal example spaces are temporary, emergent, and situated, and the only thing we can be sure of on entering is the dominance of certain images, which may themselves be culturally, historically, and biographically influenced. In chapter 4 we introduced the homespun metaphor of a larder to describe these personal example spaces, and many colleagues and learners have recognized this metaphor as describing their experience of looking for examples. The metaphor allows for different relationships to be noticed according to how the search is conducted and for what purpose.

The metaphor can be extended to include failure to find what one hoped for but with a suspicion that you can use what is there, which is what Edmund Husserl (1973) described as "in-grasp" (p. 103 ff.), to create something appropriate. When looking for a number with exactly four factors, perhaps with an initial sense only of those that have two factors and "the rest," one might come across a number with four fortuitously or one could construct it from knowledge of primes. In *Task 45a: Find a New Object* concerning particular quadratics, you may have constructed what was required from other things you know about quadratics in general. Therefore, the larder offers a structural metaphor for finding and making examples from past and forgotten experience, using what you know in unfamiliar ways, and finding the raw material with which one can tinker and glue new objects. This reminds us of diSessa et al.'s (1991) description of learners as designers and builders rather than just experimenters and of Bereiter's (2002) vision of school learning as design and adaptation in response to problems. Here, the designers and builders are stimulated by what is at hand.

When we first developed the larder metaphor, we tended to notice those for whom it resonates; but there are some for whom it does not. In some incidents described in this book it has been clear that spatial metaphors are not helpful for everyone, and a learner who generalizes rapidly in an algebraic manner may have nothing on the shelves apart from what, to the rest of us, look like opaque boxes labeled *polynomials* or *shapes* but which, to them, offer clarity and organization.

Even when it is helpful, the larder can be seen as a rather static metaphor and might not take into account what many of us do in larders when we start looking for something; that is, we begin to reorganize and recategorize the larder. It seems that as we begin the task of looking for examples, we also organize the search. We may not even call casual viewing of the contents *searching*. But as each new item is seen, we are continuously reorganizing the search by creating new categories and subspaces and even knocking down walls into the larder next door. The larder metaphor describes well the search for objects that we have met before, but it only offers the beginning of a sense of reconstruction and extension that characterizes learning and is often hard to articulate. Larder reorganization copes with restructuring, but opportunities for continuous restructuring and multidimensional networking are limited. It does not offer images to parallel the sudden collapsing of example spaces which we saw in Jim's case (refer to the Constructing New Objects for Oneself section of this chap.), where insight into generality removes the need for a cluttering of multiple examples and allows the learner to move to another level of abstraction. One abstract image takes the place of what for others might just be a collection of objects seen as somehow similar. A further omission is the learner as designer who starts from first principles, not from what is on hand. In the Constructing New Objects for Oneself section Anthony started constructing, not from the given object and all that it evoked, but from different readings of the language of mathematics, finding a reading from which he could design and build from scratch.

Nevertheless, we find the larder metaphor more informing than limiting.

SUMMARY

We probed the pedagogy of structuring example spaces more deeply and discussed three kinds of examples: central, extreme, and general classes. Then we considered effects of teachers and authors providing one or several examples for learners to think about. We explored learner responses to tasks that ask them to produce several examples, including new ones. Then we looked carefully at how it is possible to construct new objects that you have not previously considered, leading into a resolution of the learning paradox. Finally, we returned to the larder metaphor as a description of the structure of example spaces.

In the next chapter we return to the classroom to show how people have used these and similar ideas, and then we pull together the different types of tasks we have used throughout the book.

Strategies for Prompting and Using Learner-Generated Examples

In this chapter we identify strategies and task structures that have proved effective in prompting learners to construct mathematical objects. We draw on the various tasks used in previous chapters and on some further cases of classrooms, lessons, and other learning environments in which learners have been asked to construct LGEs for themselves. In each case we look for manifestation of the principles derived in chapter 3:

- Exemplification is individual and situational.
- Perceptions of generality are individual.
- Examples can be perceived or experienced as members of structured spaces.
- Example spaces can be explored and extended by the learner, with or without external prompts.

At the end of the chapter there is a list of different types of tasks used so far in the book and an exploration of how practice can be incorporated into tasks that promote exploration of structure.

CASE STUDIES

We start with Sara and Andrew using exemplification with 11-year-old students to encourage metacognition and to inform their teaching, Tim using it for revision purposes as well as for diagnostic assessment, and

Nevil using exemplification to encourage conjecturing. Next we look at the use of LGEs for undergraduate study, with one case using software to provide feedback, with the aim being both cognitive and self-assessing. Interaction between learner and text is then suggested as a means of using LGEs to explore mathematical concepts. Work associated with the Shell Centre in the United Kingdom provides instances of use of LGEs as exercises. Then we look at some practices in which generation of examples provides raw material for empirical mathematical discovery, similar to *Task 1a: Two Factors*. Next we look at two classrooms in which LGEs are part of normal practice in a variety of ways, highlighting how responsibility can shift from teacher to learner. The last classroom we describe shows how far such a shift can go, so that teaching is mainly dependent on learners' contributions, questions, and thoughts, with LGEs being one of a variety of forms of mathematical discourse for which responsibility has shifted to learners. We include many descriptions of classrooms, lessons, and snippets of practice here because much of our thinking derives from our excitement about teachers' practices, and everything offered in this chapter can be used, with some adaptation, for any age group and at any educational level.

Sara

Sara is a secondary mathematics teacher who found herself working in a school in which the teaching approach is usually traditional and textbook based. Her previous teaching experiences had been more varied and activity based, and she wanted to introduce new methods in a systematic way, evaluating the learners' reactions and monitoring their understanding (Howes, 2001).

Sara started by introducing weekly evaluation sheets on which learners could write about what they had learned during the week. She found that their responses very rapidly became stereotyped and that they were usually writing about a broad topic rather than giving information about changes in their understanding. For instance, typical responses would be "This week we did percentages." The more insightful might write "This week we did percentages. I have done them before, so this was not hard." These responses gave her no information about their learning, and she decided that the sheets she had constructed were not encouraging meaningful mathematical reflection.

Sara then asked her students to give examples of what they meant when they said "we learned about such-and-such." Interpretations of this request varied. When the topic was a technique, some would give a worked version, but some just gave an example of a question. For instance, when they had been working on finding arithmetic means, some would give a list of numbers and their mean; others would just write something like "find the mean of 3, 3, 4, and 5." When the topic was about some kind of mathematical object, learners would give an example. For instance, when they had been working on fractions, the example given might be "$\frac{3}{4}$" with no further information about how the learners see this, what they think it means, and so on. Some of these responses were helpful in communicating to Sara; others were not. Because her main aim was to monitor her teaching rather than develop their exemplification skills, Sara did not further explore this stage.

This work used the principle that exemplification is individual and that perception of generality is individual. Although some learners might have searched their example spaces, it would also be possible to use only what had already been given by Sara, thus exploration and extension was not explicitly encouraged.

Andrew

We know from Andrew Waywood's (1992, 1994) work that learners can and do explore their spaces when exemplification is the explicit focus of development. In asking learners to write journals as a metacognitive activity, he gave them a number of different requirements, including that they should "collect important examples." Younger learners tended to collect examples showing how to get answers, middle school pupils collected examples showing how to apply algorithms and formulas, and older learners used examples to illustrate ideas and serve as mnemonics for the content of a topic (1992, p. 37). Andrew constructed a hierarchy of sophistication of exemplification:

1. Give examples as appropriate practice exercises.
2. Illustrate mathematical procedures with examples of their use.
3. Display important examples that show how the mathematics works.
4. Illustrate points in the learner's discussion of the work with suitable special examples.
5. Summarize an area of mathematics by giving a range of examples, annotated to show their relevance.

The requirement to give examples became a useful form of reflection for some learners. They noticed things while writing that had escaped them during class. For example, one learner noticed that "some squared numbers had a doubling pattern to them: For example, decimal 0.142857 . . . squared is 0.020408163265 . . ." (Waywood, 1994, p. 331).

Andrew found that learners' use of exemplification improved, according to his hierarchy, during their time in his class. The fact that their journals were assessed may have helped with this, because they knew that to get more points they had to use examples to do more than just illustrate class-work techniques.

Tim

Sara's ideas were developed further by Tim, who offered a prompt sheet asking for LGEs as a revision aid to his 13-year-old students. The intention of this sheet was that learners would explore beyond what they had been given by Tim. They were asked to give worked examples of techniques and construct examples of concepts that fit certain constraints. Some of them were designed to bring learners into conflict with well-known limitations of conceptual understanding. Typical requests were as follows: Make up an example to show someone that you understand probability; make up an area problem that involves taking away three rectangles from one rectangle; give as few measurements as possible and still make it possible to calculate the area left when you take away the three rectangles.

These revision tasks recognized the principles of individuality, but because they were for learning rather than assessment purposes, it was more important that they encouraged exploration and extension. This was generally done through introduction of special constraints designed to push learners beyond their habitual boundaries, such as: Make up a number that is less than -2, greater than -3, and has 7 as one of its decimal digits, and is as large as possible.

Nevil

Nevil Hopley (2002) used LGEs to generate data for whole class discussion. Using a network of scientific calculators, each learner can send entries to the teacher's calculator which then appear on the projection screen. In this way, learners can self-check their ideas superficially by seeing if they are similar to others, and they each had to do some initial thinking about the topic before sending entries. For instance, the request "Send me a point for which the y-coordinate is double the x-coordinate" provides a set of points that should be on a straight line. If anyone sends a nonexample, only the teacher knows who it is. Furthermore, the learner sending the response is likely to see the error immediately and correct it. Common errors, such as getting the x- and y-coordinates the wrong way around, can be discussed by the whole class.

Another request could be "Send me the name of a shape that has at least one pair of parallel sides." The teacher gets immediate information about limitations of learners' current example spaces or the way they search for examples, whereas the learners are exposed to a variety of answers that may be different from their own. It also provides information needed to push further and impose more constraints to see what else learners can construct. Nevil reported that when he asked a class for the name of a shape that had an interior angle sum of 180° someone contributed the words *open circle*, and this generated some lively debate. He believed that this would probably not have happened if he had only been able to ask learners one at a time for answers.

This approach recognizes the individuality of example spaces and allows for exploration and extension. In many cases, learners have to understand some of the structures they are exploring, and it is always up to the teacher to impose constraints or special conditions to develop a sense of structure.

Chris

Chris does not use a classroom approach; he uses self-testing software. To provide an environment in which learners can explore how their understanding of important mathematical concepts may be partial or limited, Chris created banks of questions that are individually checked so that learners get instant feedback. He started by researching mathematics question types, building and using a taxonomy that informs assessment design. Questions are posed that require the following:

- Factual recall.
- Carrying out a routine calculation or algorithm.
- Classifying some mathematical object.
- Interpreting a situation or answer.
- Extending a concept.
- Proving, showing, or justifying.
- Constructing an instance.
- Criticizing a fallacy.

One question sequence is as follows:

Enter a formula for a function $p(x)$ such that:

$p(x)$ is a cubic,

$p(x)$ is a cubic and $p(4) = 0$,

$p(x)$ is a cubic and $p(4) = 0$ and $p(5) = 0$, and

$p(x)$ is a cubic and $p(4) = 0$ and $p(5) = 0$ and $p(0) = 20$.

Give an example of a cubic that satisfies the second condition but not the third condition and one that satisfies the third condition but not the fourth condition.

The procedure tests what the learner types in to see if it works and provides immediate feedback. Chris pointed out that "the creativity needed to genuinely construct an example could manifestly be replaced by the appropriate factual knowledge." Correct answers alone do not prove that learning is taking place at a deep level, because superficial recall can lead to correct answers when the person asking the question is unaware of what is already familiar for the learner. Thus, what has to be constructed afresh in one person's example space may already exist in another's. Even this task does not discriminate between deep and superficial learning, because the reason why an example may come to mind without construction for particular learners may be that they have worked so extensively in the area that they have more examples at hand. So the production of an appropriate example may be factual recall from a limited set, factual recall from a complex and well-organized space, or construction. By imposing unfamiliar constraints, the program can probe below the surface of a learner's response (Sangwin, 2003).

Another feature of his test is that learners may answer at different levels of generality. For example, some would give a particular cubic for their answer to the first condition; others might give a general formula, seeing cubics as a special case of all polynomials. There would also be variation between those who chose the figural example, $y = x^3$, and those who chose the more general one, $y = ax^3 + bx^2 + cx + d$ or $y = a(x - p)(x - q)(x - r)$. (See also *Task 28: Zeroed Functions*.)

The LGEs are stored and can be accessed and used for tutorial purposes later. Chris sees dialogue as an essential part of working productively with LGEs, which do not just play a role in assessment.

Chris is using the principles that (a) example spaces and perceptions of generality are personal, (b) they are structured in some way that relates to access, and (e) they can be explored with prompts. At the time of writing, he was finding that learners vary their responses in only limited ways when first using the system.

Patricia

Also working with undergraduates, Patricia uses assignment questions to demonstrate a commitment to LGEs as an integral part of learning advanced concepts (Cretchley, 1999). She also challenges them to justify their choices. She believes that asking for LGEs: (a) promotes reflection on specific aspects of a concept or on the concept generally, (b) encourages creative thought about mathematics, (c) assists in transferring ownership and responsibility for learning, and (d) makes it clear to learners that they should be able to demonstrate their depth of understanding and the ability to reason and communicate.

Typical tasks she prepared for learners are as follows:

- Here is an example of [some concept]. Give another example that illustrates something about the concept that this example does not show.
- Explore intersections of other sets of planes: Good examples will be selected and put on the web page.
- From each section of the problem sheets, single out one good problem—one you feel taught you the most or illustrates your understanding of the concept of that section best—explain why it was valuable for your learning.

These types of tasks engage learners actively with the concepts. Public display, such as a web page or collective review sheet, increases motivation and provides both assessment evidence and self-assessment opportunities. A few learners respond in a minimalistic way to these challenges; some devise a method that allows them to work at a moderately safe level; others play the "guess what she wants" game. Most take these prompts seriously, and students feel they become better learners as a result. Underlying the tasks are three principles: that LGEs are useful for learning about concepts, that learners can construct them and extend their example spaces, and that example spaces have structure that supports and informs qualitative judgments.

Nathan

A simpler case of exemplification for consolidation and assessment was used by Nathan with 15-year-old students. For homework he asked them to create "two good worked examples" for each rule of indices. Some learners handed in proofs of the rules written out in words, others gave verbal articulations of the rules, one learner wrote down his personal aide-mémoire, "and if the powers are next to each other they are multiplied, NOT ADDED." One learner had written that $(25^{1/2})^3 = 25^{3/2} = (25^{1/3})^2$; he also wrote $\sqrt{25} \times \sqrt{25} \times \sqrt{25} = 5 \times 5 \times 5$ which seemed at odds with $(25^{1/3})^2$ and caused confusion. However, he chose to cross out the work that led to a contradiction and stuck with his original understanding of the rule. This work was the most revealing of the whole set of homework as it told Nathan that some learners might not have a complete grasp of the necessary relationship between rule and demonstration and that rules were so paramount for these learners that examples which confounded them might be rejected, rather than use the examples to reject the rules.

A Textbook Approach

The case studies involve teachers responding to learners. Is it necessary to have an expert's response, or could something similar be achieved through textbooks? Some teaching texts invite learners to construct examples as a matter of course. For instance, in *Algebra I: A process approach* (Rachlin, Matsumoto, Wada, & Dougherty, 2001) learners are taken through a series of tasks and explorations that, one hopes, provides a rich experience of the field being studied. In a typical module, say the one on prime and composite numbers, most of the tasks are closed, but they have been structured to reveal features gradually rather than being merely for practice. A typical sequence of tasks is as follows:

- Find all integer factors of 20.
- Factor these numbers as products of primes.
- Find another number that fits the factorization lattice[30] for 20.

In the last task the learner is expected to construct a number that has the same multiplicative structure as 20. However, without teacher knowledge, there is no way to distinguish between those who find one by testing likely numbers and those who construct one by making a list of prime numbers that match the structure of $20 = 2 \times 2 \times 5$ (i.e., seeing 20 as the product of a prime and another prime squared). Further tasks and questions that would help learners who have not yet done so make this final shift to knowing about structure could be:

Task 49: Factor Lattices

Find some more numbers that have the same factorization lattice; share your results with your friends.
What do they all have in common?
What can you say is true about all numbers that have this lattice?

In ways like this (which we believe are better mediated by a teacher than left to textbook authors) such construction exercises can be directed to-

---

[30]A factorization lattice is a diagram depicting all the factors and how they are related to each other. See Appendix B for examples.

ward exploring the structure of the example space by drawing attention to multiplicative rather than additive structure.

This type of textbook exercise promotes deeper thought only when teachers also value and get involved in the tasks and when teachers are happy to work with a range of common features that learners notice, as well as the one for which the task is designed. Experience with similar exercises in a scheme widely used in secondary schools in the 1980s and 1990s in the United Kingdom suggests that, left to themselves, learners are likely to omit open questions and to construct their answers to "what do you notice?" according to what they find appearing on the next few pages of the textbook!

Such exercises use the principles that example spaces can be explored and extended with external prompting and that examples can be perceived as belonging to structured spaces. The individual nature of perceptions of generality means that what learners make of their experiences needs pedagogical input from the teacher who can respond to the particularities as they arise by prompting and probing in useful directions.

Bell and Shell

Teaching materials developed by the Shell Project in Nottingham in the 1980s and 1990s incorporated a variety of uses of LGEs that had been researched by Alan Bell (1976) in his thesis. One use of LGEs is to generate raw material for generalization. For instance, learners systematically create a range of examples of a mathematical situation, conjecture what relationships might hold in general, and then find out if this conjecture is true. *Task 15: T shapes* is an example of this approach.

One way to verify a relationship would be to test it with more examples, particularly extreme values, such as, in arithmetic, 0, 1, and −1 (Bell, 1976). Examples can be generated to check given conditions and theorems. In these ways, LGEs are being used as an integral part of the development of mathematical reasoning and proof.

Examples can be classified and ordered to obtain a complete set. For instance: Find all the different triangles which can be drawn on a 9-point square lattice grid, in which the vertices are points of the lattice. Such tasks encourage exploration and extension of the example space and raise questions about different generalities that might be perceived. Complex mathematical reasoning is required, and explicit choices have to be made to justify that the set found is indeed complete.

LGEs were used mainly as raw material for generalization, but they also appeared in some Shell-inspired worksheets in a different role. The last task on each worksheet, or in each section of a worksheet, was often "make up some questions like this of your own and give them to your neighbor to solve." In this way, learners had to be explicit about what they thought the worksheet was about; the teacher, by seeing what was understood by "like this," could evaluate their understanding. Such tasks do not always probe understanding deeply, because learners can sometimes simply substitute numbers into an existing template. Of course, any task can be approached mechanically or algorithmically, with a minimum of fresh thinking. If the kind of task learners are trying to emulate is not a worked-through technique, however, but a sequence of questions, such as those given for composite numbers in the previous section, then they have to imitate a structural argument rather than a number-crunching machine.

Silent Lessons

One kind of lesson that uses LGEs as raw material for generality, but explicitly recognizes that perceptions of generality are individual and may even be idiosyncratic, is what has come to be known as a *silent lesson*. We think this is first described by Colin Banwell, Ken Saunders, and Dick Tahta (1972/1986), and versions of it have subsequently been published in a variety of places.

> From now on—silence
> The teacher holds up the white chalk and a volunteer takes it and writes a number on the chalkboard. The teacher, having a specific function in mind, writes a corresponding number in colour. The white chalk is offered again and a number written on the board. Again the teacher writes a corresponding coloured number. Someone else writes a coloured number but this time the coloured chalk is offered to the class and a volunteer writes a coloured number. (It may be necessary for the teacher to erase an incorrect coloured number.) More white and coloured numbers are written on the board. (pp. 90–91)

The idea is that learners will automatically try to make sense of what is being offered. The first thing they have to make sense of is "why is the teacher saying nothing?" to which they soon supply the answer "because the teacher wants me to think this through for myself." Then it gradually becomes clear that they are expected to either offer numbers as examples for further evidence or offer examples to test their private conjectures. Sometimes this takes the form of "I wonder what the teacher is thinking about. . . . Perhaps it is this." Sometimes it takes the form of "what I see happening here will be demonstrated, tested, or shown to be false if I offer this example." In each case, no one else needs to know why a particular example has been offered, and all examples provide evidence toward the generalization that the teacher has in mind.

Martin Gardner (1977, 2001, pp. 504–512) described a game called *Eleusis* which is a similar activity, but it is not "silent." Participants offer examples intended to fit an unknown criterion. Once someone thinks they know the generalization or rule, they try to provide examples that will make this rule clear to others. With just one or two sessions of this game, learners discover that believing your conjecture is not sufficient. You have to try nonexamples (according to your conjecture) to try to make sure you have not made some inappropriate or unnecessary assumptions.

This kind of lesson recognizes that perceptions are individual and that example spaces can be extended, but it steers learners toward an intended generality while exposing a useful range of examples to the whole class. Discussions can arise about the value of using negative numbers and fractions as test examples, as well as the value of using special numbers such as 0.

Vicky

Vicky routinely includes getting learners to construct examples as a way to get them intimately involved in the using the structures of concepts. Here is a brief illustration of her strategy with a class of 12-year-old students whose past achievements were not outstanding. It was based on straight line equations.

Vicki started by drawing a coordinate grid on the board and some coordinate pairs next to it. Learners came to the board one by one to put the points on the coordinate grid. All the pairs had 2 as the y-coordinate, and this provided a self-checking device for those who may have misremembered the order. Vicky, however, did not mention this. Instead, she asked the learners to say what they noticed about what they had done. Several said that the points were all on a straight line parallel to the x-axis and that only the x value varied. She then asked for them to tell her some more points on the line. Their examples gave her information about their understanding. Next she asked them to suggest a name for the line. Three ideas offered were y is 2, y^2, and $y = 2$. Vicky confirmed that the last idea is the conventional notation. Then she asked where $y = 0$ would be, and many learners responded correctly. Learners were subsequently asked to write their own notes or to copy her notes if they preferred.

Before long someone called out "what about x?" and drew a vertical line in the air to indicate what she expected to happen.

In this lesson, Vicky used learners' examples of points on a given line and learners' examples of ways to represent the line; she also encouraged them to write their own notes. Possibly as a consequence of this participatory approach some had felt able to suggest further ways of working in the area, such as looking at lines of the type $x = a$.

In this lesson, examples have been used as raw material to explore a topic and build confidence. The principles being used are that exemplification is individual but that spaces can be explored and structured; with enough feedback, learners can be guided to form appropriate examples. This is in addition to the motivational and informal assessment purposes of such exemplification.

David

When being offered new ways to teach, it is a common response for teachers to say "that is all very well for others but it would not work for my students because. . . ." The reasons usually given include time pressure, they have to be made to think for themselves, they are frightened about saying the wrong thing, they expect to be told what to do, the class is too big, they are not clever enough, they are too clever, and so on.

David taught twenty 11-year-olds who had just started secondary school. They failed to achieve the national target grades in their previous year, and they knew it. It is usually assumed that these learners ought to be disheartened due to knowing they have failed and that they will regress due to transferring schools and being with a new group of peers in a new place.

David's belief is that all learners like to take part and need to have tasks that enable them to take part. He also believes that their mathematical learning will be enhanced by having a flexible and connected view of what mathematics is and some awareness of what they have learned. He has been regularly using prompts such as "if the answer is 4, what could the question be?" and has been trying to discourage learners from giving sums involving addition and subtraction and encourage more use of multiplication and division and, ultimately, to generate questions that involve other areas of mathematics. He hopes this will also have the effect of making them more confident in tackling unfamiliar questions.

He began this lesson by asking them to think about the mathematics they have been learning in recent weeks, look back through their books, and tell him what topics they think they have learned something about. There were 9 or 10 responses, and he thanked them all, giving particular praise to someone who mentioned positive and negative numbers, which they had worked on most recently. Then he asked them to respond to "if 16 is the answer, what is the question?" and to make up as many questions as they could, using anything from their work so far.

As they wrote questions, he went around the classroom to see what interesting ones were being created. He had already introduced into their classroom discourse the idea of each having "my favorite question," and they interpret this to mean "hard or complicated." Their view of what makes a question hard is, as many researchers have found, that it uses several operations or big or complicated numbers. He also includes the idea of "Mr. A's favorite question" (using his surname), and it is this strategy that allows him to direct their focus toward mathematical complexity and away from strings of simple calculations.

Eventually they were asked to select their favorite questions and write them on the board. He thanked all of them and praised some, pointing out special features. One question was "If there was a square with sides 4 cm, what was its perimeter?" He then asked what *perimeter* meant, and he gave three ways of defining or describing it. A later expression was $-6 + 22 = 16$, and this gets special praise ("I think this is going to be one of my favorites") because it arises from recent work. These learners are beginning to understand that it is praiseworthy to link what happens in different mathematics lessons and not to treat each topic as a separate item.

After several more responses, he said that he wanted to see more and more responses like his two favorites and not so many of the "8×2" type. He said "I know that you know $8 \times 2 = 16$, and you know that I know, so we don't need to share those so much now."

Next they moved to a new topic—fractions—and David started by drawing a 3×4 rectangle on a squared board and asking them to tell him how they know it is a rectangle. Again he heard several descriptions. The personalizing of the question turns it into a genuine question: He really wants to know how they see it, and this inspires them to respond. They are then asked to find as many ways as they can to shade one half of the rectangle.

In this classroom, the message is clear that learners are to explore dimensions of variation in what is offered to them. The way they choose to shade the rectangle shows David whether they are counting squares or thinking of congruent shapes or even thinking of area. From this, the lesson could go in various ways. It turns out that most were counting squares, so he could now progress to thinking about fractions of a number. However, some have drawn diagonals and can say that there was a difference in how they thought about the "counting squares approach" and how they thought about the shape-based approach. He could, instead, progress into thinking about area or congruency.

The homework was to find 10 ways to shade one third of a 3×6 rectangle and to think about what fraction is left over each time.

Most of the lesson had been interactive. The individual written work was all preparation to contribute to the interactive sequences in the lesson. There were no occasions on which only one answer was elicited or accepted by the teacher. It is clear from his response to them that all answers are welcome but some are more welcome than others. The learners themselves have generated much of the raw material for the lesson: definitions, descriptions, reasons, examples, ideas, and representations.

At every stage there is an assumption that learners' emerging example spaces are individual but can be explored and extended through prompts and experience. In particular, David appears to believe that such spaces are structured in ways that allow learners to discriminate between easier and harder examples.

Because there are only 20 students, this description of teaching may not appear to offer much to those for whom large class sizes cause problems, but many of the techniques he uses would be usable in much larger classes. In fact, most of them would work even better with more learners because there would be more ideas offered to shape the direction of the lesson.

Shannon

David's classroom illustrates that repeated experience of working in such open ways can shift the learner's idea of the norms of mathematical behavior in school. Shannon's classroom gave us some higher level (mathematically speaking) examples of the effects of practices that expect participation. In her case, learners did not need any prompting to produce examples as an integral part of their work. It was as natural to them as chewing gum. We saw a mixed-ability class of secondary school students (about 15 years old) working on functions. Displayed on the board were four linear functions and four nonlinear functions in two lists. Learners had to decide which were which and to think about rules describing how they could know something was a linear function or not. The four linear ones were not all written in the same format.

Shannon reminded them that equations can be transformed. With a learner's guidance she wrote $2x + y = 6$, $2x - 6 = -y$, and $y = 6 - 2x$. Another learner questioned this particular way of isolating y, saying "wouldn't it have been faster to subtract $2x$ from both sides?" To this, Shannon replied "it depends on whose mind you have which you think is faster."

They were asked to draw and label the graphs making use of graphical calculators as support. They were asked to transform all the equations, linear and nonlinear, into the form $y = f(x)$ to plot them. One learner was working on $xy = 10$ and said "I hate these kinds. How can you possibly find out about 10 divided by x?" She then began to test different values of x until she achieved a sense of how the function behaved, saying "okay" with satisfaction and moving on to the next task.

When they had all plotted graphs, Shannon asked them about their findings about the graphs and the original classifications. She and some of the learners took on the role of supplying counterexamples to some of the stated rules. For example, $y = 4$ is linear but did not fit some of the suggested definitions. One learner offered $y = 0x^r + 4$ as a possible version of $y = 4$, and it was agreed that, because r could be anything, its linearity had to be a special case. Later, when trying to define lines that represented direct variation, learners gave several descriptions of possible functions: 0 is the intercept; no addition or subtraction is allowed; there can only be one step, and that step will be multiplication; and x must have an exponent of 1. Later, the problem of $y = 4$ appeared as a possible special case of a quadratic where two coefficients are zero. One learner gave $y = 0x^{54} + 0x^{35} + 0x$ as a possible degenerate example of the x-axis, which produced much hilarity.

After all this, learners were asked to work backward from the examples given to try to construct a definition of a linear function.

In this classroom there are clear principles being used about learners constructing their understanding openly in discussion with others and the teacher, who provides tasks that invite conjecture and discussion. Exemplification is an integral activity for the learners, even as far as playing with boundary and possible counterexamples themselves. Exploring special values to understand $xy = 10$ was a natural activity for one learner, providing examples of definitions was expected from all of them, and offering extreme examples was a natural part of classroom discourse. There was respect given to individual constructions and understandings, yet all learners were in an environment where they would be offered objects beyond their current confidence and knowledge levels. Playfulness is encouraged.

Swan's Way

Malcolm Swan (2000) uses LGEs regularly with students who are retaking school-leaving examinations at a community college to get higher grades. He encourages them to make up their own worked examples, develop hard questions to pose to each other, invent statements to fit diagrams or graphs, and create objects that satisfy certain constraints or connect concepts or use particular representations. These students have arrived at college with low self-esteem and very negative views about learning mathematics. Previous experiences in which fluency with technique has been emphasized have resulted in them becoming passive learners. Normal college remediation methods involve "going over" or reteaching the entire syllabus but more quickly, using a transmission followed by imitation approach. Certainly in this context, such an approach has patently failed: Dropout rates are high, and pass rates are disappointing. Malcolm claims that the only positive way to move forward is to allow students time and opportunity to slow down and construct meaning for what they have already superficially encountered. Over 2 years he worked with teachers from 44 different community colleges to explore a student-centered approach to learning. Some teachers felt that it was too risky a step to take. The tension is clear: Some of the syllabus might go untaught, but what is the point of teaching if there is no learning? As one teacher said:

> One of the major pressures I feel is the obligation to cover everything in the scheme of work. It is difficult to get through everything in under three hours a week. I recall a staffroom conversation in which we sounded like we were competing to see who had managed to "cover" trigonometry in the shortest time possible. Is this effective teaching and learning? When I "speed teach," I sometimes ask myself who is covering the syllabus? Is it the students or is it just me?

As a result of this project, many of the teachers have radically changed their classroom practice and students have become excited by their learning—even in the more abstract aspects of mathematics. Lessons now involve a great deal of discussion and reflection. Sometimes not a lot is written down, but meanings are created and connections are made. There are difficulties, however. When students become creative, misconceptions and confusions surface and life gets messy. Teachers sometimes feel that they have caused this confusion, but more often they have simply revealed the confusion that was already lurking beneath the surface. Building sites are messy places! This has proved too much for some teachers who have found it impossible to change from their normal, tidy approaches. They use the activities as just another type of exercise, giving many ideas of their own and not really valuing and building on student suggestions.

What Can We Draw From These Cases?

At a very basic level many teachers recognize that asking their students to give examples is a powerful way to get them motivated and to assess their understanding. In Sara's case there is also a metacognitive role, because learners have to review their work and write about it. But they do more than that. They have to go back and organize their understanding to extract something representative. They have to decide what is worth representing and how to represent it. Sara's students end up not merely writing about the topic but thinking reflectively in order to abstract.

In David's case there is also a cognitive role in that he is explicitly asking them to construct more sophisticated meanings. They do this first by using bigger numbers or more operations, but his friendly rejection of these extensions moves learners toward more conceptual complexity: They introduce brackets, they use noninteger numbers, they draw on a range of mathematical knowledge, and they look for ways to incorporate what they find hard to learn or new.[31] In Shannon's class learners raise interesting questions by creating what they know to be boundary examples. Can one legitimately call a polynomial with zero coefficients and a non-zero constant anything other than a constant function?

Although Malcolm's teaching is successful and genuinely uses learner-generated ideas to structure lessons, we also learn that it is possible for teachers to reduce any kind of task to a mundane exercise. A common feature of the successful teaching practices just reported is a genuine shift in responsibility to the learners—a genuine commitment to the power of learners to construct meaningful mathematics.

Shifting Responsibility Even Further. Ultimately we look to learners to create these challenges for themselves. Over a period of time, learners who are trusted to make choices do respond sensibly and productively. Not only will they take responsibility for generating raw material, illustrations, counterexamples, and worked examples, but they will also take responsibility for deciding when it is appropriate to do these things, as they do in Shannon's classroom. As described elsewhere (Watson & Mason, 1998), the regular use of certain question types can further scaffold this shift, with beneficial effects on learning and self-esteem through self-identity as mathematical learners.

The work of Brown and Coles (1999, 2000) is a refreshing example of an inquirers' mathematics classroom in which the teacher, Alf Coles, has complete trust in his learners' ability and willingness to raise and explore mathematical questions for themselves, thus providing the direction, substance, and discourse of the lessons, with increasingly less and less direct input from himself. For instance, learners in his classroom naturally pose mathematical questions starting with "why?," which leads to attempts to prove conjectures, and their classification of cases with which they work naturally leads to the use of structural and algebraic descriptions. The question "what is the same and what different about . . ." becomes integrated into the classroom practice to the extent that it is shortened to the term *same–different*. In his lessons responsibility is freely taken by learners. They do not wait until asked to do so before they pose questions, suggest directions of exploration, and produce examples with which to characterize concepts. They have shifted from needing the prompt of an occasional question to taking initiative for what they now know to be mathematical behavior.

---

[31]As found in problem-posing studies (e.g., Ellerton, 1986; English, 1998; Silver & Cai, 1996), learners can create complex questions when given support and knowledge of how to do this.

What we are describing is not peculiar to mathematics. Indeed, in most subjects, learners work with examples and nonexamples simultaneously. It is only in mathematics classrooms that this natural propensity sometimes seems to be blocked or blotted out, to the detriment of learners and teacher. By prompting playfulness and a search for extremely peculiar examples, teachers can encourage learners to reveal and learn more through constructing their own examples.

SUMMARY OF STRATEGIES

Now comes the hardest part of the book for us to write. We decided to bring together in one place a list of the strategies that we have observed and used so that they can be referred to easily and compared. This was a difficult decision because we do not want to be seen as offering recipes or tricks for good teaching. If we found copies of this book in which these particular pages were very well-used and the others were not, we would feel very uncomfortable. Rather, we hope that you will find your experience enriched so that your future choices are informed through principled reflection on what you want to achieve with your learners.

When we offer our list of strategies, it is in the expectation that it provides nothing more than an *aide-mémoire* for what has gone before and that no one would use a strategy without a conscious decision about how it might aid learning, what knowledge transformations might be possible when it is used, what the teacher might do next, and what the learner might experience.

Currently in U.K. primary schools all pupils are encouraged to share their own methods with the whole class. Without a theory of how this helps learning and an idea of what the teacher might do next with all these expected, unexpected, prosaic and extreme, wonderful, or eccentric methods, such a strategy can merely become a fruitless classroom routine—a game that some learners learn to play but leaves others bewildered. No strategy can guarantee mathematical learning.

One way to think about the various styles of tasks we have offered is in terms of what learners are actually asked to do. What they are asked to do does not tell us everything about the intentions and actions associated with a task, but this list of instructions, followed by a brief elaboration of each, may serve to stimulate thought about task design:

- Make up an example.
- Make up an example with some constraints.
- Add constraints sequentially.

- Make up another or more like or unlike this.
- Make counterexamples and nonexamples.
- Confound expectations.
- Characterize all objects that satisfy specified constraints.
- Reverse.
- Explore distinctions.
- Bury the bone.
- Use features of methods or objects as starting points.
- Find.
- Use wild-card generation.

Make Up an Example

Here is an instance of this task: "Give me an example of a number between 3 and 4." This task exposes dominant images and current understandings, tells the teacher what knowledge learners have, and provides raw material for further work, including practice.

This is especially used in *Task 5: Practice Tasks* and *Task 16: Freedom* to initiate constructions exposing figural images and probing beyond assumed constraints.

Make Up an Example With Some Constraints

Here is an example of this task: "Make up a unitary fraction that has six unitary fractions bigger than it." There is nothing special about the choice of *six* except that it is more likely to promote a general approach rather than a happenstance answer found by guess-and-test. To find six unitary fractions, learners are unlikely to do a random search and are more likely to look for principles to help them find examples. Once they have a method to find these examples, they can generate as many as they like, but it is the search for the method that makes them look at what fractions are and the effect of varying the denominator. The task is about becoming aware of a method, not about learning which unit fraction has six larger than it. Some learners might produce lists that are special in some way, such as unitary fractions of the form $\frac{1}{n^2}$. Sharing examples within the class enables learners to see that there are other possibilities when you return to making up more examples with more constraints. Creating a generalization of the rules that different people have used to produce their lists would be a useful subsequent task. This method is used in *Task 13c: Inter-Rootal Distance Further Constrained*, *Task 21: First Reactions*, *Task 32: Constraining the General*, and *Task 46: Decagon*, among others.

Add Constraints Sequentially

This is the essence of many of the tasks we use in workshops and discussed in chapter 5. We find that it affords learners access to classes of examples from which to choose and, hence, to generality. It makes use of the mathematical themes of freedom and constraint: You start with considerable freedom in choice of example (e.g., write down a number or draw a quadrilateral) and then more and more constraints are imposed. Here is an example: "Create a quadrilateral. Make one with no edges parallel to edge of paper. Make it have one reflex angle. Can you make it have 2 reflex angles?" Note how increasing constraints extend awareness of what is possible. This method is used in *Task 9: Quadrilateral Sequence, Task 26: Named Decimals*, and *Task 36: Compounding Constraints*, among others.

Make Up Another or More Like/Unlike This

As well as allowing learners time to reflect on what has been happening and to try their hand at making variations, "make up more like this" also tells the teacher what the learners think "like this" means. "Make up another example that illustrates or highlights some other feature not readily detected in this example" is another way to draw attention to different dimensions of possible variation.

Patricia used this example style to support a pause for reflection and exploration of range of permissible change with respect to objects recently constructed. We also use it in *Task 7a: How Different, Task 12b: Difference of 2 Again, Task 37: Several Ways*, and *Task 43a: Another and Another Cutting Circles*, among others.

Make Counterexamples and Nonexamples

Note that these examples work only in the context of some ambient assumptions about generality. Every counterexample is an example of another class; every example in one context can act as a counterexample in another. Here is an illustration:

- In the context of primary math and the introduction to decimals, use a calculator to find some numbers for which "putting a 0 at the end" does not work when you multiply by 10.
- In the context of constructing groups from symmetries of shapes, find a group of order 4 that does not have a subgroup of order 2.
- Give an example to show that not all sets of three simultaneous linear equations with three unknowns have a solution.
- Find a property for which $y = x$ is an example; find a property for which it is a counterexample.

Counterexamples are used explicitly in *Task 18: Finding* and *Task 21: First Reactions* but they arise in many other tasks.

A nonexample displays something of the boundaries of a concept by showing that some condition or constraint is necessary. A nonexample serves as a counterexample when the corresponding conjecture is articulated. *Task 20: This But Not That, Task 24: Constrained Search,* and *Task 47: Constant Diameter* illustrate this connection.

Confound Expectations

For this to work one must begin with an expectation. For example: "Give a number for which the square is not larger than itself." Sometimes reducing constraints can have the effect of surprise. For example: Draw a hexagon that has three axes of symmetry, draw a hexagon that has only two axes of symmetry, and draw a hexagon that has only one axis of symmetry.

Here releasing constraint makes the search more difficult for some people, perhaps because we are more used to seeing and drawing symmetrical hexagons rather than irregular ones. This task sequence is designed to wrench learners away from strong images that might come to mind when the word *hexagon* appears.

When asked to predict and then graph the function

$$\frac{sin(2x)}{sin(x)},$$

many learners, even graduates, are surprised by what they discover. When asked to predict and then graph

$$\frac{cos(2x)}{cos(x)},$$

their expectations are again confounded.

We are assuming certain expectations when we say that this strategy is used in *Task 8: Comparing Squares, Task 21a and b: First Reactions,* and *Task 53: Self-Perpendicular Hexagons.*

Characterize All Objects That Satisfy Specified Constraints

This is exemplification with constraints but for the purpose of learning more about the class that results. Here is an example:

- Find numbers that are one more than the product of four consecutive integers. This requires the generation and examination of examples. Then learners can discuss other special features of some examples and how they relate to the construction instructions.
- Find triples of numbers that can be the three sides of a triangle. What can be said about them?
- Find polynomial functions that have a root of 1. What can be said about them?
- Find all the triangles you can make on a 9-point square lattice, with vertices on the lattice points.

This strategy is used in *Task 3a: Alternating Signs, Task 12d: Difference of 2 Generalized*, and *Task 50: Optimal Placements*.

Reverse

In some of our tasks we have assumed a normal order and reversed it to open up the task for further exploration. A usual task is to give an answer and ask what the associated question might be. An example is the classic task known as *the story of seven*:[32]

$$5 + 2 = 7$$
$$7 = ?$$

A specially chosen closed version of this task forces an extension of what is possible: "What could the question have been if $7 = 11 + \ldots$?" Another classic example includes: "The answer to a division problem is 5 with a remainder 2: What could the question be?" Trying to find all possible division questions with this answer leads to characterizing a class of numbers.

There are other kinds of reversal, such as working backward from some roots to a family of quadratics rather than from a quadratic to its roots. We use reversal (from an assumed "normal") in *Task 2: Mode, Median, and Mean* and *Task 47: Constant Diameter*, among others.

Explore Distinctions

This is at the heart of most mathematics and most learning concepts. Creating objects that explore the boundaries of definitions is a powerful way to learn about mathematical structures, and it also helps learners understand the reason for linguistic distinctions. We used this style in *Task 9: Quadrilateral Sequence* and *Task 33a: Four Factors*, among others.

---

[32]See, for example, Banwell et al. (1972/1986).

Bury the Bone

Start with what is normally the final stage of a procedure; then ask learners to reverse a method and hide the answer in increasingly complex ways. For example: "The solution to a linear equation is $p = 6$; what could the equation be? Make it as complicated as you can." Learners get an intimate understanding of the structure and, hence, are better able to understand the usual method of solution or invent their own.

Burying the context can give learners the experience of making up their own word problems, which provides a wider perspective on those much hated, much maligned, end-of-chapter challenges. For example: "Tell me a story about a situation in which I would have to multiply 3 by 2.5." We used this strategy in *Task 5: Practice Tasks*, *Task 12c: Least Obvious Difference of 2*, and *Task 37: Several Ways*, among others.

Use Features of Methods or Objects as Starting Points

In this strategy we do not use the answer but some by-product of the procedure, or a method itself, as a basis for reconstructing a process. Here are examples:

- Find the smallest numbers for which subtraction requires five "borrowings" or "exchanges," depending on how you think about the formal algorithm.
- For which two numbers could the Euclidean algorithm have as the sequence of remainders 7, 4, and 1?
- Which three-dimensional shapes could have a square and an isosceles triangle as silhouettes?
- Which shapes, when cut along a straight line, produce pieces whose shapes are all similar to the original?

In particular, we can use unusual features of examples as invariants to promote exploration, such as in *Task 41a: Give Me a Number With One Constraint*. We also used this strategy in *Task 13a: Inter-Rootal Distance* and *Task 54: Fraction Comparisons*, among others.

Find

Here we give a sequence of slight variations on the request "to find." Each type, we believe, triggers slightly different expectations and constructions.

Find examples of . . .	Find an example that . . .
Find the example that . . .	Find examples such that . . .
Find all examples that . . .	Find an example of . . . and another and another.
Find an example that shows that you understand how to use the technique for . . .	Find examples that . . .
Find the hardest, most complicated, simplest, easiest, most weird . . .	Find an example that is the same in this way but different in that way to . . .
Find . . .	

Here is a sample task: "Find a pair of rotations in three-space that combine to give a rotation about one axis." Tertiary school students may be familiar with the fact that combinations of two rotations in two-space have to be rotations; but in three dimensions, this is less obviously always true. Questions posed to learners are more usually about combining simple-to-imagine rotations, but this prompt expects them to end up with something simple and, hence, to work with more obscure rotations than usual ones—unless, of course, they respond to the prompt by actively searching for simple solutions.

We used this strategy in *Task 13b: Inter-Rootal Distance Constrained, Task 13c: Inter-Rootal Distance Further Constrained, Task 26: Named Decimals*, and *Task 43a: Another and Another—Cutting Circles*, among others. We discussed subtle differences between being asked to find one, two, and three examples in chapter 5.

Wild-Card Generation

Examples include dropping a ruler onto a rotating coordinate grid to get a straight line, turning around and pointing when stopped to generate directions for polar coordinates, stabbing with pencil to choose three points through which a parabola has to fit or to get points of discontinuity, and so on. Wild-card generation techniques give starting examples for further work that might not have been obvious ones to choose. Values are likely to be "nasty" numbers; simplistic techniques or rules of thumb are unlikely to be applicable. Unlike other strategies, the creation of the example does not trigger much thought, although sometimes it might extend an emerging example space. Another wild-card approach is to get a large group of people to each choose an example and then to pool results to look for patterns. Some prompts are so open that learners are likely to choose examples for a wide range of reasons. We used this strategy in *Task 22a: Write Down* and *Task 63: Square Addition Sequence*, among others.

FOCUS ON ACTION

Another approach to thinking about what learners are asked to do is to focus on the actions of recalling (e.g., reference examples and favorite examples), tinkering and gluing as bricolage, complexifying, and varying and generalizing, rather than on the structure of the prompts.

Recalling involves producing a known example as a familiar starting place for mathematical activity or as a familiar object that might be looked at in a different way, such as a member of a newly understood class.[33]

Tinkering involves adjusting one or more objects, perhaps even gluing them together in some way. The learner becomes a *bricoleur* who assembles new things from old. In the process, an idea for an entirely new object may arise, leading to new mathematical questions, new exploration, and possibly revision of previous ideas.

Complexifying is not unlike tinkering, but it is not as radical. The Burying the Bone task provides a generic example of how learners can start with something simple and then develop more and more complex versions. The version of *Task 12a: Difference of 2* that asks for the least obvious pair of numbers with a difference of 2 is working in the same direction. Sometimes searching for extreme examples (hardest, most complex, or most complicated or tricky) leads to the conclusion that they are all, in fact, easy. This reflects the learners' extension of their example space and their growing confidence through that extended space. A useful version of this for high school students is to get them to rearrange all the trigonometric identities they can find to make $sin(x)$ the subject. All the expressions so formed can contribute to an exercise in manipulating trigonometric expressions to "get back to" sine. Furthermore, in the same topic area, learners can create a set of exercises for simplifying "horrible" trigonometric expressions by complexifying a few standard ones for themselves.

Varying and generalizing are again like tinkering but in an outward direction. As learners become aware of the various dimensions of possible variation, they can try to encompass these dimensions in one or more general objects, as well as characterize all possible such objects. Many of the tasks we have devised for this book have been created using deliberate identification of dimensions of possible variation, choosing those less familiar, such as focusing on variation in digit use in numbers (as in *Task 16: Freedom, Task 23: Write Down Constrained,* and *Task 41a: Give Me a Number*

---

[33]Susan Pirie, Lyndon Martin, and Tom Kieren (1996) used the Pirie–Kieren (Pirie & Kieren, 1994) model of understanding and referred to this process as "folding back and collecting."

With One Constraint), or choosing to fix something that is usually allowed to vary (like in *Task 12a: Difference of 2* or *Task 13a: Inter-Rootal Distance*). Another feature of our task design is awareness of the range of change in each dimension, using our pedagogical experience to know what sorts of limitations generally come into play, to pose questions that encourage people to look beyond these.

PRACTICE AND FLUENCY

It hardly needs to be said that the most common use of examples in school mathematics is to rehearse techniques. However, it is not always clear what it is that needs to be rehearsed. In other fields of endeavor, practice focuses on an aspect of a complex task that has to become fluent to allow overall success. In classrooms, fluency does not seem to be the aim; learners try very hard to get right answers, and teachers observe errors to inform their future teaching of individuals and classes. Some teachers, such as Sarah in chapter 2, use LGEs for practice, and this introduces the extra possibility of reflecting on how the technique relates to the structure and solution of the question. Practice is the main priority; the reflection on structure is the side effect. These goals can be swapped to focus learners on structure and offer practice as the side effect. The following tasks offer this possibility, and they include repetitive work that can thus become fluent through practice.

Task 50: Optimal Placements

Place the digits 3, 4, 5, 6, 7, and 8 in a three-digit subtraction problem so as to minimize and then to maximize the answer.

This gets learners to rehearse three-column subtraction by exploiting what they already know. In the course of finding minimal and maximal answers they may rehearse several subtractions. If they do not need to but can arrive theoretically at the answers, then perhaps they do not need practice at all. The task can be varied to include other digits, repeated digits, and so on.

Task 51: Unit Fractions

What fractions can be the sum of two unit fractions? Three? Four? . . . What collections of unit fractions add up to 1?

Learners rehearse adding fractions, a task likely to involve them in choosing and adding plenty of fractions together, not to get the answer to be marked, but to see what is possible. Again, if they can arrive at answers theoretically, then perhaps they do not need practice.

Task 52a: Do Enough to . . .

Multiply enough pairs of expressions of the form $(x + 2)(x + 3)$ together so that you can identify whether quadratic expressions always arise as the product of two such factors.

Task 52b: Find More

Observe that $x^2 + 5x + 6 = (x + 3)(x + 2)$ and $x^2 + 5x - 6 = (x + 6)(x - 1)$ and also that $x^2 + 13x + 30 = (x + 10)(x + 3)$ and $x^2 + 13x - 30 = (x + 15)(x - 2)$.

Find as many other examples as you can that you can still factorize after changing the sign of the constant.

What is the effect of changing the sign of the coefficient of x?

This collection of tasks gets learners to expand brackets for a purpose and then to factorize quadratics for a purpose.

In posing this kind of task, teachers avoid the tendency for learners to merely fit new numbers into the template offered by a worked example (Anthony, 1994; Back, 2000). However, they may still follow templates offered by the textbook to frame their own responses. To challenge this habit, learners can be invited to make up a collection of examples that show that learners have understood how it is done, which would serve as good challenges for learners the following year or display the variety of things that can happen.

SUMMARY

We have summarized a practical–experiential approach to learner-generated exemplification. Finally we related LGEs to the common classroom activity of practice. The next chapter draws together many of the various threads.

7

Mathematics as a Constructive Activity

It is useful to use mathematics as a constructive activity, and constructing objects as an integral component of learning mathematics. We are not saying that such construction is everything needed to learn, but it is far more important than something to be left to the "hard problems at the end of the topic" which are only ever done by the very best students.

We suggest, for example, that every mathematical problem involves a construction, even if it means using a well rehearsed algorithm or technique. In fact, Hazzan and Zazkis (1997) found that some of their students tried to create algorithms when faced with an exemplification task, thus creating both a technique and a class of examples. Mathematics can be seen as a constructive and, hence, personally creative activity,

- not just simple constructivism in which learners are seen as constructors of meaning (what else could they do apart from memorize like robots?);
- not just radical constructivism in which learners are seen as actively trying things out seeking a fit with past and future experience;
- not just social constructivism, in which learners are seen as being enculturated into ways of speaking and acting by being in the presence of more experienced people engaging in relevant practices;
- but also mathematical construction in which to learn is to construct objects meeting specified constraints, so that when example spaces are triggered they are complex and confidence-inspiring, with their components richly interconnected, enabling re-construction and fresh construction as appropriate.

We begin by considering the psychological role of imposed constraints as learners engage in construction and the different ways in which awareness of constraints can be used by the teacher in constructing tasks and by learners in constructing objects. This leads us to the way in which constructing things for yourself, whether by tinkering or by extending, helps build self-confidence and personal identity. Next we gather various threads from previous chapters, leading to an elaboration of different metaphors and images that try to capture the experience of example construction. Then we deal with what is (for us) the most important outcome of our work: not more principles or abstract characterizations of tasks and constructions, but the experiences of colleagues as they worked on the tasks and reflected on their experiences. The final section consists of comments about how awareness of the constructive nature of mathematical learning has led us to consider some questions about the parameters of task design.

CONSTRUCTIVE CONSTRAINTS

Constraints are not always seen as positive because they appear to limit freedom. Yet, as many artists and creative thinkers have observed, creativity is released as a result of meeting constraints. This section considers the role of constraints in construction tasks.

Some suggestions for possible approaches appear in the comments after the third task in this chapter.

Task 53: Self-Perpendicular Hexagons

Draw a hexagon with each pair of opposite edges perpendicular to each other.

We hope there is at least a fleeting moment of surprise!

Task 54: Fraction Comparisons

Find a fraction for which adding any positive number to the numerator and adding double that number to the denominator increases the value of the fraction. Characterize all such fractions.
Find a fraction for which the same action decreases the value.
Find a fraction for which the same action preserves the value of the fraction. Find all such fractions.

This is similar in style to some other tasks we have offered. You may like to compare the three prompts in *Task 53* and think about how learners' response might be subtly different.

Task 55: Extending Sequences

State a rule in words for extending this sequence, and then find a formula that generates all the terms for 1, 3, 5, 7, ...
State a rule in words for extending this sequence, and then find a formula that generates all the terms for 1, 3, 5, 7, 33, ...

For hexagons, starting with a pair of opposite edges may be more productive than starting with consecutive edges. For fractions, using a general fraction and then imposing the constraint and specializing may be more productive than trying particular fractions. For sequences, plotting points on a graph or using a method of differences may reveal a structure that does not jump out merely when looking at the numbers.

That it is possible to meet the constraints in all of these tasks may come as a bit of a surprise. Expectation about possibility can be a significant factor: If you believe something is impossible, you may not search very hard, although you may try to prove none are possible. However, if you believe it to be possible, you may keep searching. Alternating between belief and disbelief in a conjecture is thought to be the most fruitful approach (P. Davis & Hersh, 1981).

Constructing examples with the purpose of testing whether it is possible at all and, if so, to find ones that work may lead to at least one example. Of more interest than simply one example is to find "all such" objects. This search may involve moving to a generality and then imposing the required condition on the symbols, but it can also be done by starting with any likely example and getting a sense of the dimensions of possible variation through tinkering with it in various ways.

For instance, for the hexagon you could rotate edges (using sticks perhaps) until they are perpendicular and see what this forces on other edges. For the fractions, you could see what happens if you add appropriate numbers to the numerator and denominator of any fraction and then alter your starting fraction until you get the desired effect. Treating the instruction to double in the fractions task as a dimension of possible variation opens up a world of exploration in which the initial constraint is seen as but one of a multitude of possibilities. For the sequences, you could explore the effect of adding squared terms, cubed terms, and so on to some linear expressions. Realizing that there is more than one polynomial that generates 1, 3, 5, and 7 (or any other finite set of numbers) opens a dimension of possible variation that suggests a class of such polynomials. If you were really stuck, you could plot polynomials with a free choice of their coefficients, look at their shapes (how wiggly do they have to be?), and ask yourself "Is it at all possible to make one of these go through such points as (1, 1), (2, 3) . . . (5, 33)?"

Here we show that being asked to find something that sounds unlikely can get this response: "This looks unlikely; what examples can I generate that will give me more knowledge about this kind of thing?" Learners who are used to generating examples to explore mathematics can tackle unfamiliar questions and challenges in this way. Those who are on familiar territory may move faster to a generalization.

The decision to generalize might be conscious, but it might be your automatic response. Recall Jim's designs for spatial representations of quartics in chapter 5. In Jim's case generalization was unintentional and arose as an expression of his way of seeing the problem. This showed beautifully how generalization allows us to encapsule what we see as all possible cases in one form. However, rapid generalization can obscure some features.

Others choose to look for generalizations, as we illustrated with the story of Pip in chapter 5. It was simply more interesting for him to construct a general class. In terms of the larder metaphor, it seemed that Pip was writing a label for a shelf rather than looking for individual items.

Task 56: Least Common Multiples

Find two numbers for which 24 is the least common multiple.
Find another two.
And another two.
Find all such pairs; formulate a method of finding all such pairs for
   any number.

What were the roles of exemplification and generalization when you worked on this task? What struck you about the transition from finding one pair, then another, then another, to finding all such pairs? The final prompt encourages people to look for general structures of such numbers and to ask what it is about 24 that is special and what is generalizable. Some people may start by doing that; others may start by working in an ad hoc fashion. For others again there may have been an interplay between special and general all the way through the activity, including generating examples to check that their method worked.

Constraint Watersheds

If learners are asked to come up with an object that has very little, if any, constraint but is reasonably familiar (e.g., "write down a number" or "draw a quadrilateral"), then all they can do is select something from what comes to mind. If they are aware of a wide range of possibilities, they may lack criteria for choosing. It may be too hard to choose or too tempting to choose something simple in case the next step involves complications.

If the constraints imposed suggest that no such examples are possible, or if the constraints are technically obscure or unfamiliar, then there is likely to be little thought beyond wondering what the teacher is after and perhaps playing it safe by looking for something simple. If example production is a familiar activity, then what is produced is likely to represent something of the learners' awareness of dimensions of possible variation. As constraints are added, learners may be forced into slightly unfamiliar territory, thus discovering that there are possibilities beyond those that had come immediately to mind. They may also be surprised that unexpected constraints can actually be met (e.g., opposite sides of a hexagon can be perpendicular).

When asked to explore different dimensions of possible variation (e.g., "construct a problem like this," "construct another object like that," etc.), learners are likely to modify various numbers and other features of constraints that they recognize as being open to change. They may become aware that their chosen range of change is limited and can be extended. This may reveal further aspects of the dimensions of possible variation of which they are aware. Each of these steps can be prompted by self or others or by peers or teachers.

If the object itself is unfamiliar (e.g., the sequence 1, 3, 5, 7, 33, etc.), learners are most likely to select whatever dimension first comes to mind and exhaust that dimension as a search domain before questioning the choice of domain itself. As they become experienced in example production, they may turn to bricolage or they may reverse the task by starting from a general or other object on hand and imposing constraints sequentially themselves, perhaps changing the order of imposing the constraints, to find a pertinent or appropriate object.

For instance, in the sequence task they might use the obvious fact that $(n-1)(n-2)(n-3)(n-4)$ is zero for $n = 1, 2, 3$, and 4 as a starting point to tinker to meet the unexpected constraint of 33 at $n = 5$. If they have a function f that works for $n = 1, 2, 3$, and 4, then they could construct

$$f(n) + \frac{(x-1)(x-2)(x-3)(x-4)}{(5-1)(5-2)(5-3)(5-4)} g(n),$$

where g is arbitrary, apart from $g(5) = 33$. This method uses an available function f and adapts it to meet an extra constraint. Simultaneously, this opens up the possibility of adding more values to the sequence and constructing appropriate new functions to cope with six, seven, eight and so on given terms. A learner without these skills and insights might find other ways to tinker with what they already have on hand to generate at least a sense of what might be possible. The temptation to say "it's a straight line, and then it goes up steeply" could prompt discussion about the necessity for smoothness.

At the other extreme, imposing considerable constraint on an object to be found (e.g., "solve these simultaneous equations" and "draw a triangle with two specified side lengths and a specified angle between them") is most likely to summon up a taught technique for solving such a task as long as the learners recognize the relevance of the technique. For instance, in the sequence task the method of differences might be applied. The differences between consecutive terms give you a second, new sequence, and the differences between the terms of the new sequence give a third sequence, and so on until a constant difference might be obtained. A polynomial formula for the original sequence is then generally reconstructible from the constant difference, but in this case it is rather nasty.

By seeing even these traditional task types as construction tasks, learners have access to other strategies in the absence of a taught technique that comes to mind. They can start with something general and impose constraints sequentially to get at least some sense of what is going on and perhaps to then resonate some appropriate technique, or they can remove some of the constraints for themselves and build up to the desired object. Furthermore, they may appreciate the scope and role of the taught technique by thinking of its use as a construction tool.

Contrast these *Task 57a* with *Task 57b* in terms of their possible effect on learners:

Task 57a: Differing by Two (Straight Lines)

Sketch the graphs of a pair of straight lines whose y-intercepts differ by 2. (pause)
Sketch the graphs of a pair of straight lines whose x-intercepts differ by 2. (pause)
Sketch the graphs of a pair of straight lines whose slopes differ by 2. (pause)
Sketch the graphs of a pair of straight lines meeting all three of these conditions.

We tried doing this with mental imagery alone, but sticks could be a useful aid.

Task 57b: All at Once

Sketch the graphs of a pair of straight lines for which the pair of y-intercepts, the pair of x-intercepts, and the slopes all differ by 2.

In the first case you can creep gradually toward a final product, possibly learning something about each type of constraint as you go; it tempts a dynamic, spatial approach. In the second case you can be overwhelmed by the constraints that, if they do not block progress, may suggest a lot of algebraic modeling as a starting point, followed by equation solving. In the second case the journey to get the answer can dominate; in the first case, given enough time, you are more likely to use the task as an arena for exploration.

However, the second task affords learners the opportunity to make their own choices of which constraints to impose at first, whereas the first task makes the choices for you, being more structured and thus perhaps more limiting.

Making It Harder

We have mentioned several times that many people when asked to construct an example, then another, then another, spontaneously start to challenge themselves; they start to "make things a bit harder" and more interesting. Comments include: "I tried to make my own challenge and found it more interesting. We set our own boundaries. I had to stop and think 'what can I do that's different?' " There is often a connection between "more interesting" and "harder," because these comments imply some further mental effort that may be pleasurable in itself or may lead to pleasurable outcomes. These may not match what a teacher believes to be more interesting or harder, which thus affords insight into learners' experience.

Very occasionally we have found that not everyone challenges themselves. For instance, we often use one of our favorite tasks:

Task 12 Yet Again: Difference of 2 Again

Write down two numbers whose difference is 2. (pause)
Write down another two numbers whose difference is 2. (pause)
Write down yet another two numbers whose difference is 2.

A few people respond by writing three very similar examples; in one case, one person wrote down the same example three times! But we have always found that when possibilities are shared and dimensions of possible variation opened up, people become more adventurous. Perhaps their past experience leads them to needing explicit permission to be playful, extreme, or adventurous in mathematics.

In some other cases, people tried to guess what we would find interesting, which involves them in thinking about what might be interesting to them as well. There are so many variations to consider: What if one of the numbers has to be the negative, reciprocal, negative reciprocal, or square of the other? There are cases wherein after several exposures to similar construction tasks some people voluntarily formulate challenges that take them way beyond familiar territory. Mainly we have found that people complexify the task for their own interest by relating it to other areas of mathematics, such as (in the just-noted task) looking for prime pairs, thinking about integrals whose difference is 2 more than some definite intervals, exploring shapes on square grids whose perimeters differ by 2 while the area stays the same, and so on (see a discussion of this task in chap. 3).

In fact, it is almost inevitable that something interesting will happen when three different objects are generated, as long as there is public discussion about the method of choice or generation. Even a simple collection of pairs, such as 1, 3; 2, 4; and 3, 5, can be discussed and generalized (expressed in symbols and extended to fractions or decimals). Choosing at random can open up interesting questions: What would *random* mean in such a situation? What appears at first as mere repetition for efficiency or to minimize effort proves to have mathematical interest.

Learners actually want interesting tasks, and being asked to exemplify gives them the opportunity to do this for themselves—to ask themselves what could be of interest. For some teachers this may be slightly shocking because motivation, especially of secondary students, can be a problem. As teachers we can say that we have never met learners who are not interested in what comes from their minds, pencils, or mouths and who do not respond when a teacher is interested in their creations and constructions.

Nevertheless, this kind of self-complexifying behavior can only take place in ways that the learner already knows or knows about or knows how to do. The learner knows something about what can be varied and how it can be varied, but these variations are limited by experience and knowledge.

How can learners go beyond self-imposed constraints and thereby extend their example spaces? Obviously one method is through hearing about what others do. As one session participant said: "I wouldn't have thought of negative numbers." Here someone knew about negative numbers, but this person did not perceive them as relevant for the prompt about the difference of 2. They were not seen as in the range of permissible change of numbers, but a few experiences like this may lead this learner to extend the example space in similar situations in the future. Learners are interested in extending possibilities even if they may chastise themselves about what they could have thought of but did not.

For some learners, being exposed to other possibilities is a positive emotional experience. One person noted: "The fun in the tasks seems to be related to what I would have thought about before and what I would not have thought about before." Other methods teachers can use to encourage extension were discussed in chapter 6.

We have had a lot of fun with *Task 12a: Difference of 2*, using this constraint to raise new types of question about graph sketching as in *Task 57A: Differing By 2 (Straight Lines)*.

BUILDING CONFIDENCE

Readers might think that constructing objects is out of reach for some learners. We hope that, on the basis of experience of previous chapters, you will appreciate how wrong this; any learner can construct objects if the task is appropriately structured. Even more important, constructing your own object not only refreshes your sense of the general class of which you are aware but affords pleasure due to the sense of personal control. Rather than being at the mercy of abstract generalities, learners' confidence in themselves as learners of mathematics grows with every new object they find they can construct for themselves. This is why it is valuable to push learners to construct extreme or peculiar examples.

A taste of possibilities afforded to learners concerning their personal self-confidence and identity as practitioners is offered through the following tasks. Focusing on the structure of the tasks and the commentaries may make sense even if the mathematical content is unfamiliar.

Task 58a: Three Real Roots

Write down a formula for a function that you know has three real roots. (See also *Task 28: Zeroed Functions.*)

When we gave this prompt to a class who had all recently worked with cubic polynomials, there were some interesting results. Some learners gave a general cubic, $y = ax^3 + bx^2 + cx + d$, without thinking that not all of these polynomials go through the x-axis three times. Others tried to construct specific examples in this form by substituting small numbers for a, b, c, and d. Some did nothing, and only one offered a formula in factorized form. Because this was not shared in public, it would not have influenced learners' response to the next prompt:

Task 58b: Three Real Roots Specified

Write down a formula for a graph that has roots at $x = 1, 2$, and 3.

This time there were more learners who gave a formula in factorized form, none who gave a general version, and some who still fiddled with values for a, b, c, and d. There were also some, although fewer, who did nothing. In *Task 58b* the constraint of specific roots gave some people different access to the class of cubic functions than in *Task 58a*.

It turned out that those who offered nothing were constrained by a lack of confidence at first because they had been asked an open question and were not used to having to give examples in this way. Learners may indeed be cautious about making choices when first given freedom to do so (see also Hazzan & Zazkis, 1997). Regular use of LGEs can contribute to learners becoming more confident about exploring the general classes from which they might select examples.

For those who recognized the use of a factorized formula, there were no problems with the second prompt. But it seemed that knowing *about* cubic graphs when asked about functions with three roots did not mean they could necessarily *do* anything with their knowledge, even on the level of messing around with the coefficients.

A further group of learners tried to start from $y = x^3$ and transform the graph until it cut the x-axis three times. For them three roots turned out to be too hard, so they simplified to asking about 2, 1, and 0 roots: "Oh! Zero roots are not possible!"

Eventually these approaches were publicly shared, and there was a mixture of groans as some realized they could have used factorized forms; others realized they did know enough to produce examples but had been fearful of doing so. Interestingly, those who chose to transform from $y = x^3$ reported more realizations as they searched than those who had chosen to alter coefficients. Coefficient altering had been confined to positive and negative small integers: No one used peculiar values such as 0 and ± 1 or tried to make one coefficient very large to dominate the function. This was a clear case of an inappropriately constrained range of change or an unfamiliarity with the power of constructing peculiar, extreme, and boundary examples.

Concerning psychological aspects of exemplification, this incident suggests that confidence might be a major issue in example construction that is as important as ways of seeing knowledge and knowing what could be done. Yet, in all our requests for three examples, everyone who was present participated. Perhaps the role of the first example is that it should be easy enough to get people started, to counteract confidence either by giving everyone something to do or by creating an "I can do that" reaction through public sharing.

In our experience confidence cannot be established separately from success with a task. What is undoubtedly true is that the benefits of example construction cannot be attained vicariously. No amount of being told or listening and watching others can substitute for the personal experience. David Clarke and Joanne Lobato's (2002) reexamination of injunctions to "tell" or "not to tell" is useful here. They wrote that "telling" or "not telling" are oversimplifications of the teacher–student relationship. Focus is too much on the form of teachers' statements rather than the function—that is, the structure of what is said rather than how it is perceived and acted on by the learner. A learner who is told something directly when it is useful may respond to it in a very active, sense-making way; a learner who is not told something useful at an appropriate time may become stuck. Clarke and Lobato preferred the notions of initiating and eliciting. It seems to us that the actions of initiating and eliciting can be taken by both teachers and learners. A teacher can legitimately initiate a sense-making activity and exploration or can provide an environment in which learners can initiate their own mathematical activity. If exemplification and other typical mathematical actions are commonplace norms in the classroom, there is more likely to be flexible responsibility for initiating activity and eliciting response.

As learners develop a sense of themselves as *constructors*, as possessing the requisite powers to participate in and make choices about the objects used as examples, their personal identity develops alongside. Confidence breeds confidence; identity feeds identity.

Confidence to Work With New Ideas

The conundrum Clarke and Lobato (2002) raised is related to the learning paradox (see chap. 5). In their articulation, if telling is not a useful way to teach, then how are new ideas to be introduced? This is seen as particularly problematic for teaching methods that appear to advocate "not telling," such as collaborative learning or discovery methods. However, much is hidden in the detail of what teachers actually do in these situations. Clarke and Lobato suggested that teachers could combine eliciting and initiating so that although the function is telling, the form is not. This is not a new idea. Close examination of Plato's story of Meno, which is often held to be an example of scaffolding a pupil's insights, could suggest that "telling" was going on in a less than subtle way. The untutored slave boy was being led carefully and step-by-step toward a particular insight. The learner recovers the knowledge from the interaction, and in this case it is the knowledge the tutor intended. For the slave boy, it may have felt as if he was thinking it out for himself or it may have felt like being driven down a narrow path in a fog.

The same conundrum arises when we think about LGEs. We would not call the use of LGEs a method of teaching; it is just a strategy to use when it seems appropriate.[34] We certainly would not make global claims for the effectiveness of getting learners to construct examples. What we do say is that it provides an arena for active construal, and the more structured or constrained the arena is, the more interesting the learning, as far as the watershed of overconstraint described earlier.

It might seem that LGEs are inappropriate when new topics are being introduced, but we have found that they have very particular uses in the introduction of new ideas. Mathematical ideas are so interwoven that any new topic can and must be linked to previous knowledge, so relevant ideas can be elicited from learners at the start of a topic. Learners can also be challenged to construct examples that happen to illustrate the new concept or the new idea that will motivate their interest through raising mathematical questions about the range and scope of their construction. Many new topics can be introduced by going to the boundary of some previously understood concepts or by seeing what happens in special cases that have arisen elsewhere. Learners are not being asked to create examples that they know nothing about; but they can be asked to create examples that contain specific puzzles and problems. For example, learners who have been studying multiplication and are about to study division can be asked to make up some examples in which a pile of counters or chips is split into smaller piles of equal size. Learners who have been studying the removal of brackets can shift to studying factorizing by making up an interesting example using their previous work. Learners who have solved simultaneous equations algebraically can be asked to write down a worked example and keep the numbers in columns instead but do not write down the variables. Thus, they can describe some matrix methods for themselves before knowing much about matrices. Further, learners

---

[34]LGEs can be used not only for supporting concept development but also for assessment (Bell & Swan, 1995; Stoyanova, 1998; van den Heuvel-Panhuizen et al., 1995). Many authors have commented on the motivational effects of learners constructing their own questions, problems, and tests (Cudmore & English, 1998; Stoyanova, 1998; Streefland & van den Heuvel-Panhuizen, 1992; Waywood, 1992, 1994).

could be asked to construct objects according to instructions involving choices at certain points, but they need not know what they are making or why they are making them until they have seen the similarities and differences of their finished products.

Learners' informal and invented mathematics contain many important ideas that may later be formalized and made explicit. Speaking of young children, Herbert Ginsburg and Kyoung-Hye Seo (1999) said "these ideas may be innate, constructed for the purpose of adaptation, or picked up from an environment that is rich in mathematical structure, regardless of culture" (p. 115). Here we go further and suggest that such crude ideas develop as a learner studies mathematics as well as from other environments that move toward formalization: "Teachers then can use these crude ideas as a foundation on which to construct a significant proportion of classroom pedagogy" (Ginsburg & Seo, 1999, p. 115). Recall Jeff's practice in chapter 2. He encouraged learners to create the process of graphing as a way to represent their knowledge of functions. Notations and representations are an integral aspect of learning new mathematics.

DiSessa et al. (1991) sought to understand what it was about the learning environment that had led learners to be able to invent graphing for themselves as a way to represent motion. Their hope was that, by understanding the context, they would be able to create situations in the future that would encourage learners to create mathematical representations for themselves, rather than using given methods automatically. Learners compared their individual attempts to represent motion with each other, exploring the payoff between simplicity and information. After this, learners further developed their representations. There was no attempt at this stage to get everyone to use the same approach. Later, the teacher initiated discussion of the same kinds of issues, focusing on particular features of the motion being graphed. By this kind of sharing and questioning of ideas produced by the class, learners eventually constructed the usual, conventional, representational type of graph although their previous experience of graphing as modeling was almost nonexistent.

DiSessa's learners had immense emotional commitment because they were working on refining their own creations. The teacher helped them organize, focus, and characterize their creations and also acted as a model for mathematical critique by generating questions about strengths and weaknesses of ideas. The lesson reports show that the style of questioning set up by the teacher enabled learners to use similar questions to compare their work and challenge each other's ideas. This was perhaps underplayed by diSessa and colleagues (1991) who focused instead on peer explanation, peer with peer discussion, avoidance of overt teacher judgments, and so on. These classroom norms are important in providing a framework in which nonthreatening, real discussion can flourish, but of at least equal importance are the type of questions used by teachers to model what can be asked in mathematics. The teacher in this study categorized responses, named them, and examined what they could and could not do (p. 155), and learners picked up these habits for themselves.

For us, this study confirms two aspects of the use of LGEs that we have been advocating. First, children are builders of knowledge, in particular of mathematics, given the right tools. "They can, and indeed, *must* (re)invent even those things that are *presented to them* in the classroom" (diSessa et al., 1991, p. 158). Second, learners will model their methods of mathematical inquiry on those presented, used, and expected of them by the teacher. The teacher, therefore, has a role in providing a model of mathematical questioning and example creation as well as organizing learning in such a way as to encourage it.

The sociomathematical norms of the classroom in the aforementioned study are similar to those in the classrooms studied by Schwarz and Hershkowitz (1999, 2001). In their work, learners used given examples as *prototypes* to build new examples of functions in an interactive software environment. They stated that "intensive production and use of representatives improved the learning of the function concept" (p. 256).

The computer environment seemed to encourage experimentation in the form of building objects. Learners who did not have computer experience did not develop their own new examples. The presence of possibly irrelevant attributes in individual examples was beneficial and lead to exploration, but this was only true for those using dynamic graphing tools.

What is the mechanism by which this happens? Dealing with multiplicity and example construction leads to the construction of meaning. For these learners, interweaving a variety of examples constructed by altering prototypes led to extraction of invariant properties. Ambiguities and dilemmas posed by comparing examples were clarified. The critical community of learners may also have played a role as it created a need to explain, resolve differences, and be explicit.

But it is also clear that the use of software made a difference. This has also been true in some of our teaching. Learners with graphical calculators report that they can easily overcome the emotional block of expecting the teacher to provide examples because it is so easy to try some themselves; however, software use might block the experiences of actually building examples and being aware of the role of its constituent parts. There is a complex interaction among confidence, software as an enabling tool, taking risks involved in making examples yourself, understanding the construction process, and learning about the concept.

Status of Examples in Building Confidence

What role do examples play in the learner's mind? Having been appropriately prompted, scaffolded, and supported to produce examples, what happens next? As we have pointed out before, it is usual for the authority that gives examples to have one idea about their status and learners to have quite different ones, but we have also suggested a range of contributions that self-generated examples make to learning.

There is, of course, the confidence generated by having created something successfully for yourself, particularly if it is then taken up by a teacher and used as the foundation for future work. There is ownership and a focus for interest in the example. The fact that many teachers adopt and use LGE practices enthusiastically attests to the motivational effect on learners. Whether an LGE survives as a central image and becomes a dominant example for them depends on how learners develop the example spaces into which it fits. If it was already a dominant image developed from past teaching, then it is likely to continue in that place. Otherwise, you might hope that continual reorganization of the space might alter its role as it is seen to relate to other examples, either similar or different. In studies by Schwartz and Hershkowitz (1999) and diSessa et al. (1991), deliberate comparisons were made in class about LGEs, allowing example spaces to be challenged immediately and ideas to be shared.

If we vary the parameters of an example, we can decide if it is generic, in the sense that it provides a paradigm for a class, or if it has some special features that make it rather more particular or special in some way. What is important here is whether it is appropriate for the example to occupy a pole position in the space or whether it should be seen as special and possibly representative of a subclass. For example, unit fractions form a special subclass of fractions, but when you add or subtract them, you go outside that class. So it is not sensible to think that limiting your work to unit fractions is informative about fractions in general. In calculus, the relationship between definite integration and area can be explored and unwise generalizing avoided by using functions that have real roots within the integration interval. In terms of techniques that can be used, functions that do not have roots in the integration interval can be seen as one particular kind, whereas those that do have roots can be seen as another kind. To emphasize some of the conditions needed for integration to work, a peculiar example of a step function that rises and falls could be introduced. This can lead either to a new, more detailed, description of techniques or to the introduction of the word *continuous* into the previous description. In the former approach, this peculiar example is incorporated as a new subclass; in the latter approach, it is barred as a kind of "Lakatosian monster" to be excluded.

Examples that have very unusual features have been called *peculiar* (Bills, 1996). It is important for learners to know, through feedback, if they are clinging to a peculiar example thinking it might be generic or ignoring a peculiar example whose behavior challenges their assumptions. When teachers refer to examples as temporary or overspecific rather than as right or wrong, learners are supported in seeing themselves as developing rather than as performing.

This sense of status of examples can be deliberately developed in the classroom by an aware teacher, or it can happen haphazardly over time as the learner becomes more and more acquainted with the concept and its associated words. A teacher who is making distinctions among roles of examples can choose to emphasize the status of a particular example with more clarity than a teacher for whom examples are an unclassified muddle.

In some situations, such as algebraic manipulations or geometric diagrams, an example is something whose structure may give insight into properties and behaviors of a whole class of examples. In other situations an example may be used with several others as raw material for inductive reasoning. In some of the tasks in this book we have not been explicitly clear about what you might do with an example once you have found it. This is because, for the purposes of this book, attending to details of the search itself and the learning and reorganizing that it entails is maximally important, but in a classroom context, the particular mathematical ideas, properties, or relationships are likely to be of greatest importance. Other tasks, such as *Difference of 2* (*Task 12a*), can be done fairly easily without effortful searching. What is the purpose of getting all these examples of differences of 2? The experience of self-challenge seems to be important in this kind of exercise, relaxing learners into looking for more extreme and peculiar examples for themselves and affording opportunities for meta-cognitive awareness of how decisions are made.

At the heart of the use of examples is the learner discerning variation. Nitsa Movshovits-Hadar (1988) wrote that surprise is an underused element of mathematics teaching, yet many theorems and properties in mathematics can be expressed as surprises. The fact that the squares of sides of right-angled triangles have a special relationship can be seen as a surprise result among sums of squares of the shorter two sides of triangles that are not right angled. The fact that square numbers have an odd number of factors can be seen as a surprise among the pairs of factors generated by other numbers. The fact that the diagonals of a kite do not bisect each other can be seen as a surprise among the diagonals of many other symmetrical quadrilaterals; thus, this may lead to exploration of other symmetrical quadrilaterals that challenge such simple expectations. But if mathematics is seen as a motley collection of unconnected facts and techniques, it is hard to be surprised by anything.

Can you be surprised by your own constructions? Probably not, unless they turn out to have more properties than initially imagined. But you can be surprised to be asked to construct something that seems impossible and whose existence challenges assumptions. Many of the tasks in this book contain the potential for surprise, but to be surprised you need to have an expectation, and expectations arise from past experience and conjecturing. You might like to think again about this prompt from *Task 22*, which we use frequently:

Task 22 Yet Again: Write Down Continued

Write down an example of . . . that no one in this room will write down or you think no one in the world has ever written down before!

After initial shock, people tend to become very creative with this task and finally believe it to be possible or at least possible in principle.

LEARNING AS CONSTRUCTION

We have been unable to find significant awareness in the literature of the potential power of LGEs in promoting profound understanding of mathematical structures. Yet our experience suggests that it can be a major influence in concept development. As Hazzan and Zazkis (1997) said, "we believe that a construction of a specific mathematical object described by its properties, may help students in the mental construction of the relevant mathematical notions on a higher level of abstraction" (p. 306).

Problem Posing

Learner generation of problems has been recommended widely, particularly in relation to motivation and promoting understanding, yet the literature about whether it helps, how it could help, and what else is needed to make it help is surprisingly thin. Ed Silver and Jinfa Cai (1996) found a clear relationship between learner facility in solving problems and the complexity of problems they created, but they warned that this result should not be taken to imply that skills are transferred between the two situations: At best there may be some correlation. They preferred to emphasize that complex problem posing in its own right was a valuable mathematical activity. In a searching and insightful survey of the problem posing of some 13- and 14-year-old learners, Elena Stoyanova (1998) found that problem solving and problem posing required different skills.

The link between the two was not at all obvious in her view. She found learners using identifiable strategies to invent new problems. They could swap the given for the goal (e.g., undo; if this is the answer, what is the question?), increase operational and structural complexity, model their own life experience, extend the structure by adding new elements, and work at a more general level than the original problem. But she could not point to significantly improved problem-solving skills as an outcome.

In very few cases are improvements in general mathematical achievement researched and reported. Yoshihiko Hashimoto (1987) found that learners who had rewritten story problems improved in their subsequent ability to solve word problems, but Silver's (1994) extensive research, despite the result just described, does not consistently support this outcome. However, it is possible that learners' experience of problem posing generated a sense of learning that teachers could not observe.

Ramakrishnan Menon's (1997) thesis highlights this beautifully in his use of teacher and learner comments. Teachers typically talk about benefits in motivation and the information generated for informal assessment purposes, showing amazement at the range of questions produced, claiming the activities improved motivation and concentration, and that it was easier to see where there had been a change in students' learning. On the other hand, learners typically talked about being made to think and being better able to answer other people's questions, claiming that it helped them understand how to make problems and get their own answers.

It seems as if the learners had some sense of cognitive challenge, but teachers were mainly aware of affective benefits and the opportunity for informal assessment.

What Then Is Learning?

We say that constructing examples of objects promotes and contributes to learning because we see learning as improving constructing and reconstructing generalities. And we are in good company:

> Children engage, unconstrainedly and continually, in reflective inspection and testing for the sake of what they are interested in doing. Habits of thinking thus generated may increase in amount till they become of importance on their own account. It is part of the business of the teacher to lead students to extricate and to dwell upon the distinctively intellectual side of what they do until there develops a spontaneous interest in ideas and their relations with one another—that is, the genuine power of abstraction, of rising from engrossment in the present to the plane of ideas. (Dewey, 1933, pp. 225–226)

> When the subject-matter has been psychologized, that is, viewed as an outgrowth of present tendencies and activities, it is easy to locate in the present

some obstacle, intellectual, practical, or ethical, which can be handled more adequately if the truth in question be mastered. This need supplies motive for the learning. An end which is the child's own carries him on to possess the means of its accomplishment. But when material is directly supplied in the form of a lesson to be learned as a lesson, the connecting links of need and aim are conspicuous for their absence. What we mean by the mechanical and dead in instruction is a result of this lack of motivation. The organic and vital mean interaction—they mean play of mental demand and material supply. (Dewey, 1902, pp. 19–32)

Seymour Papert (1993) maintained that learning is most effective when learners are constructing things through actions they perform, although his focus is largely on computers and computer-driven robots.

Constructionism is built on the assumption that children will do best by finding ("fishing") for themselves the specific knowledge they need. Organized or informal education can help most by making sure they are supported morally, psychologically, materially, and intellectually in their efforts. . . . the goal is to teach in such a way as to produce the most learning for the least teaching. (p. 139)

Philip Fisher (1998) related learning to wondering, claiming that wondering is a result of experiencing a state of wonder, which by its very nature can only arise in extraordinary ways. He said: "To characterize wonder we are forced to look at its alternative, the ordinary, and paradoxically what we end up saying is that there cannot be any experience of the ordinary. . . . The ordinary can not or does not turn itself into experiences" (p. 20).

In other words, it takes surprise or other forms of disturbance to have an experience of something. There must be some sort of distinction made to distinguish the foreground from the background. In Marton's view, response only happens when there is some variation to discern. How can learners' attention be structured toward noticing and discerning variations in mathematics? This is what Leon Festinger (1957) was getting at when he coined the term *cognitive dissonance* and what Movshovits-Hadar (1988) was getting at with her notion that most mathematical theorems contain a surprise. The van Hiele levels of geometric thinking elaborate subtle differences in application of the same idea.[35] Put differently, *learning* is the name we give to experiencing a shift in the structure of attention (Mason, 1989), that is, in how we attend to specific situations and what we

---

[35]van Hiele levels can be summarized as visualization (wholeness); analysis and description, using language developed at previous level (discerning details); abstraction, using language for distinctions developed at previous level (relationships); informal deduction (properties); and rigor and formal deduction (properties as axioms; see Burger & Shaughnessy, 1986; Fuys, Geddes, & Tischler, 1985; Usiskin, 1982; van Hiele, 1986).

are sensitized to notice through attending and distinguishing. A slightly more general version sees learning as reasonably durable and generalizable change (Johansson, Marton, & Svensson, 1985).

Any view of learning also presupposes a particular view of knowledge. If mathematical knowledge is taken to consist of factual information and procedural instructions, then this kind of dynamic, constructive, active, and messy learning may be perceived as a waste of time, as indeed it is by many school and college students who have to take mathematics as a service subject. Ed Dubinsky (1991a) took the view that "knowledge and its acquisition are not easily distinguishable, if at all" (p. 161), a view that can also be seen in the definition of *procept* (Gray & Tall, 1994). Ernst von Glasersfeld (1991), summarized thousands of years of educational thought as follows: "Knowledge is the result of a learner's activity rather than the passive reception of information and instruction" (p. *xiv*).

This view simultaneously defines mathematical knowledge and learning: Knowledge is the result of activity, so learning is the activity and the development of greater facility in engaging in similar activity in the future. Enactivists such as Humberto Maturana (1988), Tom Kieren (1998), and Brent Davis (1996) go so far as to identify knowledge with action: It is not that knowledge enables action or that action leads to knowledge; it is the performing of actions that constitutes knowledge. Thus, the messiness of action and the messiness of learning coexist.

We have almost completed a circular relationship, but von Glasersfeld's (1991) description omits the transformation processes that ensure that the activities the learner can pursue become more and more complex. By actively constructing examples, you experience and thereby learn about structures; by actively working on examples, you learn about classes of objects; by actively working on problem posing, you learn about how problems are designed; by actively construing, you learn how meaning is constructed; and by actively constructing objects that meet specified constraints, you learn how objects are constructed and thus come to appreciate the concepts that they exemplify. You learn how to learn.

LGEs for Concept Development

Efforts to translate construction into pedagogy abound, particularly in the internationally influential reforms of the mathematics curriculum in the United Kingdom, Australia, Israel, and the United States, but often these efforts have been at the level of promoting an investigative approach, problem solving, social norms of mathematical work, assignment and assessment of extended tasks, and so on. When detailed pedagogical practices have been specified, such as scripted lessons, three-part lessons, and the use of specific tools such as the empty number line, there has been widespread adoption by teachers, although this is sometimes done more mechanically than thoughtfully. There have been few articulations of pedagogy in which the structures of ways of working directly scaffold the structures of mathematics. We found one in the work of Patricia Sadovsky (1999), who almost accidentally provided a task structure that asks for LGEs and results in improvements in understanding. She asked questions like the following (p. 4-147):

Task 59: Divisors and Dividends

How many division operations (problems?) are there that give a dividend of 32 and a remainder of 27?

If you think there are less than three, write them all down and explain why there are no other ones.

If you think there are more than three, write down at least four of them and explain how other solutions can be found.

She used this generic form of questioning in several different ways. The numerical dimensions of variation in a division sum are the divisor, dividend, quotient, and remainder. She chose various subsets of these dimensions to constrain the information given to the learner. In Task 59 she fixed the dividend and the remainder. Her sequence of questions started with some that only have one answer (e.g., divide 26 by 12 and give the remainder) and moved toward some that have infinitely many solutions. Her aim was to "get data to characterise a possible articulation space between arithmetic and algebraic practices" (p. 4-145). Of particular interest to us is her unexpected outcome that "these problems are simultaneously a chance to find the limits of the arithmetic practices and enrich the conception of Euclidean division" (p. 4-148). For us the concept enrichment was utterly expected given our convictions about LGEs. To give examples one has to either mimic given examples (but Sadovsky gave none, so this easy method was not available) or construct, manipulate, inspect, and transform knowledge structures of the concept or modify familiar objects. As always, the challenge is in the detail: to make it happen deliberately, as Dubinsky (1991a) did when he wrote of the constructive intention of his own teaching: "I design instruction intended to induce students to perform the constructions which [a decomposition of the concept] specifies, and then I observe the students as they try to make sense out of this instruction" (p. 185).

Teaching materials and research emanating from the work of Alan Bell and others at the Shell Centre throughout the 1980s and 1990s showed that they appreciated the complexity of LGEs. They used a wide range of techniques for getting learners to take responsibility for various kinds of exemplification. For instance, materials produced for the South Nottinghamshire Project (a curriculum development project) frequently prompted learners to create examples (Bell, Swan, Shannon, & Crust, 1996). Initially, this was introduced as a self-assessment strategy, but the authors were clearly aware that the production of an example for assessment purposes might also cause further thought and deeper understanding. In other words, assessment activities were seen as teaching and learning activities as well. They regularly asked learners to "make up more questions like these. If they work, give them to a neighbour to solve" and found that this improved motivation to work and awareness of question types. Questions were then discussed in class, particularly if they turned out to be too easy. Sometimes constraints were placed on a question, such as asking learners to invent questions that led to a specific or interesting answer. Occasionally, the prompt would not be to create a question but to create examples of classes of objects, such as "make up two straight line equations, and find out if and where they cross." In one sequence of tasks they used "piles of stones" as a euphemism for unknown numbers and asked learners to build up equations with "piles of stones" on each side. This approach may remind you of Ed in chapter 2.

Can LGEs Be Used for the Introduction of a New Topic?

A deliberate use of LGEs in the introduction of new concepts is reported by Dahlberg and Housman (1997). They were interested in how mathematics undergraduate learners might construct concepts for themselves, rather than depend on formal concept definitions and examples provided by authorities. They studied significant changes in the development of the personal concept image as revealed by learners' expressions of their understandings in verbal and written forms of learner–teacher communication.

Learners were given a definition and asked to construct examples as follows:

Task 60: Fine Functions

Definition: A function is called *fine* if it has a root (zero) at each integer.
Give an example of a fine function and explain why it is a fine function.
Give an example of a function that is not fine and explain why it is not fine.
In your own words or pictures, explain what a fine function is.

This exercise was a precursor to being asked to classify some given functions as *fine* or *not fine*. In the spirit of the rest of this book, we suppose you will have immediately tried to adapt these generic forms of question into something more appropriate to your own level of teaching.

The lesson being studied was the first time a new concept had been introduced in this way, and teachers found that, for some learners, having to create an example from the definition was the most significant aspect of their learning; for others, personal reformulation of the given definition was the most significant. This agrees with the work of Cécile Ouvrier-Buffet (2002), who found that the creation of definitions by learners necessarily coemerged with conceptual understanding, rather than preceding or following.

Dahlberg and Housman (1997) reported on a learner who was able to visualize suitable graphical images and recognizing that expressing them in algebra was beyond this learner. It was noticeable, in their study, that all learners had to evoke a graphical image, rather than an algebraic one, to generate a class of suitable functions successfully. Using visualization to extend one's example space, and thus to create a need to extend representation and articulation of the example space, seems at least valuable and perhaps vital. Those learners who employed example generation consistently in the study made more progress in their understanding and were more able to use examples to extend and develop their concept usage than their colleagues.

Hazzan and Zazkis (1999) studied learners' mathematical and emotional difficulties in constructing examples. Their working hypothesis was that "while students are working on generating particular examples of a mathematical concept which satisfies certain properties, they construct a more general notion in their mind" (p. 4). They used tasks like the following:

- Give an example of a six digit number divisible a) by 9; b) by 17.
- Give an example of a function which has a value of -2 at $x = 3$.
- Give an example of a system of equations that has $(3, 7)$ as a solution

They concluded that "give an example" problems not only promoted deeper learning but enabled learners to make links among concepts. In our experience, it takes more than one simple example for learners to begin to appreciate the range of choices available to them. So, in asking for a six-digit number, learners are pushed out of their immediate example spaces. Task structures such as "another and another" and "something others will not write down" have a similar effect.

The research we just referenced and our own experience lead us to grant LGEs a fundamental role in conceptual learning. After reading some of this research, Annie and John Selden (1998) wrote:

Granted the inherent epistemological difficulties of finding examples for oneself, are we, in a well-intentioned attempt to help students understand newly defined concepts, ultimately hobbling them, by providing them with pre-digested examples of our own? Are we inadvertently denying students the opportunity to learn to generate examples for themselves? (p. 4)

In learning more about mathematical concepts, going far beyond the generation of questions and problems to exemplification of all kinds in mathematics, we have come to the following conclusions:

- The construction of examples necessarily requires some generalization of a learner's experience so far and some organization of knowledge to fit the present requirements, hence promoting reorganization.
- The construction of examples, with properties that are new to the learner and characteristics, leads to significant extensions of personal example spaces.
- The notion of extending example spaces provides an incremental approach to new structural knowledge.
- Because much of mathematics is about exploring classes of objects, their features, and relationships, exemplification is a major cognitive strategy that teachers can scaffold for learners, which eventually fades when learners seek examples habitually for themselves.

GATHERING THREADS

Through the use of various tasks we have offered students and colleagues, their reported experience, our own experience, and from relevant literature, we have not so much come to conclusions but have been led to articulate significant threads. For us these threads are more than abstract summaries. They are articulations of what amounts to aspects of the psychology of example construction, providing access to what it is like to construct and reconstruct examples as part of learning mathematics.

Psychology of Example Construction

In chapter 3 we discussed four principles:

1. Exemplification is individual and situational.
2. Perceptions of generality are individual.
3. Examples can be perceived or experienced as members of structured spaces.

4. Example spaces can be explored and extended by the learner, with or without external prompts.

We also encountered a number of related observations that go some way to describing the experience of example construction:

1. The same example can be seen as representing classes or as a special case by different learners—regardless of the teacher's intention. Some special cases turn out to be examples of generalities that are new to the learner.
2. Example creation can give a sense of structure. You have to search structures to find classes of examples. You may have images of certain examples as if they belong to certain structures. To sense structure you may need an experience of the infinite, such as being "shot through with infinity."
3. Spaces can be explored by considering dimensions of possible variation and their associated ranges of permissible change. That is, learners can find out what can vary and how far it can vary, identify new variables, work from first principles, build objects from definitions, and use alternative modes of representation to see what is possible in one example and relating it to another and in other ways.

In chapter 5 we considered various kinds of examples: central, generic, and dominant; extreme, special, and pathological; and generalizations as general classes. We discussed different ways in which examples can be constructed, most of which end up in some form of generalization, despite whether starting from the general and imposing constraints or start from several examples and seeking what is general about them.

Through the variety of tasks we have offered we have suggested a number of different strategies for exemplifying that were summarized in chapter 6: recalling (reference examples and favorite examples), tinkering and gluing, complexifying, and varying and generalizing. These were elaborated to show the wide range of task types that teachers can use to engage learners in appropriate actions:

- Make up an example.
- Make up an example with some constraints.
- Add constraints sequentially.
- Make up another or more like or unlike this.
- Make counterexamples and nonexamples.
- Confound expectations.
- Characterize all objects that satisfy specified constraints.

- Reverse.
- Explore distinctions.
- Bury the bone.
- Use features of methods or objects as starting points.
- Find.
- Use wild-card generation.

Metaphors

In chapter 4 we broached metaphors for example spaces (the larder, the landscape, and toolshed) and for example construction (tinkering and cooking), which we and colleagues have found helpful in contacting experience.

Example Space as Larder.   As we mentioned, looking for examples is like going to the larder and either immediately picking out something familiar or having to look for it for a while or recognizing that something else that catches your eye will do the job perfectly well. At other times, something has to be made from what is there—either by adapting familiar items or putting things together in a range of ways to make an appropriate mathematical object.

Example Space as Landscape.   As we noted, looking for examples is like scanning a landscape. The tendency is to look in regions that are close to hand and more familiar (like low-lying pastures and well-worn tracks), but if these regions prove inadequate, then trips into the higher ones along less well traveled tracks are possible.

The metaphor of landscape is an interesting way to look at knowledge, although it does tend to emphasize the overview map aspect rather than what it is like to be in the landscape itself. You can have an overview, an intimate knowledge of particular areas, or a knowledge of how areas fit together to make the overview without necessarily having all three kinds of knowledge. It is almost a probabilistic model, suggesting that you are most likely to recall those things with which you have had a larger variety of experiences in the past. Thus, what we have been calling central or dominant images might (in the metaphor) be associated with the peaks.

The landscape metaphor unfortunately reinforces the experience of locating an example as a form of search of what already exists or getting an overview of a landscape as a kind of map to locate a region likely to contain what you seek. Often we find examples come to us ready formed or as a taste of a possibility that is triggered by the situation. They rise up out of our experience. Sometimes they are fully formed; other times they are but fragments of possibilities that need to be integrated or built into a construction. The larder metaphor gives at least a hint that the contents can be treated as raw material for further construction.

Example Space as Toolshed.   As we stated, tools that are used frequently are close at hand; things that might prove useful accumulate in the nether regions, and the whole layout gets rearranged according to the season and which tools are most needed.

The toolshed offers potential in that tools and their possible uses are inseparable. Because tinkering and adjusting and taking things apart and gluing things together is such a common experience, example construction is usefully thought of as a process of bricolage—of using what is on hand in our triggered example space but going beyond what is already extant.

Example Construction as Bricolage.   As we mentioned, this is taking two or more ideas or objects usually thought of as distinct and combining them in some way.

We propose that example construction contributes to that overlaying of new experience onto intuitions, as described by Fischbein (1987). That is, it contributes to the enrichment of the example space that comes to mind in a situation and, hence, to the confidence with which you set about tinkering, conjecturing, checking, and so on. Example construction and reconstruction affords access to more complex examples and, through these examples, to general classes of objects. In other words, the richness and complexity of your example space in a given situation is enhanced through your own imaginative construction.

Example Construction as Cooking.   We like Schoenfeld's (1998) image of creating a recipe by imagining the possibility of doing to Ingredient B what you are in the habit of doing to Ingredient A and vice versa. This neatly combines the metaphors of the larder and bricolage. Thus, if the search fails, you can begin to create with what is on hand, using methods and heuristics that have proved useful in the past, albeit with other raw materials.

There are, of course, other metaphors that people use, but all are fundamentally position based. As George Lakoff and Mark Johnson (1980) together as well as separately (Lakoff, 1987; Johnson, 1987) pointed out so persuasively, the movement of our bodies in space provides the most common and most informative metaphors, because our primal experience is of movement in and through space.

Example Spaces as Islands.   A colleague of ours, Scott Lucas (2002), described children's knowledge of numbers as a lake with islands of certainty between which children can choose according to the problem at hand, and then they can navigate between the islands to construct new facts from known facts.

This image was also used by Ivan Peterson (1990) for whom "islands of truth" are those pieces of mathematics that you can be sure about, whereas all else is open for speculation and exploration. Certainty takes the place of familiarity in his metaphor. In chapter 4 we referred briefly to an ecological metaphor elaborated by Greeno (1991) in which he likened the development of familiarity with numbers and arithmetic to the way in which you become familiar with a new location: At first there are isolated patches of confidence, but over time these begin to connect together.

There seem to be various kinds of images that learners find useful and relate to the experience of searching for examples. So far we have talked about the search itself—the description of what it feels like to search for an example. The image of islands in a lake enables us to understand access and navigation through the space (including the invisible undertow of currents that drag us unknowingly in particular directions). For instance, we can go to a number and then look around for ways to use it to answer a question at hand just as we can go to an island and then use it as a base camp from which to explore the environs. If we are looking for factorizable numbers, we might go to 24 as a familiar place and from it see that 36 or 60 might also be significant. The connections between these numbers are structured by how the learner makes sense of them through their experiences with numbers. However, learners are usually offered a very different image—a number line—that encodes the number properties of proximity and relative size using a geometric representation. In this image, 24 is always near 23 and 25, rather than 36 and 60. Learners may adjust this "given" image to make it more adaptable and to allow access at different points along it and to different sections and scalings of it. Here we are not talking about being taught to scale and zoom, as happens with the use of an "empty" number line which is calibrated according to the current task but retains the same scale along its length, but ad hoc adaptations made in response to experience and personal sense making. Diagrams of learners' number images revealed to Brenda Carter (1983) show number lines that are jagged, curly, and sometimes almost logarithmic in the way they selectively scale and intertwine number relations. These were all constructed spontaneously by learners (see Fig. 7.1).

Willingness to go somewhere a little unfamiliar and then to explore around it can be supported through adoption of the idea of larder, landscape, islands in a lake, the number line, and the understanding that there are other images from which you can choose. Each image imbues mathematical objects with meaning in relation to other objects, and these relational meanings are different in different metaphors.

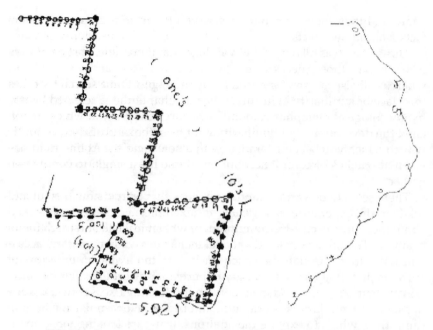

FIG. 7.1.   Tarun and Lucy's number lines. From "Number Lines," by B. Carter, 1983, *Mathematics Teaching, 103,* pp. 2–3. Copyright © 1983 by the Association of Teachers of Mathematics. Reprinted with permission.

Despite how it is visualized, an example space has to afford instant access by being open to rapid inspection by the person searching for examples. Something familiar and useful can be spotted or structured so that an appropriate idea can come readily to mind as a starting point. But this can also be problematic. It is our experience that people generally do not start with a broad sweep, but rather with one dominant object or type, and this dominant example can sometimes act figurally as a barrier to seeing wider choices. A role of the teacher (or other source of questions) is to direct learners toward other possibilities.

Dynamic Example Spaces

Metaphors may be powerful, but their use needs care, for unexpected and unintended associations may be carried by the metaphor much as unintended properties are carried by figural examples.

The larder, the landscape, and the islands in a lake could be taken to imply a rather static or stable nature. In conversations, Mike Ollerton and Adrian Pinel reminded us of the scene in the film *Butch Cassidy and the Sundance Kid* (Foreman & Hill, 1969) when Sundance fails to shoot straight while he is standing still, which captures nicely the sense that creative construction is not an algorithmic process. Sundance asks to be allowed to shoot on the run, as he is more likely to succeed in a dynamic situation than in an artificially static one. Therefore, we need to use dynamic spaces for reference to emphasize what can vary and, if possible, to show it varying.

Our experiences working with learners suggest that a search for examples almost inevitably leads to a reorganization of the space. An example space is almost self-extending and self-developing because as you consider specific objects within it, there is at least the opportunity, if not the tendency, to ask "what if" questions and so extend the examples in new directions. Each contribution from others also has a similar effect of opening up new dimensions of possible variation.

How the larder is reorganized and reconfigured and how this impacts the search for an example to meet specific criteria is very fluid and depends on how the current example space was stimulated and the situation in which it is functioning. This has parallels with connectionist models of brain function. Rather than perceived as a pursuit along a preexisting decision tree, in which the firing of each node sends the "thought" down a particular pathway, the brain is seen as functioning like a network that is constantly restructured so that an experience at one point of the path through the net leads to a reorganization of what follows. Someone is running ahead and switching the points as our journey progresses. This apparently nightmare scenario, beloved of fantasy adventures, makes very good sense in terms of larder searching, because it is a common experience to recategorize things in ways influenced by the current search. During the search you find new ways to group objects by concatenating previous distinctions or creating new ones—in other words, by reorganizing knowledge. Indeed, connectionist research suggests that loss of one part of the path triggers adaptation of other parts of the network to fulfill the same function—in our context this would be like creating appropriate examples from what is at hand. The model also accounts for people learning the same thing in different ways, thus supporting our claim that example spaces are individual and situated (Harré, 2002, p. 201). This contrasts strongly with Michener's (1978) model of a preexisting directed graph of a mathematical concept that may be more helpful when describing teaching than learning.

Inductive Generalization From Examples.   Exemplification is sometimes seen as a necessary but implicit part of inductive generalization. Dave Hewitt (1992) described activities that provide raw material for generalization, usually the development of a formula for the nth term of a sequence (as in *Task 15: T Shapes*). How that formula is constructed is often a mystery. One approach that is commonly taught as a technique is to find differences between successive terms in the hope that this will enlighten the search. Other teachers encourage learners to look for connections between the function values they have generated and familiar sequences, such as square numbers, triangle numbers, and so on. This stage of the work involves creating examples of functions that might fit by using past knowledge and experience and anything else that comes to mind. There is no systematic all-purpose method, and many learners are left to their own devices; those who are successful relying on insight and fiddling or, if lucky, finding a formula from a structural feature of the work rather than from the function values.

Several of the metaphors suggest that systematic searching may not necessarily be the most efficient way to go about things. These suspicions are supported by Lisa Haverty and others (Haverty, Koedinger, Klahr, & Alibali, 2000), whose research into learners applying inductive reasoning to find general formulae showed very little difference between data-collecting and pattern-searching habits of successful and unsuccessful learners. In fact, they found that the systematic and orderly generation of function values was not a necessary feature of success (i.e., tables of values being "tables of no value"). It is not the construction of the table that matters but the underlying structure that might be accessed by paying attention to how the table values are being constructed to get a sense of what might be happening in general.

We suspect that one of the difficulties with this approach to algebra, which expresses generalities of number sequences, is not the symbolization but the lack of acknowledgment that there is no algorithm for finding the formula; learners have to fiddle around with what they already know, deciding what might turn out to be useful. Making this approach an explicit part of the task, with all the necessary messy work, might help more learners understand the full nature of the task and be successful at it. In the work of Haverty et al. (2000), a major difference was that those who succeeded, having looked for obvious step sizes and relationships, then went further and thought up more quantities and combinations to use for comparative purposes. Those who succeeded brought more ideas into play as subgoals, did not give up when obvious approaches failed, and drew on a wider range of prior knowledge of what is possible. This research suggests several possible ways for teachers to move forward, but for our purposes the multiple role of exemplification, both for generating data and for generating possible functions, deserves recognition.

It is a common experience in our crossword solving that we start on a systematic alphabetical search but give up because the temptations to go down other lines of enquiry are too strong and, ultimately, more likely to lead to insight. For example, we might use metonymic chains of reasoning and personal word association to navigate among islands. Similarly, we contend that it is a common practice of mathematicians to try to generalize from one example and then see what happens for extreme examples (e.g., 0, 1, and ∞) or something particularly interesting in the context, rather than trying other ordered well-behaved numerical values. Indeed, working with a sequence of consecutive cases might obscure underlying structure by emphasizing incremental change.

Another dynamic feature of example spaces is the way that ideas and possibilities just come to mind without fanfare or advance warning. One moment you cannot think what to do, the next minute something shows up that can be tried, modified, or adapted.

Although being deliberately unsystematic may be an unfamiliar behavior for a mathematics student, reorganizing the larder is not.[36] It is "knowledge transformation" as described by Bereiter (1985); it is "accommodation" as described by Piaget (1971). The power of using the larder metaphor here is that teachers can make transformation more likely to happen by finding out what is already at hand in the larder and asking for more—for more general, more constrained, and slightly different objects.

In this discussion we are not implying that example spaces exist outside of the learner, to be entered and searched by them as visitors; our experience of example construction leads us to see example spaces as personal, dynamic, evolving, and situated, but also as doorways into worlds of exploration and opportunities for creativity.

Task 61: Folding Shapes

What shapes can be made by folding a piece of paper once, twice, and three times?

What proportions of a sheet of paper would mean that folding in half produced a sheet with the same proportions (thus scaling down).

For those unfamiliar with mathematical exploration, this may seem impossibly open; for those who are familiar, it suggests a rich starting point.

CONSTRUCTED OUTCOMES

The threads gathered in the previous section may be of some use, but we are convinced that what is of most use is the experience gained and the things noticed from engaging in the tasks we have offered and in trying

---

[36]U.K. school students are given credit for churning out systematic results of investigations, but their examiners treat intuitive insight with suspicion (Morgan, 1998).

out variations with others. Future choices in classrooms and during lesson preparation and task construction will be informed by the thoughts and awarenesses that come to mind in the moment, not from checklists provided by some external agency. So we draw this book to a close by reporting on a workshop conducted with educational researcher colleagues at a conference, and we use their observations to underline our contention that far from having sorted out the role of LGEs in the teaching and learning of mathematics, we have at best offered stimulus to further development through providing some structured experiences.

We had been working for a long time on the effects of and distinctions between different types of task that prompt LGEs, and we were concerned that the distinctions we had been making might be overelaborate and obsessive, so we needed to test out responses with others. Would other mathematics educators see the differences we saw and get the same sense of their importance and power? In a workshop session at an international conference (Mason & Watson, 2002), we posed five task sequences to hear the reactions of other experienced mathematics educators and researchers. All the tasks were accessible for all participants, including those who concentrate on elementary mathematics. To our delight, we found that the features we saw in the tasks were recognized by others and that their comments, both oral and written, affirmed both the differences and potential powers that we had either observed elsewhere or intended in the task design. Furthermore, different people reacted differently to different tasks, depending on their past experience, their confidence, their preferences, and so on—just as we had expected. Although some were tempted to reject a task as being tedious or pointless, others found the same task spurred interesting work. Whereas some felt a task was directed, others found it liberating. One person perceived no structure in the tasks themselves but was struck by affordances and constraints that enabled relationships to be noticed.

Task 62: Another Quadrilateral Sequence

Draw a quadrilateral with four equal sides
    and another
    and another.
Draw a quadrilateral with one pair of opposite sides perpendicular.

Our aim with this task was first to give experience of the "and another" structure that we introduced in chapter 5, but this was overshadowed by reactions to the last two prompts that were intended to trigger discussion about mathematics as a constructive activity.

At our workshop, Ron Tzur reported that he had rejected the word *perpendicular* and substituted *parallel* without being aware he had done so. In our view, his activity was so firmly embedded in what he felt was a familiar example space that he subconsciously leapt to something obvious and familiar within that space. This observation carries far-reaching messages for classrooms and for how teachers traditionally blame students for not listening or not reading the question. A misreading might be an expression of what is familiar and what is not, and a sensitive teacher can use it as a way to recognize that a learner needs more extensive experience. Ron, however, was sufficiently knowledgeable to put himself right!

The second task was as follows:

Task 63: Square Addition Sequence

Draw a square.
Draw another square beside it to make a rectangle.
Here is an action: Extend any rectangle by adjoining a square to make a new rectangle.
Repeat this action a few times, and write down the dimensions of your final rectangle and your starting square.

We then collated the various dimensions of the final rectangle, together with the size of the starting square, as data for conjecture and generalization.

In this task, the intention was to look at how LGEs can provide the raw material for looking at a whole class and constructing descriptions of properties and, perhaps, theorems about the class. However, it is also a construction task in a geometrical sense, and it has superficial similarities with *Task 62: Another Quadrilateral Sequence*; but whereas in *Task 62* the final product is likely to a class of spatial objects, in *Task 63* the final products are conjectures about numbers. We have sometimes called this *reverse Euclid* to suggest connections with Euclid's algorithm.[37] But for many, *Task 63* spoke very strongly to learners of Fibonacci numbers, because one set of choices can help you construct a Fibonacci spiral, and may have been blocked to other possibilities as a result. These people were happier on the unfamiliar territory of *Task 62* because they believed *Task 63* was not offering them anything new.

---

[37]See Appendix B for help with Euclid's algorithm and Fibonacci's spiral.

For us, these comparative comments were the most interesting. Some saw the first task as not engaging because it had a very open start; others claimed it was indeed very engaging because they needed to work very hard to get an image. Some saw the second task as uninteresting because they were just following instructions to construct; others saw it as providing structure within which to mathematize.

A neat distinction was drawn by one participant between constructions that lead to principles and principles that lead to constructions. For another, the work in one task was to find images and in the other task to use images. We were also taken by Peter Liljedahl's comment at the workshop that in one task he was constructing examples from structure and in another constructing structure from examples. However, similar comments were made by several people but not always about the same tasks! Even in this relatively mathematically sophisticated group, people saw the tasks in many different ways. The claims they made about which task was of which type turned out to be as much about their perceptions and dispositions as about the wording of the task itself.

This was also true of the final task:

Task 64: Sequence Sequence

Write down two sequences that go on forever such that the ratio of corresponding terms is constant.
Write down another pair so that the ratio rises.
Write down another pair so that the ratio falls.

Our intention had been to provide a way to compare sequences that people may not have thought about before (choosing an unusual constraint to explore what the possible variations could be). Although accepting that the case of equal ratios may not yield anything of great mathematical interest, we felt that such comparisons (especially with decreasing ratios) could provide examples for class discussions about ratios and convergence and, for some people, theorems about limits, choices of suitable sequences to apply for the comparison test[38] of convergence, and so on.

As we have found elsewhere, some approached the tasks by trying rapid generalization and then challenged themselves to look for interesting subclasses of objects or extreme cases. This was the case with *Task 64*, although instant generalization to u_n and $k\,u_n$ was enough for some, producing the reaction: "Where's the problem?" Others generated several ex-

---

[38]The comparison test is a test for convergence of one sequence by comparing it with another known to converge.

amples and then searched for patterns and relationships and made small discoveries of their own to report which were interesting in their own right, although the discoveries may collapse as trivial under the generalization. For many there was an awareness that you could choose how and where to start between specialization and generalization, and these learners experienced a piquant interplay between the two. At the workshop Gaye Williams commented that the task gave her an open and conceptual arena within which she could "strive for elegance."

We leave the last word of this section, and of the workshop, to Adrian Pinel, who told us that what he found in our tasks was "a way to combine choice and infinity."

EPILOGUE: CONSTRUCTING TASKS

One of our by-products of "gathering threads" of our activities and reflections over a period of time is the emerging awareness that we were also developing some criteria for evaluating exemplification tasks that seemed to provoke others active engagement with mathematical activity. Then we realized that these qualities apply to any task offered to learners.

We asked ourselves what makes an exemplification task effective, and we have found considerable resonance with colleagues who have engaged in tasks with us. The result is a list of questions that we can use to interrogate tasks for any teaching style. In particular, there is no implied best task type in the list that follows. We also reemphasize that different learners respond to the same task in different ways and that a uniform diet will inevitably lead to mechanical rather than creative responses.

- Does the task encourage open exploration or focused exploration?
- What constraints and freedoms are afforded?
- Is there a specified goal or is the learner to provide a goal?
- Is there the potential for surprises?
- What usual examples will learners have experienced? Are they usefully generic or excessively generic? What experiences beyond these examples would it be useful for learners to have?
- Are images going to be easily available, or does work have to be done to create images?
- Is the task challenging, or does the challenge come afterwards as a reflective activity?
- Is explanation an integral part of the task, or does it come later?
- Does the task depend on something familiar or on creating something new?

- Are learners passive or active?
- Is conflict (between expectation and demand as well as between assumption and possibility) inherent in the task or not?
- Is the task type familiar?
- Are there instructions to follow to generate examples, or do learners have to make their own instructions?
- When do learners feel safe, and when do they have to take risks?
- Does example construction lead to noticing properties, or does working with properties lead to construction?
- Does exemplification arise from structure, or does structure lead to exemplification?
- Do learners draw then think—or think then draw?
- Do learners have to find or create?
- Do they start from a generality and gradually impose constraints or start with a limited example and gradually remove constraints? Do they start from properties or prototypes?
- How might learners be brought into contact with extensions to their existing example spaces through their own explorations and acts of construction?

So our examination of uses of learner generated examples, and the development of tasks that promote their construction, has led us to explore significant questions about pedagogical task design in general.

Appendix A: Some Historical Remarks on Teaching by Examples

In this appendix we focus our attention on historical records. We look at the ways in which examples have been used for teaching mathematics. The earliest mathematical records (Egyptian papyri, Babylonian tablets, and later copies of original Chinese manuscripts) all make extensive use of worked examples to illustrate procedures, or what came to be called *algorithms* or *rules* in medieval and later texts. By the 16th century European authors of mathematical texts had begun to justify the presence of examples in their texts and to comment both implicitly and explicitly on the role and use that examples play for learners.

When authors comment explicitly on their choices we get access to explicit pedagogical theories. Otherwise we have to gauge implicit pedagogical theories from the different ways in which different authors organize their material. General rules can be described, stated in words, or sometimes expressed in symbols; worked examples and exercises can be grouped together by type, or different types can be mixed together. Rules, worked examples, exercises, and commentary can be placed in different orders. Over the centuries, all reasonable arrangements have been tried: putting the general rule first, then worked examples, then exercises; starting with worked examples, then exercises, then summarizing with general rules; and starting with worked examples, then stating general rules before providing exercises. None have proved universally popular or successful, although some texts have remained in use for nearly a century. Some authors scramble different types of problems or different looking problems, presumably to engage the learner in recognizing the type, whereas others collect exercises according to the technique needed, perhaps to promote a sense of the general class but more probably to focus on fluency of performance.

By the late 19th and early 20th centuries, pedagogical principles became more and more explicit in some cases, perhaps only to attract teachers to new pedagogical approaches and hence to buy yet another book. Principles gradually turned researched enquiry into efficacy, with the burgeoning of mathematics education in the 20th century, particularly in the second half of the century. Recent research into learners' perceptions of examples adds further insight. This appendix tracks some of these developments, with the aim of charting subtle differences in how worked examples and examples of mathematical objects have been conceived and used.

EARLY PRACTICES AND IMPLICIT THEORIES

Robson (2000) reported that from around 2500 BC onward there is evidence of "school" clay tablets consisting of documents written for practice rather than for working use:

> Some of the tablets from Shuruppak state a single problem and give the numerical answer below it. There is no working shown on the tablets, but these are more than simple practical exercises. They use a practical pretext to explore the division properties of . . . numbers such as 7, 11, 13, 17 and 19 . . . which are prime but not 2, 3, or 5. (p. 151)

Other tablets show calculations following the problems, and sometimes there are pointers to generality from brief statements, such as "the doing as it occurs," "the manner of the reckoning of it," "do it thus," and "thus is it done" (Gillings, 1982, p. 10, pp. 182–183, p. 233, respectively). It is reasonable to suppose from this that scribes were aware of general methods and that the examples were intended as demonstrative templates to be used for other practice exercises by novices. Because cuneiform tablets are not verbose, we can conjecture that the effort in making them meant that only comments considered particularly important were recorded. Consequently the inclusion of "the doing as it occurs" is likely to be more than an offhand remark. Such comments suggest that the author was pointing to something more than the specific answer and that the object of attention was not just the specific calculation but the method used. But methods are not easy to point to: all the novice can see is the particular example. Methods are procedures to be carried out, and they are intended to become practices. But novices tend to become immersed in details and, in this state, are less likely to notice the overall procedure as a procedure.

It has become popular to refer to the need for metacognitive shifts (Flavell, 1979), occasioned by metacomments (Pimm, 1994), through which learners are prompted to stand back from the immediacy of immersion in tasks to become aware not just of what they are doing but how they are doing it and in what other situations similar methods might be useful. The timing and formulation of metacommenting is itself a complex pedagogical issue.

Immanuel Kant had a similar perspective, which can be summarized as: A succession of experiences does not necessarily add up to an experience of that succession. In other words, just doing exercises and just following templates cannot be relied on to produce a spontaneous metacognitive shift into awareness of how the "doing" illustrates or exemplifies a general method. To see a generality through one or more particular cases requires something more. In other words, one thing we do not seem to learn from experience is that we seldom learn from experience alone.

Something more is required. Many authors have tried to capture this important aspect of learning when something you do becomes a method that can be examined in and for itself. Piaget (1972) coined the term *reflective abstraction* for standing back from the action and becoming aware of the performance of the actions. Ed Dubinsky and Gary Levin (1986) and Dubinsky (1991b) developed Piaget's notion into APOS theory, referring to *actions* subsequently being identified as *processes* that, through repetition, become *objects* that are then signified *symbolically*. These transitions imply and require discernment of features, relationships, and properties, as outlined by Pierre van Hiele (1986). Sfard (1994) used the word *reification* to describe an action or process becoming an object of mathematical study in its own right. Mason (1989) tried to capture this process of abstraction as a "delicate shift of attention." Eddie Gray and David Tall (1994) coined the term *procept* to express the development of a process into an object. For example, adding two numbers is a process; the sum, especially when expressed symbolically as $x + y$, holds the process while also being an object, namely, the answer. Numerous other authors (Bruner, 1966; Floyd, Burton, James, & Mason, 1981) have constructed very similar cycles involving action, articulation, and symbolization to inform the construction of teaching materials.

It is not enough for novices to engage in the process for it to become an object for them, just as counting on from a number as a process does not necessarily itself become "counting on" as a thing one can do, even when the label "counting on" is used by the teacher working with the learner. This dual perception of an expression as both a process to be carried out and as the answer is fundamental to modern mathematics.

EXPLICIT THEORIES AND IMPLICIT PRACTICES

Medieval authors were not averse to injunctions similar to those found by Richard Gillings (1982) in Egyptian and Babylonian sources. For example, Girolamo Cardano (1501–1576), writing in Latin in his famous work *Artis Magnae Sive de Regulis Algebraicis* (1545/1969), includes phrases such as

> In accordance with these demonstrations, we will formulate three rules and we attach a jingle in order to help remember them; We have used a variety of examples so that you may understand that the same can be done in other cases and will be able to try them out for the two rules that follow, even though we will there be content with only two examples; It must always be observed as a general rule . . . ; So let this be an example to you; by this is shown the *modus operandi* in questions of proportion, particularly; in such cases. (pp. 36–41)

It seems that learners were expected to discern dimensions of possible variation in a given range of examples so as to appreciate full generality. Cardano also implicitly acknowledged that sometimes it is too confusing to state a general method, as in this quote: "There follows an example of this [a problem which requires the use of two unknown quantities] which we could otherwise explain only with difficulty" (p. 71).

Robert Record (1542/1969a), who wrote the earliest arithmetic and geometry texts in English, was very concerned that people without access to institutions should nevertheless have access to arithmetic and the power that entailed. His dialogue style, use of carefully laid out and developed examples, and use of the vernacular all contribute to his aim: "For instructors, for whose sake I have plainely set foorth the examples, as no booke (that I have senne) hath done hytherto, which thing shal be greate ease to the rude reader" (p. v).

It was recognized that attempting to say in words precisely how you do long multiplication or even multidigit subtraction reveals that sometimes a process is best encountered as a practice into which one is initiated through apprenticeship rather than being told what to do. Such apprenticeship might include the notion of practice exercises, as Record (1557/1969b) described in *The Whetstone of Witte*, in which he developed the metaphor of a whetstone:

> Though many stones doe beare greate price,
> The Whetstone is for exersice
> As neadefull, and in woorke as straunge:
> Dulle thinges and harde it will so chaunge,
> And make them sharpe, to right good ease: . . .
> . . . Here if you lift your wittes to whette,

Moche sharpenesse therby shall you gette.
Dulle wittes are fined to their fulle ende,
Not to proue, and praise, as you doe finde,
And to your self be not unkinde. (Title page)

With the development of more and more widely available printed texts, authors began to justify why they were offering yet another arithmetic or algebra book to the already extensive range of texts. Justification often involved asserting pedagogical principles. For example, in *The Arte of Vulgar Arithmetic*, Thomas Hylles (1600) saw examples playing a crucial role in learning rules: "the varietie of examples is one of the chiefest lights in learning" (Hylles, quoted in Yeldham, 1936, p. 58).

This sense of the importance of variety is also found in the *Schoolmasters Assistant* of Thomas Dilworth, which was used extensively for some 100 years both in England and in North America, so extensively that a 13th edition appeared in 1765. In his preface Dilworth said:

> In all Places where it could be done conveniently, I have given Directions for varying examples by way of proof; because it not only discovers the reason of the operation, but at the same time produces a new Question, and proves the old one. And sure I am, that varying the Question, when it may be done under the same Rule, contributes very much towards a thorough Understanding of it, and making good Accomptant, as every one's Experience will teach him. (p. v)

So here we have the advice to vary questions to see why a technique works, a strategy that many teachers have used throughout the centuries but has in recent decades come to be seen as the responsibility of the textbook author rather than the teacher. Yet awareness of dimensions of possible variation being offered to learners seems to be a crucial feature of effective pedagogy.

In his lectures on algebra from 1673 to 1683, published in 1707 as *Arithmetica Universalis*, Isaac Newton (see Whiteside, 1972, pp. 129–157) presented 19 worked problems juxtaposing the words of the problem on one side with a translation into algebraic notation on the other, solving each type generally and with specific numbers. After the first one he remarked: "However, so that I may develop an intimacy with this method of reducing problems of this sort to an equation and make it clear—and since skills are more easily learned by example than precept—I have thought it right to append the solutions of the following problems" (p. 135). Newton thus acknowledged the value and role of worked examples. He then presented his problems in general and resolved them in general, yielding a formula. It seems reasonable to conclude that Newton was aware that generality might be difficult for some readers and that working through the strategy in a demonstration case was efficacious.

John Ward (1713) was also sensitive to learners' difficulties and so justified the use of a variety of worked examples:

> Now the knowledge of this difficult part of the work [determining algebraic expressions for the conditions of the problem], is only to be obtained by Practice, and a careful minding of the Solution of such Leading Questions as are in themselves very easie. And for that Reason I have inserted a collection of several Questions; wherein there is a great variety. (p. 176)

We take Ward's "Leading Questions" to mean paradigmatic exemplars. But still there is no explicit reference to what it is that a learner might do to learn from the examples, apart from working through them diligently. The diligent learner would copy the worked examples and try to use them as templates for any exercises that followed. For several hundred years, up to the mid-18th century, learners learned by memorizing rules and, in many cases, by writing them out several times in draft form in preparation for entering them in copperplate handwriting into their copybook (e.g., John King's 1795 arithmetic book published by his great-great-grandson, John King, 1994).

Exercises, as examples for learners to work through, have at least two functions: the achievement of fluency and conceptual understanding. Constructing and arranging sets of exercises was a central concern for 19th century authors of mathematics texts who may have recognized this dual purpose even when much lesson learning was done by rote. For example in Quebec, the Reverend D. MacVicar (1879) outlined the pedagogy of many hundreds of years by saying (in the preface to his rearranged version of his collaborative work with Dr. M. MacVicar in the United States) that:

> The entire drill and discussions are believed to be so arranged, and so thorough and complete, that by passing through them the pupil cannot fail to acquire such a knowledge of principles and facts, and to receive such mental discipline, as will prepare him properly for the study of higher mathematics. (p. iv)

But some also knew that exercises on their own do not necessarily lead to understanding. For example, in his preface Walter Borchardt (1905) wrote:

> This volume is intended to stand between the complete textbook of Arithmetic and the mere compilation of examples. Each exercise is preceded by a model worked out according to methods approved by modern teachers, and

explanatory notes are added where necessary; but the proof of the method, in many cases, is purposely left to be supplied by the teacher. (p. v)

In other words, provisions of worked examples and exercises in a text-book cannot take the place of a teacher.

A model of a more interactive approach to teaching mathematics was given by Record (1542/1969a, 1557/1969b) who usually started with rules stated without adornment of special or awkward cases and then, through dialogue, revealed wrinkles and extra difficulties that may arise. For example, after one short illustration of addition, the scholar (Record's learner) set himself a problem: "There came through Cheapside two droves of cattell: in the first was 848 sheep and in the second was 186 other beasts. [The implication is that we are to find the total]" (p. xx). The scholar was recorded as writing "14" in the units column but then was immediately corrected by the master. Perhaps we have here one of the earliest recorded instances of a suggestion that it is useful for scholars to construct their own problems, although it would seem that they need to have a teacher nearby to direct them when the problems they set themselves are more advanced than can be addressed using the rules they have learned to date. The scholar has been made to choose numbers that will display a common confusion or error, something that might not happen if scholars were content to stick to numbers with which they were confident.

Interestingly, Cardano (1545/1969) wrote at about the same time: "Now let us pose our own problems" (p. 41). Perhaps Cardano was suggesting that he himself benefitted from constructing his own problems and that others might therefore gain from the same experience. This suggestion was mirrored by George Polya (1981) who, following long sequences of exercises building up generalizations from a simple starting idea, ended the chapter with this quote: "Devise some problems similar to, but different from, the problems proposed in this chapter—especially such problems as you can solve" (p. 98).

It is perhaps not surprising that in the midst of so much other valuable advice Polya gave, this advice has not been given prominence. In addition, without further support in which attention is drawn explicitly through metacognitive shifts to the process through which Polya achieved his insightful generalizations, it is probably unclear to most readers what Polya had in mind.

Augusta Monteith (1928) came close to advocating learners exploring and, hence, constructing objects for themselves:

> The exercises in reasoning afforded by arithmetic can have their full value or force only when the *child himself* investigates and draws inferences—when he fully realizes the conditions of the problem, and is able to search for ways

and means of solving it. It is in fact the method that is important—not the facts learnt, but the way in which they are learnt. (p. 12)

So active engagement of learners with examples, mainly through exercises and problems, has been advocated several times throughout the history of mathematics teaching. There are even early instances, as we have seen, of writers advocating problem posing and other forms of example creation.

THE INDUCTIVE METHOD

De Morgan (1831) transformed the teaching of mathematics in England. In particular he felt strongly that learners should make theoretical observations about mathematical phenomena, should be engaged actively with mathematics, and could choose examples for themselves. Paying attention to what happens when learners substitute their own choice of numbers is seen to be important in gaining understanding. As de Morgan noted, "not at once for every number, but by taking some example, by reasoning upon it, and by producing a result . . . equally good for all numbers" (p. 56) and "by placing numbers at pleasure instead of letters in the expressions, and calculating their values to learn the difference between similar algebraic expressions which are often confused, such as $(a + b)^2$ and $a^2 + b^2$" (p. 66).

Generalization is the end and purpose of working particular examples. De Morgan (1831) stated: "In geometry . . . any proposition may be safely demonstrated by reasonings on any one particular example . . . not so in algebra which presents a mixture of general and particular statements" (p. 192). De Morgan advocated the teaching of principles instead of directions for special cases, and he urged authors to include more exercises for practice and to provide "better facilities for correcting for the teacher were wanted" (cited in Yeldham, 1936, p. 126). In contrast to John Bonnycastle (1806) and many others before him, de Morgan "suggested that it was better teaching to begin by suggesting a problem and arguing the rule from it" (cited in Yeldham, 1936, p. 111).

His sympathy with the teacher regarding the problem of finding sufficient exercises for pupils and correcting them led to his writing:

I have also added 6 or 7 examples to each rule accompanied by the answer. These will be enough for any single pupil, but may not be considered sufficient for a School. To obviate this objection, I proceed to collect some expeditious modes of forming questions of which the answers should be readily known. (cited in Yeldham, 1936, p. 116)

His suggestions include varying the question for half the class (without affecting the answer) and making use of published tables of squares, cubes, roots, interest, and the like. He also recommended keeping a book in which the first boy [sic] to solve a problem may copy his solution and sign his name. "Besides the emulation thereby excited, a collection of [worked] examples would be obtained for future use" (Yeldham, 1936, p. 116).

In 1825 Warren Colburn published an algebra text in the United States based on the inductive method of instruction, which was perhaps the first to use the term *inductive* to refer to learners detecting and expressing similarities and differences for themselves and, hence, reaching and expressing their own generalities. This, he said, was in contrast to a *deductive* approach in which "definitions, rules or principles, to be committed to memory, followed by a few illustrative examples; what was learned or committed was applied to exercises" (Nietz, 1967, p. 93).

As noted earlier, recitation from memory characterized much of mathematics learning for many many centuries. The inductive approach meant starting from simpler cases and building up to more complex cases, using mental and then slate-based exercises. Following principles adumbrated by Johann Pestalozzi (1951), Colburn (1825) tried to engage the learner explicitly in making generalizations:

> The manner of solving the examples in each section is particularly explained. All the most difficult of the practical examples are solved in such a manner, as to show the principles by which they were performed. Care has been taken to select examples for solution, that will explain those which are not solved. Many remarks with regard to the manner of illustrating the principles to pupils, are inserted in their proper places.
>
> The reasoning used in performing these small examples is precisely the same, as that used in large ones. And when any one finds a difficulty in solving a question, he will remove it much sooner and much more effectively, by taking a very small example of the same kind, and observing how he does it, than by resorting to a rule. (pp. 109–110)

Colburn's (1925) view was that "the best mode seems to be, to give examples so simple as to require little or no explanation, and let the learner reason for himself" (cited in Nietz, 1966, p. 50). After many many simple examples, the learner was taught to generalize particular cases, and to form rules. Unfortunately, there is no further indication of how the learner was taught to generalize.

The inductive approach, working from simple examples toward complex ones, contrasts with the proposal that starting with more complex problem situations and more complex numbers not only provides an opportunity for learners to simplify for themselves to see what is going on but also provides an opportunity for learners to appreciate more fully the scope of generality implied by the particular exemplars. Furthermore, learners are not deceived by the attraction of doing simple computations with small numbers rather than attending to underlying structure.

It seems that in the early part of the 19th century, authors expanded the number examples and the scope and detail of explanations. The inductive method gave way to a mixed approach of explanation, demonstration, and examples (Nietz, 1967) and to attempts at completeness. For example, Joseph Ray (1807–1857) produced *Algebra, Part First* (1848) in which he claimed to demonstrate every rule and analyze every principle. He referred to combining the explanatory methods of French mathematicians with the practical exercises of the English and German (Nietz, p. 53).

Meanwhile, exercise collections grew and grew: George Wentworth (1835–1906) published *Elements of Algebra* (1881) in which "he included some 4000 examples that had been selected, arranged, and tested in the recitation room" (Nietz, 1967, pp. 55–56). The metaphor of exercising mental muscles rather as one exercises ordinary muscles began to dominate both theory and practice. Practice, practice, practice seems to have become the principal pedagogy—the last resort of frustrated teachers who have explained everything as clearly as they possibly can. The preface to *The Science of Arithmetic* (Cornwell & Fitch, 1878) begins with the following observation:

> This book differs from others bearing a similar title in several important details. . . . The investigation of the principle on which a rule of Arithmetic depends always precedes the statement of the rule itself. . . . if self evident they are illustrated by simple numerical examples; if otherwise, a short demonstration is added. (p. iii)

This is evidence that authors were still searching for a teacher's version of the philosopher's stone: some approach that would produce understanding rather than trained behavior.

TOWARD THE MORE ACTIVE LEARNER

The work of John Seeley Brown and Kurt van Lehn (1980; but see Ginsburg, 1996, for precursors) revealed the enormous ingenuity that children show in keeping going in the face of uncertainty when they get stuck on an arithmetic problem. They showed that children construct algorithms for themselves, pieced together from fragments of methods exemplified by their teachers in different problems, partially misremembered, partially forgotten, and partially ignored. By thinking of learners as active meaning makers, trying to make sense and to work out what to do, teaching becomes less a matter of direct instruction in methods and more a matter of harnessing learners' creative powers. Put another way, what sorts of examples and experiences are most effective in supporting the active mentation of learners in coming to appreciate and make use of methods of solution to problems? The fact that learners need, expect, and depend on worked examples to understand the generality has been part of pedagogical awareness from earliest times. There has been renewed interest among researchers. For example, Michelene Chi and Miriam Bassok (1989) suggested that a worked example can be much more than a template to follow: "An example of a worked-out solution presents an interpretation of the principled knowledge presented in the text in terms of procedural application" (p. 265). As we have indicated elsewhere, although many teachers tell us that they sometimes get learners to make up their own questions, it is not something regularly observed in lessons and not very often found in textbook schemes. For example, relatively modern Chinese texts follow a pattern seen elsewhere, with numerous exercise problems for learners. In the samples provided to us through personal communication, concerning distance–speed–time over 3 years of schooling, problems such as these stand out:

- First, please restate the relationship between the quantities in the following problems, then answer it.
- Xiaoqiang can walk 4,500 meters in an hour. How far can he walk in 2 hours?
- Please create a condition where the knowns are speed and time and the required is the distance covered.

The implied tone (here translated as *please*) is remarkable, as is the request for learners to make up their own similar problems. But, as with other indications that learners are sometimes invited to construct their own similar examples, such prompts seem to be few and far between. A most notable exception is in the work of the Shell Centre over 20 or more years, in which active, creative approaches to mathematics were constantly encouraged.

Reflecting on his long and creative career in mathematics, Paul Halmos (1983) stressed over and over again the importance of actively searching for examples and, in so doing, echoed mathematicians through the centuries:

> If I had to describe my conclusion [as to a method of studying] in one word, I'd say *examples*. They are to me of paramount importance. Every time I learn a new concept I look for examples . . . and non-examples. . . . The examples should include wherever possible the typical ones and the extreme degenerate ones. (p. 62)

The importance of active engagement is also reflected by Richard Feynman (1985): "I can't understand anything in general unless I'm carrying along in my mind a specific example and watching it go" (p. 244).

Richard Courant (1981), himself a famous and influential mathematician, described the overt way of working of his sometime colleague, David Hilbert, who had a profound influence on the development of 20th century mathematics:

> He [Hilbert] was a most concrete, intuitive mathematician who invented, and very consciously used, a principle; namely, if you want to solve a problem first strip the problem of everything that is not essential. Simplify it, specialize it as much as you can without sacrificing its core. Thus it becomes simple, as simple as can be made, without losing any of its punch, and then you solve it. The generalization is a triviality which you don't have to pay much attention to. This principle of Hilbert's proved extremely useful for him and also for others who learned it from him. Unfortunately, it has been forgotten. (p. 161)

What Hilbert appeared to be doing was creating an example for himself that was as simple as it could be, yet still retained the crucial features, by stripping away inessentials. So where else do the invaluable examples sought by famous mathematicians for their own understanding come from?

> Where can we find examples, non-examples, and counter-examples? Answer: the same place where we find the definitions, theorems, proofs and all other aspects of mathematics—in the works of those who came before us, and in our own thoughts. . . . We find them first, foremost, and above all, in ourselves, by creative thinking. (Halmos, 1985, p. 64)

It is not necessary to be an experienced mathematician to recognize the value of examples, especially examples that are sufficiently confidence inspiring and familiar to be seen as exemplary. On working through examples in a mathematics text, we heard an elementary school teacher on an in-service course remark: "when the author gives an example, I am supposed to generalize; when he gives a generalization, I am supposed to create an example."

SUMMARY

Worked examples and exercises as examples for the learner to work through have played a central role in the teaching (and, hence, learning) of mathematics throughout history. Whether based on experience of learning, experience of teaching, or both, many authors have chosen to begin with worked examples and then to move to the more general ones, although there have been times when authors preferred to offer the general ones first and then to illustrate them with examples. Some authors have strongly favored one approach over than the other, although most use a mixture without explicit justification of choices made. Indeed modern textbooks seldom justify the assumptions underlying the way the text is structured. It is intended, we think, that worked examples should offer the learner ways to recognize classes of problems and questions and work with them. However, it is also clear that authors hope learners will gain some understanding of generalities by reading examples or doing exercises for themselves.

Another strand in the literature is the great importance of using examples to learn more about a concept, theorem, or proposition. It seems that authors have always invited learners to engage with examples in some way or other, but rarely invited them explicitly to induce generalities or explicitly to make up and use their own examples in ways advocated by significant mathematicians.

Appendix B: Suggestions About Some of the Tasks

TASK 1A: TWO FACTORS

It is conventional in mathematics to include both 1 and the number itself as factors of a positive number and to require all factors to be positive. To exclude the number itself, one usually speaks of proper divisors. A number is prime if its only factors are itself and 1. However, by convention, 1 is not a prime number.

TASK 1B: MORE FACTORS

One of the ideas lurking behind *Task 1b: More Factors* is that numbers that have an odd number of factors are of a commonly recognizable type. Exploring the number of factors of numbers leads to thinking about numbers as products of primes and, hence, as being related if they have the same multiplicative structure (e.g., $12 = 2^2.3$ and $18 = 2.3^2$).

TASK 2: MODE, MEDIAN, AND MEAN

The mode is the most frequently occurring number. There can be more than one mode. The median is the middle value when the data is arranged in order or the average of the two middle values if there is an even number of data points. The mean is the arithmetic average.

TASK 3A: ALTERNATING SIGNS

A rule need not be formal: It can be a written explanation.

TASK 13A: INTER-ROOTAL DISTANCE

Roots of a polynomial function are the values of the variable that make the function value zero. For example, the roots of $x^2 - 5x + 6$ are 2 and 3. These are *real* roots; that is, they can be seen as points where the graph of the function crosses or touches the x-axis. The inter-rootal distance in this example is $3 - 2 = 1$.

TASK 24: CONSTRAINED SEARCH

This task asks you to construct an oscillating graph on a segment of the x-axis excluding its endpoints, which appears to have a limit to its height but does not actually reach that limit.

TASK 48A: WHAT IF SOMETHING ELSE?

The multiplier itself could be some other familiar type of progression, such as an arithmetic or geometric progression. You could also replace the constant difference of an arithmetic progression with a changing difference, such as a geometric progression. The process could continue by using the new sequence as the multiplier or as the difference.

TASK 48B: WHAT IF SOMETHING ELSE?

To avoid the plane, the edges of the triangles will have to be curved. This might suggest looking at surfaces. Starting with three angles of, say, 65°, try to imagine the angles joined together with curved lines.

TASK 49: FACTOR LATTICES

The factor lattice displays all of the factors and joins two factors if one is a factor of the other. Thus, the factor lattice for 12 is

which can also be depicted as

TASK 55: LEAST COMMON MULTIPLES

The least common multiple of 6 and 4 is 12: the smallest number that is a multiple of both 6 and 4. The least common multiple of 2, 4, and 8 is 8: the smallest number that is a multiple of 2, 4, and 8.

TASK 63: SQUARE ADDITION SEQUENCE

Euclid's algorithm is a method for finding (constructing) the greatest common divisor (highest common factor) of a pair of positive integers. So thinking about the results of this task in terms of common factors may be illuminating.

If you choose 1 as a starting unit, then one sequence you can get is 1, 1, 2, 3, 5, . . . (the Fibonacci sequence). If you draw a smooth curve through the squares in this order, you get a Fibonacci spiral. There are, of course, still choices to be made, which we have left up to you to play and explore.

References

Anthony, G. (1994). The role of the worked example in learning mathematics. In A. Jones, A. Begg, B. Bell, F. Biddulph, M. Carr, J. McChesney, et al. (Eds.), *Science and math education papers* (pp. 129–143). Hamilton, NZ: University of Waikato.

Askew, M., & Wiliam, D. (1995). *Recent research in mathematics education 5–16.* London: Her Majesty's Stationery Office.

Back, J. (2000). Inducting pupils into mathematical discourse. In T. Rowland & C. Morgan (Eds.), *Research in mathematics education: Vol. 2. Papers of the British Society for Research Into Learning Mathematics* (pp. 33–44). London: British Society for Research into Learning Mathematics.

Baddeley, A. (1998). Recent developments in working memory. *Current Opinion in Neurobiology, 8,* 234–238.

Banwell, C., Saunders, K., & Tahta, D. (1986). *Starting points.* Diss, UK: Tarquin. (Original work published 1972)

Bateson, G. (1973). *Steps to an ecology of mind.* London: Granada.

Bauersfeld, H. (1994). Theoretical perspectives on interaction in the mathematics classroom. In R. Biehler, R. Scholz, R. Strasser, & B. Winkelmann (Eds.), *Didactics of mathematics as a scientific discipline* (pp. 143–146). Dordrecht, Netherlands: Kluwer.

Beckett, S. (1958). *Endgame: A play in one act; followed by Act without words: A mime for one player.* London: Faber & Faber.

Bell, A. (1976). *The learning of general mathematical strategies.* Unpublished doctoral dissertation, University of Nottingham, UK, Shell Centre.

Bell, A., & Swan, M. (1995). Learning how to learn. *Mathematics Teaching, 153,* 14–17.

Bell, A., Swan, M., Shannon, A., & Crust, R. (1996). Pupils' awareness of their learning. *Mathematics Teaching, 154,* 6–9.

Benbachir, A., & Zaki, M. (2001). Production d'exemples et de contre-examples en analyse: Étude de cas en première d'université [Production of examples and counter-examples in analysis: Case study in first year of university]. *Educational Studies in Mathematics, 47,* 273–295.

Bereiter, C. (1985). Toward a solution of the learning paradox. *Review of Educational Research, 55,* 201–226.

Bereiter, C. (2002). *Education and mind in the knowledge age.* Mahwah, NJ: Lawrence Erlbaum Associates.

Bills, L. (1996). The use of examples in the teaching and learning of mathematics. In L. Puig & A. Gutierrez (Eds.), *Proceedings of the 20th Conference of the International Group for the Psychology of Mathematics Education* (pp. 2-81–2-88). Valencia, Spain: Universitat de València.

Bills, L., & Rowland, T. (1999). Examples, generalisation and proof. In L. Brown (Ed.), *Making meaning in mathematics: Visions of mathematics 2. Advances in mathematics education* (Vol. 1, pp. 103–116). York, UK: QED Press.

Boaler, J. (1997). *Experiencing school mathematics: Teaching styles, sex and setting.* Buckingham, UK: Open University Press.

Boaler, J. (2002). *Experiencing school mathematics* (rev. ed.). Mahwah, NJ: Lawrence Erlbaum Associates.

Bonnycastle, J. (1806). *An introduction to algebra: With notes and observations; designed for the use of schools and places of public education.* Philadelphia: Crukshank.

Borchardt, W. (1905). *Arithmetical types and examples.* London: Rivingtons.

Bowden, J., & Marton, F. (1998). *The university of learning: Beyond quality and competence in higher education.* London: Kogan Page.

Brousseau, G. (1997). *Theory of didactical situations in mathematics: Didactiques des mathématiques, 1970–1990* (N. Balacheff, M. Cooper, R. Sutherland, & V. Warfield, Trans.). Dordrecht, Netherlands: Kluwer.

Brown, J., & van Lehn, K. (1980). Repair theory: A generative theory of bugs in procedural skills. *Cognitive Science, 4,* 379–426.

Brown, L., & Coles, A. (1999). Needing to use algebra: A case study. In O. Zaslavsky (Ed.), *Proceedings of the 23rd Annual Conference of the International Group for the Psychology of Mathematics Education* (Vol. 2, pp. 153–160). Haifa, Israel: Technion.

Brown, L., & Coles, A. (2000). Same/different: A 'natural' way of learning mathematics. In T. Nakahara & M. Koyama (Eds.), *Proceedings of the 24th Conference of the International Group for the Psychology of Mathematics Education* (Vol. 2, pp. 153–160). Hiroshima, Japan: Hiroshima University.

Brown, S., & Walter, M. (1983). *The art of problem posing.* Philadelphia: Franklin Institute Press.

Bruner, J. (1966). *Toward a theory of instruction.* Cambridge, MA: Harvard University Press.

Bruner, J., Goodnow, J., & Austin, A. (1956). *A study of thinking.* New York: Wiley.

Burger, W., & Shaughnessy, J. (1986). Characterizing the van Hiele levels of development in geometry. *Journal for Research in Mathematics Education, 17*(1), 31–48.

Burn, R. (1993). *Numbers and functions: Steps into analysis.* Cambridge, England: Cambridge University Press.

Burn, R. (1996). *Pathway into number theory.* Cambridge, England: Cambridge University Press.

Campbell, S., & Zazkis, R. (Eds.). (2002). *Learning and teaching number theory: Research in cognition and instruction.* Westport, CT: Ablex.

Cardano, G. (1969). *Ars magna or the rules of algebra* (T. Witmer, Trans.). New York: Dover. (Original work written 1545)

Carter, B. (1983). Number lines. *Mathematics Teaching, 103,* 2–6.

Charles, R. (1980). Exemplification and characterization moves in the classroom teaching of geometry concepts. *Journal for Research in Mathematics Education, 11,* 10–21.

Chi, M., & Bassok, M. (1989). Learning from examples via self-explanation. In L. Resnick (Ed.), *Knowing, learning, and instruction: Essays in honor of Robert Glaser.* Hillsdale, NJ: Lawrence Erlbaum Associates.

Clarke, D., & Lobato, J. (2002). To 'tell' or not to 'tell': A reformulation of 'telling' and the development of an initiating/eliciting model of teaching. In C. Malcolm & C. Lubisi (Eds.), *Proceedings of the 10th Annual Conference of the South African Association for Research in*

Mathematics, Science and Technology Education (Vol. 2, pp. 15–22). Durban, KwaZulu-Natal, South Africa: University of Natal.

Claxton, G. (1984). *Live and learn: An introduction to the psychology of growth and change in everyday life*. London: Harper & Row.

Colburn, W. (1825). *An introduction to algebra: Upon the inductive method of instruction*. Boston, MA: Hilliard, Gray.

Cornwell, J., & Fitch, J. (1878). *The science of arithmetic: A systematic course in numerical reasoning and computation, with very numerous exercises*. London: Simpkin, Marshall.

Courant, R. (1981). Reminiscences from Hilbert's Gottingen. *Mathematical Intelligencer, 3*, 154–164.

Cretchley, P. (1999). An argument for more diversity in early mathematics assessment. In W. Spunde, P. Cretchley, & R. Hubbard (Eds.), *The challenge of diversity: Proceedings of the Delta '99 Symposium on Modern Undergraduate Mathematics Teaching* (pp. 75–80). Laguna Quays, Queensland, Australia: The Δ '99 Committee.

Cudmore, D., & English, L. (1998, April). *Using intranets to foster statistical problem posing and critiquing in secondary mathematics classrooms*. Paper presented at the annual meeting of the American Educational Research Association, San Diego.

Dahlberg, R., & Housman, D. (1997). Facilitating learning events through example generation. *Educational Studies in Mathematics, 33*, 283–299.

Damasio, A. (1999). *The feeling of what happens: Body and emotion in the making of consciousness*. London: Heinemann.

Davis, B. (1996). *Teaching mathematics: Towards a sound alternative*. New York: Garland.

Davis, P., & Hersh, R. (1981). *The mathematical experience*. Brighton, UK: Harvester.

de Morgan, A. (1898). *On the study and difficulties of mathematics* (4th ed.). La Salle: Open Court. (Original work published 1831)

Dewey, J. (1902). The child and the curriculum. In *The child and the curriculum and the school and society* (pp. 19–31). Chicago: University of Chicago Press.

Dewey, J. (1933). *How we think*. London: Heath.

Dewey, J. (1943). *Productive thinking*. New York: Harper.

Dienes, Z. (1963). *An experimental study of mathematics learning*. London: Hutchinson.

Dilworth, T. (1765). *The schoolmaster's assistant, being a compendium of arithmetic both practical and theoretical, in 5 parts* (13th ed.). London: Henry Kent.

diSessa, A., Hammer, D., Sherin, B., & Kolpakowski, T. (1991). Inventing graphing: Meta-representational expertise in children. *Journal of Mathematical Behaviour, 10*, 117–160.

Dörfler, W. (2002). Formation of mathematical objects as decision making. *Mathematical Thinking and Learning, 4*, 337–350.

Dubinsky, E. (1991a). Constructive aspects of reflective abstraction in advanced mathematics. In L. Steffe (Ed.), *Epistemological foundations of mathematical experience* (pp. 160–187). New York: Springer Verlag.

Dubinsky, E. (1991b). Reflective abstraction in advanced mathematical thinking. In D. Tall (Ed.), *Advanced mathematical thinking* (pp. 95–123). Dordrecht, Netherlands: Kluwer.

Dubinsky, E., & Levin, P. (1986). Reflective abstraction and mathematics education: The genetic decomposition of induction and compactness. *Journal of Mathematical Behavior, 5*, 55–92.

Duffin, J., & Simpson, A. (1999). A search for understanding. *Journal of Mathematical Behavior, 18*, 415–427.

Dweck, C. (2000). *Self-theories: Their role in motivation, personality and development*. Philadelphia: Psychology Press.

Eco, U. (1983). Horns, hooves, insteps: Some hypotheses on three types of abduction. In U. Eco & T. Sebeok (Eds.), *The sign of three: Dupin, Holmes, Peirce* (pp. 198–220). Bloomington: Indiana University Press.

Ellerton, N. (1986). Children's made up mathematics problems: A new perspective on talented mathematicians. *Educational Studies in Mathematics, 17,* 261–271.

English, L. (1998). Children's problem posing within formal and informal contexts. *Journal for Research in Mathematics Education, 29,* 83–106.

Festinger, L. (1957). *A theory of cognitive dissonance.* Stanford, CA: Stanford University Press.

Feynman, R. (1985). *"Surely you're joking, Mr. Feynman!": Adventures of a curious character.* New York: Norton.

Fischbein, E. (1987). *Intuition in science and mathematics: An educational approach.* Dordrecht, Netherlands: Reidel.

Fischbein, E. (1993). The theory of figural concepts. *Educational Studies in Mathematics, 24,* 139–162.

Fisher, P. (1998). *Wonder, the rainbow and the aesthetics of rare experiences.* Cambridge, MA: Harvard University Press.

Flavell, J. (1979). Metacognition and cognitive monitoring: A new area of cognitive–developmental inquiry. *American Psychologist, 34,* 906–911.

Floyd, A., Burton, L., James, N., & Mason, J. (1981). *EM235: Developing mathematical thinking.* Milton Keynes, UK: Open University.

Foreman, J. (Producer), & Hill, G. R. (Director). (1969). *Butch Cassidy and the Sundance Kid* [Motion picture]. United States: 20th Century Fox.

Fuys, D., Geddes, D., & Tischler, R. (Eds.). (1985). *English translation of selected writings of Dina van Hiele-Geldof and Pierre van Hiele.* Brooklyn, NY: Brooklyn College School of Education. (ERIC Document Reproduction Service No. 289 697)

Gardner, M. (1977, October). Mathematical games. *Scientific American,* 18–25.

Gardner, M. (2001). *The colossal book of mathematics.* New York: Norton.

Garofalo, J., & Lester, F. (1985). Metacognition, cognitive monitoring, and mathematical performance. *Journal for Research in Mathematics Education, 16,* 163–176.

Gattegno, C. (1970). *What we owe children: The subordination of teaching to learning.* London: Routledge & Kegan Paul.

Gattegno, C. (1984). Infinity. *Mathematics Teaching, 107,* 19–20.

Gelbaum, B., & Olmsted, R. (1964). *Counterexamples in analysis.* San Francisco: Holden-Day.

Gillings, R. (1982). *Mathematics in the time of the pharoahs.* New York: Dover.

Ginsburg, H. (1996). Toby's math. In R. Sternberg & T. Ben-Zeev (Eds.), *The nature of mathematical thinking* (pp. 175–202). Mahwah, NJ: Lawrence Erlbaum Associates. ·

Ginsburg, H. (2002). Little children, big mathematics: Learning and teaching in the preschool. In A. Cockburn & E. Nardi (Eds.), *Proceedings of the 26th Annual Conference of the International Group for the Psychology of Mathematics Education* (Vol. 1, pp. 3–14). Norwich, UK: University of East Anglia.

Ginsburg, H., & Seo, K.-H. (1999). Mathematics in children's thinking. *Mathematical Thinking and Learning, 1,* 113–129.

Gray, E., & Tall, D. (1994). Duality, ambiguity, and flexibility: A proceptual view of simple arithmetic. *Journal for Research in Mathematics Education, 25,* 116–140.

Greeno, J. (1991). Number sense as situated knowing in a conceptual domain. *Journal for Research in Mathematics Education, 22,* 170–218.

Greeno, J., & Middle School Mathematics Through Applications Project Group. (1998). The situativity of knowing, learning and research. *American Psychologist, 53*(1), 5–26.

Halmos, P. (1983). *Selecta: expository writing* (D. Sarasen & L. Gillman, Eds.). New York: Springer-Verlag.

Hamilton, E., & Cairns, H. (Eds.). (1961). *Plato: The collected dialogues including the letters.* Princeton: Princeton University Press.

Harré, R. (2002). *Cognitive science: A philosophical introduction.* London: Sage.

Hashimoto, Y. (1987). Classroom practice of problem solving in Japanese elementary schools. In J. Becker & T. Miwa (Eds.), *Proceedings of the US–Japan Seminar on Mathematical Problem Solving* (pp. 94–119). Carbondale, IL: Southern Illinois University.

Haverty, L., Koedinger, K., Klahr, D., & Alibali, M. (2000). Solving inductive reasoning problems in mathematics: Not-so-trivial pursuit. *Cognitive Science, 24*, 249–298.

Hazzan, O., & Zazkis, R. (1997). Constructing knowledge by constructing examples for mathematical concepts. In E. Pehkonen (Ed.), *Proceedings of the 21st Conference of the International Group for the Psychology of Mathematics Education* (Vol. 4, pp. 299–306). Lahti, Finland: University of Helsinki.

Hazzan, O., & Zazkis, R. (1999). A perspective on "give an example" tasks as opportunities to construct links among mathematical concepts. *FOCUS on Learning Problems in Mathematics, 21*(4), 1–13.

Hershkowitz, R. (1989). Visualization in geometry—two sides of the coin. *Focus on Learning Mathematics, 11*(1), 61–76.

Hershkowitz, R., Dreyfus, T., & Schwarz, B. (2001). Abstraction in context: Epistemic actions. *Journal for Research in Mathematics Education, 32*, 195–222.

Hewitt, D. (1992). Train spotters' paradise. *Mathematics Teaching, 140*, 6–8.

Hopley, N. (2002). Calculator network. *Micromath, 18*(1), 37–38.

Howes, S. (2001). *Developing pupils' awareness of their learning in mathematics.* Unpublished diploma dissertation, University of Oxford, Oxford, UK.

Husserl, E. (1973). *Experience and judgement: Investigations in a genealogy of logic.* London: Routledge.

Hylles, T. (1600). *The arte of vulgar arithmetic.* London.

Johansson, B., Marton, F., & Svensson, L. (1985). An approach to describing learning as change between qualitatively different conceptions. In L. West & A. Pines (Eds.), *Cognitive structure and conceptual change* (pp. 233–257). New York: Academic.

Johnson, M. (1987). *The body in the mind: The bodily basis of meaning, imagination, and reason.* Chicago: University of Chicago Press.

Khaleelulla, S. (1982). *Counterexamples in topological vector spaces.* Berlin, Germany: Springer-Verlag.

Kieren, T. (1998). Towards an embodied view of the mathematics curriculum in a world of technology. In D. Tinsley & D. Johnson (Eds.), *Information communications technologies in school mathematics.* London: Chapman Hall.

King, J. (1994). *John King 1795 arithmetic book.* Twickenham, UK: J. K. Enterprises.

Krutetskii, V. A. (1976). *The psychology of mathematical abilities in school children* (J. Kilpatrick & I. Wirszup, Eds.; J. Teller, Trans.). Chicago: University of Chicago Press.

Lakatos, I. (1976). *Proofs and refutations.* Cambridge, England: Cambridge University Press.

Lakoff, G. (1987). *Women, fire, and dangerous things.* Chicago: Chicago University Press.

Lakoff, G., & Johnson, M. (1980). *Metaphors we live by.* Chicago: University of Chicago Press.

Lakoff, G., & Nunez, R. (2000). *Where mathematics comes from: How the embodied mind brings mathematics into being.* New York: Basic Books.

Leung, A. (2003). Dynamic geometry and the theory of variation. In N. Pateman, B. Dougherty, & J. Zilliox (Eds.), *Proceedings of the 2003 joint meeting of PME and PMENA* (Vol. 3, pp. 197–204). Honolulu: University of Hawai'i.

Levi-Strauss, C. (1962). *The savage mind.* Oxford, UK: Oxford University Press.

Lucas, S. (2002). *Mathematical thinking in children: Integrating two research paradigms.* Unpublished master's dissertation, University of Oxford, Department of Educational Studies, Oxford, UK.

MacHale, D. (1980). The predictability of counterexamples. *American Mathematical Monthly, 87*, 752.

MacVicar, D. (1879). *A complete arithmetic, oral and written: Designed for the use of common and high schools and collegiate institutes.* Montreal: Dawson Brothers.

Maher, C. (2002). How students structure their own investigations and educate us: What we've learned from a 14 year study. In A. Cockburn & E. Nardi (Eds.), *Proceedings of the 26th Annual Conference of the International Group for the Psychology of Mathematics Education* (Vol. 1, pp. 31–46). Norwich, UK: University of East Anglia.

Martin, G. (1991). *Polyominoes: A guide to puzzles and problems in tiling.* Washington, DC: Mathematical Association of America.

Marton, F., & Booth, S. (1997). *Learning and awareness.* Mahwah, NJ: Lawrence Erlbaum Associates.

Marton, F., & Tsui, A. (Eds.). (2004). *Classroom discourse and the space of learning.* Mahwah, NJ: Lawrence Erlbaum Associates.

Mason, J. (1989). Mathematical abstraction seen as a delicate shift of attention. *For the Learning of Mathematics, 9*(2), 2–8.

Mason, J., Burton, L., & Stacey, K. (1982). *Thinking mathematically.* London: Addison Wesley.

Mason, J., & Pimm, D. (1984). Generic examples: Seeing the general in the particular. *Educational Studies in Mathematics, 15,* 277–290.

Mason, J., & Watson, A. (2002). The psychology of object construction. In A. Cockburn & E. Nardi (Eds.), *Proceedings of the 26th Annual Conference of the International Group for the Psychology of Mathematics Education* (pp. 1–249). Norwich, UK: University of Norwich.

Maturana, H. (1988). Reality: The search for objectivity or the quest for a compelling argument. *Irish Journal of Psychology, 9*(1), 25–82.

McLeod, D., & Adams, V. (Eds.). (1989). *Affect and mathematical problem solving: A new perspective.* New York: Springer-Verlag.

Menon, R. (1997). *Writing to learn mathematics: Student journals and student-constructed questions.* Geelong, Australia: Deakin University, Centre for Studies in Mathematics, Science and Environmental Education.

Michener, E. (1978). Understanding understanding mathematics. *Cognitive Science, 2,* 361–383.

Monteith, A. (1928). *The teaching of arithmetic in the infant and junior school.* London: Harrap & Co.

Morgan, C. (1998). *Writing mathematically: The discourse of investigation.* London: Falmer.

Movshovits-Hadar, N. (1988). School mathematics theorems—an endless source of surprise. *For the Learning of Mathematics, 8*(3), 34–40.

Nietz, J. (1966). *The evolution of American secondary school textbooks.* Rutland, VT: Tuttle.

Nietz, J. (1967). Evolution of old secondary-school arithmetic textbooks. *The Mathematics Teacher, 60,* 387–393.

O'Connor, M. (1998). Language socialization in the mathematics classroom: Discourse practices and mathematical thinking. In M. Lampert & M. Blonk (Eds.), *Talking mathematics in school: Studies of teaching and learning* (pp. 17–55). Cambridge, England: Cambridge University Press.

Ouvrier-Buffet, C. (2002). An activity for constructing a definition. In A. Cockburn & E. Nardi (Eds.), *Proceedings of the 26th Annual Conference of the International Group for the Psychology of Mathematics Education* (Vol. 4, pp. 25–32). Norwich, UK: University of East Anglia.

Papert, S. (1993). *The children's machine: Rethinking school in the age of the computer.* New York: Basic Books.

Pascual-Leone, J. (1980). Constructive problems for constructive theories: The current relevance of Piaget's work and a critique of information processing simulation psychology. In R. Kluwe & H. Spada (Eds.), *Developmental models of thinking* (pp. 263–296). New York: Academic.

Pestalozzi, J. (1951). *The education of man: Aphorisms.* New York: Greenwood.

Peterson, I. (1990). *Islands of truth: A mathematical mystery cruise.* New York: Freeman.

Piaget, J. (1971). *Biology and knowledge.* Chicago: University of Chicago Press.

Piaget, J. (1972). *The principles of genetic epistemology* (W. Mays, Trans.). London: Routledge & Kegan Paul.

Pimm, D. (1994). Spoken mathematical classroom culture: Artifice and artificiality. In S. Lerman (Ed.), *Cultural perspectives on the mathematics classroom* (pp. 133–147). Dordrecht, Netherlands: Kluwer.

Pirie, S., & Kieren, T. (1994). Growth in mathematical understanding: How can we characterise it and how can we represent it? *Educational Studies in Mathematics, 26*(2–3), 165–190.

Pirie, S, Martin, L., & Kieren, T. (1996). Folding back to collect: Knowing you know what you need to know. In L. Puig & A. Gutiérrez (Eds.), *Proceedings of the 19th International Conference for the Psychology of Mathematics Education* (Vol. 4, pp. 147–154). Valencia, Spain: Universitat de València.

Polya, G. (1957). *How to solve it.* New York: Anchor.

Polya, G. (1981). *Mathematical discovery: On understanding, learning and teaching problem solving* (combined ed.). New York: Wiley.

Rachlin, S., Matsumoto, A., Wada, L., & Dougherty, B. (Eds.). (2001). *Algebra I: A process approach* (2nd ed.). Honolulu: University of Hawaii.

Ray, J. (1848). *Algebra, part first on the analytic and inductive methods of instruction: With numerous practical exercises designed for common schools and academies* (rev. ed.). Cincinnati, OH: Winthrop Smith.

Record, R. (1969a). *The ground of arts: Teaching the perfect worke and practise of arithmeticke, both in whole numbers and fractions.* The English experience: Its record in early printed books published in facsimile, 174. Amsterdam: Da Capo Press. (Original work written 1542)

Record, R. (1969b). *The whetstone of Witte.* The English experience: Its record in early printed books published in facsimile, 142. Amsterdam: Da Capo Press. (Original work written 1557)

Robson, E. (2000). Mesopotamian mathematics: Some historical background. In V. Katz (Ed.), *Using history to teach mathematics: An international perspective* (pp. 149–158). Washington, DC: Mathematical Association of America.

Rowland, T. (1998). Conviction, explanation and generic examples. In A. Olivier & K. Newstead (Eds.), *Proceedings of the 22nd Conference of the International Group for the Psychology of Mathematics Education* (pp. 4-65–4-72). University of Stellenbosch, Stellenbosch, South Africa.

Rowland, T. (2000). *The pragmatics of mathematics education: Vagueness in mathematical discourse.* London: Falmer.

Runesson, U. (2001). What matters in the mathematics classroom? Exploring critical differences in the space of learning. In C. Bergsten (Ed.), *Proceedings of the Third Nordic Conference on Mathematics Education* (pp. 2–3). Kristianstad, Sweden: Linköping Universitet.

Sadovsky, P. (1999). Arithmetic and algebraic practises: Possible bridge between them. In O. Zaslavsky (Ed.), *Proceedings of the 23rd Conference of the International Group for the Psychology of Mathematics Education* (Vol. 4, pp. 145–152). Haifa, Israel: Technion.

Sangwin, C. (2003). New opportunities for encouraging higher level mathematical learning by creative use of emerging computer aided assessment. *International Journal for Mathematical Education in Science and Technology, 34,* 671–686.

Schoenfeld, A. (1985). *Mathematical problem solving.* New York: Academic Press.

Schoenfeld, A. (1989). Explorations of students' mathematical beliefs and behavior. *Journal for Research in Mathematics Education, 20,* 338–355.

Schoenfeld, A. (1998). Making mathematics and making pasta: From cookbook procedures to really cooking. In J. Greeno & S. Goldman (Eds.), *Thinking practices in mathematics and science learning* (pp. 299–319). Mahwah, NJ: Lawrence Erlbaum Associates.

Schoenfeld, A. (2002). Making mathematics work for all children: Issues of standards, testing, and equity. *Educational Researcher, 31*(1), 13–25.

Schwarz, B., & Hershkowitz, R. (1999). Prototypes: Brakes or levers in learning the function concept? The role of computer tools. *Journal for Research in Mathematics Education, 30,* 362–389.

Schwarz, B., & Hershkowitz, R. (2001). Production and transformation of computer artifacts toward construction of meaning in mathematics. *Mind, Culture, and Activity, 8,* 250–267.

Selden, A., & Selden, J. (1998). *The role of examples in learning mathematics, research sampler 5, Mathematical Association of America Online.* Retrieved January 2003, from www.maa.org/t and_l/sampler/rs_5.html

Selden, A., Selden, J., Hauk, S., & Mason, A. (2000). Why can't calculus students access their knowledge to solve nonroutine problems? In A. Schoenfeld, J. Kaput, & E. Dubinsky (Eds.), *Issues in mathematical education: Vol 8. Research in collegiate mathematics education IV* (pp. 128–153). Providence, RI: American Mathematical Society.

Sfard, A. (1994). Reification as the birth of metaphor. *For the Learning of Mathematics, 14*(1), 44–55.

Sfard, A. (2002). *On real life and school mathematics—can they help each other?* Talk given at Matematikbiennalen, January 24, 2002, Norrköping, Sweden. Retrieved January 30, 2003, from http://construct.haifa.ac.il/~annasd/sfard.htm

Silver, E. (1994). On mathematical problem posing. *For the Learning of Mathematics, 14*(1), 19–28.

Silver, E. A., & Cai, J. (1996). An analysis of arithmetic problem posing by middle school students. *Journal for Research in Mathematics Education, 27,* 521–539.

Skemp, R. (1969). *The psychology of mathematics.* Harmondsworth, UK: Penguin.

Sowder, L. (1980). Concept and principle learning. In R. Shumway (Ed.), *Research in mathematics education* (pp. 244–285). Reston, VA: National Council of Teachers of Mathematics.

Steen, L. (1970). *Counterexamples in topology.* New York: Holt, Rinehart & Winston.

Stoyanova, E. (1998). *Extending and exploring learners' problem solving via problem posing: A study of years 8 and 9 learners involved in mathematics challenge and enrichment stages of Euler Enrichment program for young Australians.* Unpublished doctoral thesis, Edith Cowan University, Perth, Australia.

Streefland, L., & van den Heuvel-Panhuizen, M. (1992). Evoking pupils' informal knowledge of percents. In W. Geeslin & K. Graham (Eds.), *Proceedings of the 16th International Conference for the Psychology of Mathematics Education* (Vol. 3, pp. 51–57). Durham: University of New Hampshire.

Swan, M. (2000). GCSE mathematics in further education: Challenging beliefs and practices, *The Curriculum Journal, 11,* 199–223.

Tall, D., & Vinner, S. (1981). Concept image and concept definition in mathematics with particular reference to limits and continuity. *Educational Studies in Mathematics, 12,* 151–169.

Thompson, A. (1992). Teachers' beliefs and conceptions: A synthesis of the research. In D. Grouws (Ed.), *Handbook of research in mathematics teaching and learning* (pp. 127–146). New York: Macmillan.

Tirosh, D., Hadass, R., & Movshovitz-Hadar, N. (1991). Overcoming overgeneralizations, the case of commutativity and associativity. In F. Furinghetti (Ed.), *Proceedings of the 15th Conference of the International Group for the Psychology of Mathematics Education* (Vol. 3, pp. 310–315). Assissi, Italy: Università di Genova.

Tsamir, P., & Tirosh, D. (2003). Errors in an in-service mathematics teacher classroom: What do we know about errors in the classroom? In J. Novotna (Ed.), *International Symposium Elementary Mathematics Teaching: Proceedings* (pp. 26–34). Prague, Czech Republic: Charles University.

Usiskin, Z. (1982). *Van Hiele levels and achievement in secondary school geometry.* Chicago: University of Chicago Press.

van den Heuvel-Panhuizen, M., Middleton, J. A., & Streefland, L. (1995). Student-generated problems: Easy and difficult problems on percentage. *For the Learning of Mathematics, 15*(3), 21–27.

van Hiele, P. (1986). *Structure and insight: A theory of mathematics education*. London: Academic.

Vico, G. (1990). *On the study methods of our time* (E. Elio Gianturco, Trans.). Ithaca, NY: Cornell University Press.

Vighe, P. (2003). Pre-conceptions about the triangle. In J. Novotna (Ed.), *International Symposium Elementary Mathematics Teaching: Proceedings* (pp. 152–157). Prague, Czech Republic: Charles University.

von Glasersfeld, E. (Ed.). (1991). *Radical constructivism in mathematics education*. Dordrecht, Netherlands: Kluwer.

von Glasersfeld, E. (1998, September). *Scheme theory as a key to the learning paradox*. Paper presented at the 15th Advanced Course, Archives Jean Piaget, Geneva, Switzerland.

Vygotsky, L. (1978). *Mind in society: The development of the higher psychological processes*. Cambridge, MA: Harvard University Press.

Ward, J. (1713). *The young mathematicians guide, being a plain and easie Introduction to the mathematicks in Five Parts* . . . London: Thomas Horne.

Watson, A. (2001). Low attainers exhibiting higher-order mathematical thinking. *Support for Learning, 16*, 179–183.

Watson, A., & Mason, J. (1998). *Questions and prompts for mathematical thinking*. Derby, UK: Association of Teachers of Mathematics.

Waywood, A. (1992). Journal writing and learning mathematics. *For the Learning of Mathematics, 12*(2), 34–43.

Waywood, A. (1994). Informal writing-to-learn as a dimension of a student profile. *Educational Studies in Mathematics, 27*, 321–340.

Wen, L. (2001). A nowhere differentiable continuous function constructed using cantor series. *Mathematics Magazine, 74*, 400–402.

Wentworth, G. (1881). *Elements of algebra*. Boston: Ginn & Heath.

Whiteside, D. (Ed.). (1972). *The mathematical papers of Isaac Newton: Vol. V 1683–1684*. Cambridge, England: Cambridge University Press.

Wilson, P. (1986). Feature frequency and the use of negative instances in a geometric task. *Journal for Research in Mathematics Education, 17*, 130–139.

Winograd, K. (1997). Ways of sharing student-authored story problems. *Teaching Children Mathematics, 4*, 40–47.

Wise, G. (1993). *Counterexamples in probability and real analysis*. Oxford, UK: Oxford University Press.

Yeldham, F. (1936). *The teaching of arithmetic through four hundred years*. London: George Harrap.

Zaslavsky, O. (1995). Open-ended tasks as a trigger for mathematics teachers' professional development. *For the Learning of Mathematics, 15*(3), 15–20.

Zaslavsky, O., & Peled, I. (1996). Inhibiting factors in generating examples by mathematics teachers and student teachers: The case of binary operations. *Journal for Research in Mathematics Education, 27*, 67–78.

Zaslavsky, O., & Ron, G. (1998). Students' understandings of the role of counter-examples. In A. Olivier & K. Newstead (Eds.), *Proceedings of the 22nd Conference of the International Group for the Psychology of Mathematics Education* (Vol. 4, pp. 225–233). Stellenbosch, South Africa: University of Stellenbosch.

Author Index

Subject Index

A

Ability, 12, 20, 100
Abstraction, 8, 80, 176, 199
Affect, 36, 94
Algebra, 45–49, 54, 88, 190
Algorithm, 111, 124–125, 160, 197
  Euclidean, 155, 193, 212
APOS theory, 199

B

Bricolage, 80, 157, 164, 186

C

Cognitive dissonance, 178
Constraint, 6, 11, 21–24, 52, 98–103,
    116–119, 125–128, 153, 164, 171
Counterexample, 68, 75, 95, 208
Creativity, 21, 116–118, 161

D

Dimension of possible variation, 5, 57, 70,
    81, 86, 118, 128, 164

E

Example
  boundary, 70
  central, 62
  extreme, 7, 25–30, 100–103
  figural, 62, 188
  generic, 96, 105
  hard, 13–14, 157, 166
  model, 47, 64
  pathological, 92, 100–103
  peculiar, 42–45, 88, 168–169, 174–175
  reference, 7, 64, 95–97
  types of, 3, 7, 64, 92–103
  worked, 3, 60, 149, 159, 197–198
Example space
  collective, 76, 113
  conventional, 62, 64, 76
  global, 61, 76
  local, 61, 76
  metaphors for, 61–62, 130–132, 185–191
  personal, 61, 71, 76, 130
  potential, 51, 61, 76
  structure of, 5, 58, 92
  types of 7, 61, 76, 82

F

Figural concept, 63, 96